SURPRISED BY GOD

SURPRISED BY GOD

How I Learned to Stop Worrying and Love Religion

DANYA RUTTENBERG

BEACON PRESS, BOSTON

Beacon Press
25 Beacon Street
Boston, Massachusetts 02108-2892
www.beacon.org

Beacon Press books
are published under the auspices of
the Unitarian Universalist Association of Congregations.

11 10 09 08   8 7 6 5 4 3 2 1

This book is printed on acid-free paper that meets the uncoated paper
ANSI/NISO specifications for permanence as revised in 1992.

Text design by Susan E. Kelly
of Wilsted & Taylor Publishing Services

Library of Congress Cataloging-in-Publication Data

Ruttenberg, Danya.
  Surprised by God : how I learned to stop worrying and love religion /
Danya Ruttenberg. — 1st ed.
     p. cm.
  ISBN 978-0-8070-1068-6
   1. Ruttenberg, Danya—Anecdotes. 2. Jewish women—United States—
Religious life—Anecdotes. 3. Jewish youth—United States—Religious
life—Anecdotes. I. Title.

BM729.W6R88 2008
296.7092—dc22   2007045469

FOR LAURA

and

FOR NIR

AUTHOR'S NOTE

This is a memoir; this means that the stories are recorded as I remember them—often, but not always, with the help of old journals. They're all true, but certainly filtered through my own memory and understanding of what happened. (If you figure out where they keep objective reality, please be sure and let me know.)

The people in the stories are real, as are the things that they said, but some names and identifying characteristics have been changed, and some locations and specific events have been renamed or ever so slightly altered as well. (Many have not.) In cases where I couldn't reasonably cover up a person's true identity, and in which the folks in question are public figures, I used their real names.

It's almost Shabbat. As usual, the last few hours of Friday afternoon are a whirlwind: cooking, cleaning, straightening the mess in the living room, and trying to move forbidden objects—pens, a laptop, some loose change, and a couple of CDs—to less obtrusive locations. I throw myself into the shower with a calculated twenty minutes on the clock; I've got this routine down to a science by now. Up until the very last second I'm in motion, putting on shoes and jewelry and trying remember where I left my keys. When I can't put it off for another moment, I finally dash over to the pair of white tealights waiting for me on some tinfoil in the kitchen. I stop. I take a deep breath. I take a second breath. Okay.

I ignite a match, and fill my lungs with oxygen, slowly, again. I kindle the two wicks, drop the match on the tinfoil, and make three circular, sweeping motions with my arms, drawing the light inward. I then cover my eyes with my hands and feel the glow of the candles begin to surround me, feel some clenched part of me start to open like a flower to the sun.

Finally I whisper, "Blessed are You, God our Deity, Ruler of the Universe, who has sanctified us with His commandments, and commanded us to light the candles of Shabbat."

The light is so big. My eyes are closed but I can feel it. I'm bathing in it. I want to remain in this moment, in this monastery of light, for as long as I can. But I have to get going. I take one more deep breath and open my eyes; the fire is flickering serenely. I'd love to stay and hang out with the candles, but I can't. I'm leading tonight; I can hardly get away with showing up late.

I grab my prayer book and my coat, and dash out into the Jerusalem night.

I look like a lot of the other people scurrying to and fro. I've got long brown hair and glasses, I'm wearing a black skirt that reaches midcalf; a long, flowy shirt; and sparkly beaded earrings. Living in Jerusalem these last few years has brought out my inner hippie. Sometimes people nod and wish me a Shabbat Shalom as they pass, sometimes they glance down at the ritual fringes swaying from underneath my shirt and don't say anything. Sometimes I'm aware of them turning around after I've passed, and I know they're taking in the fact that I'm wearing a yarmulke. It's not such a common sight in these parts, a woman wearing male ritual garb. I smile, say, "Shabbat Shalom," and go through the service in my head, humming chunks of melodies and transitions.

I get to the apartment building, double-check the number, and climb up a few flights of stairs to number 6. The large living room has been rearranged so that chairs and the sofa line the walls, and soft mattresses have been put on the floor for people to sit on. I greet the hosts, grab a glass of water, and take my seat, try to enjoy a last moment or two alone in my own head as people around me—friends, acquaintances, co-conspirators, and some folks I've never seen but will no doubt meet later, over the potluck dinner—are chatting their hellos. A couple of minutes later, it's time; the room is already threatening to overflow, and a good number of people will be coming in late, because they always do.

I quietly begin singing a wordless melody—two notes in, the rest of the room identifies it as an old favorite and joins in. We, all together, begin yi-di-di-ing our way up and down the spectrum, letting the intensity of the music build and release, following some unspoken, shared sense of how to unwind the notes, one after the other. The music blossoms and explodes, bounces over the walls and pushes through us as we sing from a place beyond any of us and bigger than all of us. It's so beautiful.

As the melody runs its course and begins to ebb, I move into the first piece of the liturgy, a medieval love poem full of longing for union with the Divine.

Beloved of my soul, compassionate parent, draw Your servant to Your will. Let Your servant run like a gazelle to bow down before Your splendor. Let Your affection be sweeter than a honeycomb or any other taste. Splendorous one, most beautiful radiance of the world, my soul is sick with love for You.

And so we sing in the Hebrew, sweeter and sweeter. The feeling I had when I was standing in front of the candles earlier—the sense of being surrounded by light—is stronger now, thicker, multiplied by the sixty people packed into the front of someone's apartment. God's presence vibrates in the room.

This is home.

I wonder, sometimes, what my combat-booted, hardcore music fan-girl teenage self would think of all this religion. I wonder how she'd view my observance of Shabbat, my keeping kosher, my praying several times daily, studying Torah, and, most especially, all this God stuff. Sometimes I think that the younger me would be horrified. Atheism had been such an oddly significant part of my identity for so many years, and when I gave it up, I didn't do so lightly. But on the other hand, perhaps if my sixteen-year-old self knew how much serious thinking about hard questions was demanded by the process of coming to a religious practice, and how grueling the internal work required really is—if she knew how much was entailed, I'd like to think that she'd respect the undertaking, at least.

Maybe she'd get it if I explained to her that she already had the starting point. That is to say, maybe she'd understand if I told her that the same feeling I used to get by immolating myself in drums and guitar at Fugazi shows was honed and developed thorugh a spiritual discipline. That religion took this sense of bliss and used it to make me more sensitive, more ethical, more connected to the world around me, and more in touch with the sacred than I ever thought possible. I'm sure she would have been impressed by my time in the glitter carnival of dot-com-era San Francisco—Halloweens on the Castro, elaborate and outrageous theme parties, drinking smuggled absinthe with wealthy geeks, and plotting the revolution with feminist zinemakers. Maybe she would have appreciated the tension that I began to feel between the life I loved and my desire to follow my deepening religious practice as far as it could take me. I'm sure it would be at least some consolation for her to know that I still listen to the Pixies and the Replacements from time to time.

At each stage of a long and crazy road, over and over again, I watched my self and sense of self change and fall away, distilling slowly down to something much more essential and quiet than I would have imagined. I found, lost, and found again communities of like-minded seekers, all the while taking a winding, semireluctant path through traditional Jewish practice that eventually took me to the rabbinate. This is, in part, the tale of how that happened, a religious coming of age from the mosh pit to the Mission District and beyond.

Over the years, I've inhaled countless stories of the spiritual awakenings of Catholic saints, Buddhist nuns, and Hasidic masters. It didn't take long to notice that their struggles with discipline and integration were startlingly like mine despite apparent differences in era, culture, and sensibility. The same issues came up again and again: being forced to rethink relationships with friends, family, the self, and one's connection to the wider culture. Facing the nasty goo of the subconscious as old fears and pain are laid bare. Grappling with desire—which is *never* fun. This process is confusing, angst inducing, painful, and utterly, improbably, magical.

The core tropes of spiritual awakening appear again and again in texts both ancient and modern. And yet, many of the stories that most inspired me were written by Buddhist and Christian monastics or Sufi masters, or by Jews who lived exclusively in religious Jewish society—the people for whom certain distractions from hard spiritual work had been carefully removed. Me? I was trying to live in the world, to make sense of this path without renouncing my friends as bad influences, without denouncing my past with the regret of conversionary zeal.

And there was another complicated twist. Over time, I began to wonder if, perhaps, this age-old process of taking on a religious discipline might not be even more difficult today than it's been in the past. Contemporary America is, after all, the most consumer-oriented culture in history. The same forces that have encouraged us to consume $5 trillion worth of goods and services per year and landed us in 60 percent more credit card debt than we had ten years ago have had a strong impact on how we think about what it means to take on a spiritual practice.[1] It's inevitable that living in a strongly individualistic, highly materialistic culture is going to affect the way we navigate classic religious challenges like confronting attachments, distinguishing between what we want and what we need, and allowing the discrete self to identify with others, find its place in community, and, eventually, accept the tremendous responsibility that comes with simply paying attention. Though the wisdom found within our ancient religious disciplines has never been handed out on a silver platter, now, perhaps, it's harder than ever to access, because there are so many real obstacles in the way—obstacles that are sometimes difficult to notice or identify because they have become our culture's default setting.

For me, the work of the religious life has been about reconfiguration and reintegration. It's been about determining which parts of my life I'd outgrown and which could grow with me, as well as figuring out how to allow the Divine to work in and through me and learning to accept the inevitable grief and losses that come with spiritual health. The people who were my closest friends during my San Francisco Camelot years remain among my closest friends today, and many of the ideas I valued back then have remained central to my work—even as they've changed in form, and in delivery. This path does not require shedding one's old life completely, though it does demand much letting go along the way.

Though this is my story, hopefully something beyond my own experience can be glimpsed in glimmers here and there. And yet, as theologian Rabbi Elliot Dorff writes, "I think that we human beings have no unmediated knowledge of God but that we rather have to construct our conceptions of God on the basis of the experiences we have."[2] None of us has real claims to absolute truth—only God can know what God is like. Divine wisdom may reveal itself to us, but what we grasp of it will necessarily always reflect the imperfect filters through which we view the world—filters created, in part, by our situations, opportunities, time, and place. As I share my story, my own lenses and my limitations will become abundantly clear; you may very well see things that are outside my peripheral vision. After all, we all have pieces of the puzzle. Here are the ones that I've gathered so far.

SURPRISED BY GOD

It was Rosh Hashanah, the Jewish new year. It was the September after my bat mitzvah—which had been, insofar as I could tell, a big party that my parents had thrown for their business associates. Now, the synagogue was packed with well-heeled midwestern suburbanites surreptitiously eyeing one another and shifting uncomfortably in the velvet-covered theater chairs. The choir droned on in four-part harmony. We had already done dinner: brisket and green beans almandine. Each year demanded the acquisition of four new outfits to get me through piety season, and while my matching skirt and top weren't horrible, the pantyhose and low heels pinched and chafed. Worse yet, I was too old to get away with hiding in the ladies' room with my Hebrew school friends for the entire duration of the service, so I was stuck with the rest of my family, surveying the crowd from our balcony seats.

The bearded man at the front of the enormous room put his hands out, palms up, and raised them. We all stood on cue, like well-trained dogs. After a few incantations he lowered his hands, palms down, and we sat back down. This happened a number of times. It was very irritating, having to keep standing up and sitting down like that. By the end of the service, I could barely contain my contempt. After all, these people in their Brooks Brothers and Escada suits didn't know what they were doing, or why. More than that, they didn't particularly seem to care. Why should I care? The truth claims offered by the book we were holding were too patently absurd to consider.

When I was six, the Sunday school teacher had asked us to draw what we thought God looked like. We had all come forth with the same old man sitting among the clouds in a white robe.[1] He supposedly kept an eye on our every deed and had the power to grant wishes. Now, just starting the eighth grade, I realized that this whole pageant had been organized around the supposition that the cartoon was real. Did people really believe that?

In my house, we didn't talk much about the cartoon. A couple times a year we celebrated holidays, but it was more about new clothes and brisket and, at Passover, my mother and her friend Cynthia getting silly after a few glasses of white zinfandel. At Sunday school they had tried to engage us in mushy conversations about the Bible and morality, but to my relief I had managed to get out of going as soon as my last bat mitzvah check had been cashed.

I gazed out at the sea of bankers and lawyers and tennis-playing housewives standing up and sitting down in perfect synchronization. I decided that Marx must have been right about opiates and, on that very same Day of Judgment, I declared myself an atheist.

I grew up in a Chicago suburb just as it was being made famous by John Hughes films. Not everybody in my town was as rich or obnoxious as the kids in *Pretty in Pink*, *The Breakfast Club*, and *Sixteen Candles*, but enough were to give the usual suburban conformism of the town culture a decidedly upscale cast. I had been a bookish little kid and, though I suppose nobody really does, I didn't weather the transition to adolescent girlhood particularly well. I didn't understand the constantly shifting list of clothing brands that had to be worn, amulet-like, to guard against social ostracism. I was totally ignorant of permitted and forbidden ways of doing my hair or folding the bottoms of my jeans. My undoing, though—the mistake that proved my social downfall in the fifth grade—was that I voluntarily chose solitude when I could have had the protection of a clique. For this, there was no absolution.

One day, for reasons I didn't totally understand, I left behind the safe harbor of my usual lunch table and began eating alone. It was social suicide, but suddenly the kids with whom I had been friends since forever seemed so... boring. I itched for some kind of thrill, some kind of stimulation I wasn't finding at Central School, and for some reason I chose to go it alone until I figured out what that was. The next couple of years were fated to be lonely and miserable. It wouldn't be until the summer after seventh grade—just a few months before I cast a critical eye over a congregation of sharply dressed Jews at the Theater of Atonement—that I would discover the world that I had been seeking so desperately.

His name was Zev Klotzick. He had braces and a skater haircut, he drew skulls on the back of his hand during summer camp activities, and he told me about bands with names like Bauhaus and Love and Rockets and Black Flag and Sonic Youth and Public Image, Ltd. and the Minutemen. There were so many. Joy Division and the Sugarcubes, Hüsker Dü, and this incredible new bald woman named Sinéad O'Connor. He copied tapes for me. He made me a mix.

It wasn't Zev, though his adolescent charms were considerable. Rather, it was the thrilling new world he opened for me—this edgy, critical place where creativity, freakiness, and boundary pushing were primary values. Punk's cultural norms were a revelation; girls were required to be neither "nice" nor "pretty." They could be tough, sassy, rough, smart, crazy, weird and follow their own impulses, and they'd be considered all the cooler for doing so. I felt, for the first time, that I was given permission to experiment, to wear ridiculous clothing, to try something, anything. To release Whitman's barbaric yawp, insofar as a thirteen-year-old was able to let loose and yawp about anything.

Of course, I would eventually discover punk's petty dogmas and trite formulas. Yet, for me, as for so many kids, it served as an indispensable first language of cultural critique and the first intimation of possibility, of redemption. And the music! The music to swoon over, each band more fresh and exciting than the last.

When my parents picked me up from the airport at the end of

the summer, my hair was bleached orange (I'd been shooting for blond). A rubber rat, speared on an earring hook, was dangling from one of my lobes, and there was a silver spider in the other. I began to wear mostly black, grateful that a store at the mall called Le Château was able to help augment my wardrobe with acid-green or purple tights, spiky purses, and big, clunky shoes. I used the word "nonconformist" liberally, oblivious to any irony.

By 1988, the aesthetic I was embracing had been well established in the broader culture. At Central Junior High, however, my sartorial choices were little short of revolutionary. A newfound confidence made me more aggressive, baiting teachers I didn't like and tearing away at my opponents in classroom debates. When the popular girls cornered me, I would snarl retorts rather than, as I had in the past, slinking away as quickly as possible. It wasn't the most comfortable existence, but it got me through the eighth grade more or less intact.

High school arrived not a moment too soon. I graduated from a junior high class of 90 to a high school in which I was—in my grade alone—one of 650. There were more than enough people for everybody to find their cultures and their subcultures; in study hall, I met a girl with black lipstick named Rina. I wound up sitting next to Kath, who sported purple hair and torn fishnets, in algebra. There was a kid in gym class with big army pants and a Buzzcocks T-shirt. We made eye contact the first day, started talking shortly after that. My own combat boots, thrift store wardrobe, and artificially black hair were useful semiotic tools for navigating such an enormous school, tickets into the social scenes I was hoping to penetrate. Of course, shared tastes in fashion and music didn't always lead to deep, satisfying bonds of friendship, but it gave us a starting point— one that I, like most teenagers, really needed.

A couple weeks into September, Kath invited me out for that next Friday night. She and her friends were going to Medusa's, which was all ages until midnight; afterward, she said, I was welcome to crash with her at her dad's in the city, since he didn't really care about curfews.

I'd heard about Medusa's. It was a club in the city, up on Belmont. In the late eighties, Belmont was Chicago's punk rock terrain, and it was where we suburban kids went to buy our cred: The Alley sold band T-shirts and posters, red plaid bondage pants, and black leather motorcycle jackets. Music came from Reckless, vintage clothes from Flashy Trash and Beatnix, jeans and T-shirts from the dollar-a-pound place that smelled like mothballs. The prospect of going there at night was entirely thrilling.

We—me, Kath, and a couple of her friends from the city—met at Kath's dad's house. We decked out in our punk prettiest, white tank tops and short black skirts, stripy knee-highs, and big, big boots. We smeared heavy black around the eyes and did our lipstick in the in-famous Blackberry, the color of dried blood. We were fourteen and fierce. We hit the club.

Medusa's was amazing. I loved being within the dark gritty walls covered in velvet and candles and crosses and graffiti, amidst torn couches and the parade of every conceivable trend and subculture, ripped and dyed, safety-pinned and pierced, all so much older and so, so cool. There was a corner of the dance floor where the skin-heads and serious goths would circle each other like vultures as-sessing the kill, hands behinds their backs and feet smashing hard against the tile. There was another corner where the girly girls would shake their hips and take drags from clove cigarettes in time with the music. There were mohawked peacocks, couples making out furiously, and dour, gauzy boys in black who seemed less like they were dancing than swaying aimlessly, out of time with the music.

Chicago was the capital of industrial music in those days, and at Medusa's, the beats were synthesized and brutal. This was mu-sic for pounding, stomping, slamming, shoving and getting lost. This was music for dancing hard, legs and hips and pelvis and neck. Even that first night I left the safety of my group, swam out to an uninhabited square on the dance floor and let the drum machine push me out to sea until the sweat and mascara ran thick down the sides of my face, till I was panting hard, shirt stuck to my back. I pushed myself deep into the music until I didn't know where I ended and the beats began, until my thoughts disappeared and my body got blurry and all I knew was the sharp clear *thum thum thum* surrounding everything. It was like getting lost, but better. It was like getting found.

Years later I would hear about the practice of using music to enter a trancelike state; Sufis, Hasidic Jews, Lakota Native Americans, and gospel choirs (to name a few) do it all the time to reach elevated states of ecstasy, to annihilate the small self in the attempt to unify with something bigger. As twentieth-century Sufi leader Hazrat Inayat Khan wrote, "It seems that the human race has lost a great deal of the ancient science of magic, but if there remains any magic it is music."[2]

At Medusa's, as Nitzer Ebb and Front 242 crashed around me, I danced into the heart of someplace mysterious. The center of my chest was open—perhaps for magic, maybe just for the music itself. Everything else melted. "Every thought, every word has its form. Sound alone is free from form," writes Khan. "Every word of poetry forms a picture in our mind. Sound alone does not make any object appear before us."[3] Maybe he's right. Maybe the secret of music and dance is that they have the ability to liberate us from the usual external forms to which we are accustomed.

Words, in particular—the incessant flow of chatter and commentary in our brains—keep us hyperaware of the separations between our individual selves and everything else. It's across those separations that, sometimes, the alchemy happens. Words, after all, are all about making distinctions between things. As Kabbalah scholar Daniel Matt puts it, "The appropriateness of [a] name lulls me into thinking that there really is a separate object called a 'leaf,' as if the leaf were not part of a continuum: blade-veins-stem-stipule-twig-branch-limb-bough-trunk-root."[4] Music, for some reason, manages to help quiet the part of the brain that does all that distinction making, the part that uses words to talk about how "I" am separate from what Rumi calls the "slow and powerful root that we can't see." When we get caught in music and let go of all the linguistic distinction making, it becomes easier to experience ourselves as part of the bigger continuum, to feel the ways in which everything is interconnected—including ourselves and the Big Big-ness, whatever you want to call it. This experience is often called immolation, union, reunion, transcendence . . . Whatever and wher-ever it is, it's beyond language.

At the time, I certainly never thought about this stuff. I would go to Medusa's and soon enough find myself transported off to this *place,* this somewhere, but eventually I'd come back to my usual self-conscious self (I was a teenager, so let's make that "hyper-self-conscious") and once again assess the social space and my place in it.

Kath's friends mostly didn't dance. They preferred to lean against the balcony and flirt, to smoke, and, I learned later, work the crowd in search of acid. Kath would dance a little and talk on the balcony a lot. I didn't want to talk, and it was only partly shy-ness. I knew that if I stuck tight to Kath and let her introduce me around, I could get in with some of these kids who seemed just so unreachable. But I couldn't, I wouldn't. All I wanted to do was dance, to let time get blurry and the music take over—to get to the place I would later, as an adult, chase again and again.

Midnight hit and those of us without ID spilled out onto the street. We lined the sidewalks of Clark and Belmont ("Hellmont"), talking more, smoking more, some putting small pieces of paper on their tongues and waiting for the colors to kick in. The ready avail-ability of drugs didn't interest me, but it was of great significance to a lot of people there. I would later hear of acquaintances insti-tutionalized briefly after bad trips, and my friendship with Kath would wind up taking a serious downturn right around the time she started dealing after school at the local IHOP. But that was later. The Hellmont scene was both much less and much more in-nocent than that, given the range of people who loitered on that corner until the wee hours. I met lots of kids from all over the area—many like me, privileged kids with crayon-box hair who loved the ethos and the music, and some who were much more punk rock in the sense that they had already had hard, painful lives or lived in difficult circumstances. I wasn't sorry then and I'm not sorry now that I hadn't had the material suffering necessary to grant a person real credibility in this scene. Mostly I was just glad to hang around other people who cared about all of this as much as I did.

The humanities courses I took freshman year involved grouping one class together for both English and history, creating a sort of subculture of humanities geeks who all got to know each other a little too well. Conversations with them tended to be less about bands and more about the meaning of life, or any of the big questions as we articulated them then.

One day Helene Strauss recommended this amazing book she was reading. She thought I might dig it. Really? I asked. Who's it by?

"This woman Ayn Rand. It's called *The Fountainhead*."

I inhaled the book. While I found Rand's ideas vaguely creepy— a few years later I'd have stronger words than that for them—at the same time, they captivated me. She took concepts I thought I understood and dramatically reframed them, forcing me to think through old assumptions in new ways: What if *selfish* did mean "one who has a self"? What if *selfless* meant "lacking in self"? What would the implications be for altruism or self-absorption as we know it? However critical I may be today of Rand's relentless individualism and valorization of the ego, she was my first exposure to philosophy, and it blew my intellectually itchy fourteen-year-old mind. I was agog at the potential to see the world through entirely new lenses. "Philosophy," Plato suggested, "begins in wonder." Wonder. Whether or not I would ultimately embrace these ideas or any others, they caused me to stop, to have to reconsider who I was and how I might approach certain questions.

That same year, we read *Demian,* Hermann Hesse's Gnostic/ Jungian novel about the process of opening up to one's unconscious, and I was hooked. Anything with a philosophical bent was fair game. I wanted as much exposure to as many new ideas as possible and I didn't care if I agreed with them or not. I quickly worked my way over to the Beats and their wild, unmitigated desires, to Robert Pirsig, Milan Kundera, anybody I could find. I hounded teachers and bookstore owners for recommendations and sat for hours at Café Express with a book and my journal. I fell hard for the existentialists, carried around my dog-eared copy of *The Stranger*, and tried, like its hero Meursault, to lay "my heart open to the benign indifference of the universe."

The atheist or nontheist underpinnings of most of these writers helped me to flesh out my own increasingly vehement rejections of God and religion in ways I found deeply satisfying. Sartre, for example, wrote in his essay/lecture "Existentialism Is a Humanism,"

> *Dostoevsky once wrote: "If God did not exist, everything would be permitted"; and that, for existentialism, is the starting point. Everything is indeed permitted if God does not exist, and man . . . cannot find anything to depend upon either within or outside himself . . . One will never be able to explain one's action by reference to a given and specific human nature; in other words, there is no determinism—man is free, man is freedom.*[5]

Like punk, philosophy gave me new tools for crafting my life. The famous existentialist "burden of freedom" made me giddy. If we were, truly, only who we chose to become, then I was looking at an open road, an utterly blank canvas. This struck me as good news, despite the fact that I had no idea what I would do with such permission.

I didn't understand all the implications of my new friends' ideas, though. As fiercely on board as I was about the no-God thing, and as easy as it was for me to talk about the meaninglessness of life in the face of death's inevitability, I hadn't quite pushed this understanding of the world to its extreme logical conclusion. *The Stranger* portrays the world of the absurd, in which life has no absolutes, no reason, no virtue, no human dignity—a harsh proposition indeed. For Camus, if life truly was absurd, murder could be portrayed as a morally neutral act. (Though I didn't know it at the time, Camus himself was not an absurdist; he actually believed that there was meaning in the world and was quite outspoken in his protests against totalitarianism.)

And for all of my infatuation with the burden of freedom, Sartre intended something a bit more complex than whatever I imagined as a high school student still fenced in by curfews. For, he explains, every choice that each of us makes has profound reverberations for all of humankind, and this responsibility weighs heavily on anyone who fully understands it. Moreover, I began to understand years later how oddly ambivalent Sartre was about his staunch atheism, and how strange it was that his work constantly referred to the Divine, in which he did not believe. In *Being and Nothingness*, he writes that "To be man means to reach toward being God." Elsewhere, he confesses that he "finds it extremely embarrassing that God does not exist."[6] More telling still is his recollection of a childhood incident in his autobiography:

> I had been playing with matches and burned a small rug.
> I was in the process of covering up my crime when suddenly God
> saw me. I felt His gaze inside my head and on my hands. I whirled
> about in the bathroom, horribly visible, a live target. Indignation
> saved me. I flew into a rage against so crude an indiscretion,
> I blasphemed, I muttered like my grandfather: "God damn it,
> God damn it, God damn it." He never looked at me again.[7]

Even years later when he sat down to write his memoirs, Sartre described the experience as an accurate record of reality. He doesn't write that he "felt that God saw him" or that he "believed that God saw him." In the story, God's objective presence in the room was revealed. Sartre successfully pushed this God aside, but God would haunt him for the rest of his life. As it turned out, Sartre and I had at least this in common.

I'm not sure why I was so invested in my atheism; religion certainly hadn't been a central enough part of my upbringing to be a notable site of mutiny. My mother claimed that having children caused her to believe in God, but she never tried very hard to make it through a whole Yom Kippur fasting. Sure enough, she was much more unnerved by my wardrobe and choice of friends than by my ideological posturing. My father was slightly more into the ritual stuff—at least he made it through Yom Kippur—but only on the condition that Judaism didn't bother him more than twice a year. He was even less troubled than my mother by my unbelief.

So rebellion wasn't it. And I can't remember any childhood experience of the Divine that would have, as it did Sartre, so unsettled me that I would have felt the need to develop some sort of philosophical God repellent. A lot of what bothered me about religion was the adherence to dogma, the suggestion that I might have to accept someone else's idea rather than thinking for myself. (Not even Camus and Sartre were exempt from this; by my junior year of high school I was savaging the "pseudo-existentialists" along with all other espousers of doctrine.)

In a different way, though, certain kinds of questions were simply there with me, from a fairly young age. When I had to pick paper topics in junior high and high school, I inevitably went for the Christian symbolism, rather than the political context, of *The Grapes of Wrath*, or for Tolstoy's understanding of redemption rather than his depiction of tragedy. Maybe I proclaimed my atheism so loudly because, based on whatever quirk there was in my personality or soul, I simply couldn't escape the questions that drew me to it. And, once I had formulated a conclusion, it felt like such a relief to have things settled at last.

When I was in high school, Sartre had seemed so right in arguing, "Existentialism is nothing else but an attempt to draw the full conclusions from a consistently atheistic position."[8] Like Meursault, I had no interest in wasting what time I had in this life on God—and as I declared my atheism stridently and often, I tried to make sure that everyone around me understood this.

Cornell had a summer program that allowed high school kids to take college-level classes. I begged my parents to let me take an introductory course in philosophy the summer before my senior year.

My social scene and musical interests had shifted somewhat over the previous few years; by this time, I spent much less time on the dance floor than at shows. My friends and I would haul into the city to see local acts like Screeching Weasel or Naked Raygun, or go to see acquaintances' bands in some basement crammed with sweaty kids trying to mosh despite the fact that there was rather obviously no room for anything remotely resembling a pit. This was before Nirvana broke: We would slam, one against the other, hard and fast to the music. It was ferocious, sweaty, endorphin-drenched, and dizzying, physical and transcendent, but it wasn't violent. People were always very good about removing spiked bracelets beforehand, and if someone fell, there were always a million hands to lift them up.

Being a short chick was not a liability, which was good because I was not interested in wearing delicate clothing and hanging at the back like some of the girls I knew. Rather, I'd go to a show well armored in boots, T-shirt, flannel tied around my waist, keys and ID safety-pinned securely into my jeans pocket. The music would blare and the bodies would slam and float in a ballet of action and reaction; the guitars would create a sort of fog that got thicker and thicker until I couldn't see anything else—only the music as it reverberated inside me. Just as at Medusa's, it was like time stopped, and there were only guitars and my body. Or not even a body: just guitars. I'd emerge at the end of the show with my hair plastered to my face and bruised with battle scars, glowing like there'd been an exorcism.

I was sorry to miss a full summer of shows. I was even bummed to miss the hours I would have passed on the curb outside Café Express with Jimmy J. and ADP (Adam Da Punk) and Kath and Rina and the rest of the kids, waiting for something to happen, listening to the clack-clack-clack of skateboards on concrete. But that wasn't enough to miss digging into all those new ideas and, perhaps, getting a little change of scenery.

At Cornell we lived in the dorms, segregated by gender. My roommate was a perky girl with a penchant for flowery dresses and hairsprayed bangs that she teased and puffed for hours. One day we switched clothes and took charge of each other's hair and makeup. Everyone laughed hysterically when they saw me. Almost nobody recognized her.

We got to take two classes. Sociology was interesting enough, but it didn't hold a candle to Intro to Philosophy. It was, naturally, a survey course, cramming in as many of Western thought's greatest hits as possible within six weeks. I'd stay up late in the student lounge, reading and underlining and trying to follow the intricate concepts. Plato was thick and rich, like heavy cream. Anselm's proof of God-cum-clever-rhetorical-backflip impressed me even as I was certain that he'd gotten it wrong. Descartes forced me to sit up straight and pay attention. He was doing interesting things and I was determined to understand them, if for no other reason than to figure out where the holes were—he was a theist, after all. Nietzsche, well, he called religious people "lying little abortions of bigotry." That was certainly enough to get him into my good graces. The teacher didn't cover his superman theory or its influence on Nazism; mostly what I got from Nietzsche that summer was a handful of acidic quotables from the man who wrote God's obituary.

In that same essay—the one I read at Cornell—the angry Prussian rails against the notion that religious people take the "greatest problems of existence . . . life, the world, God, the purpose of life . . . 'truth' 'love' 'wisdom' " and discuss them with "impudent levity . . . as if they were not problems at all, but the most simple things which these little bigots know all about!!!"[9]

This, then, was the core of my own objection to God and to the people who (as I saw them) served as God's slobbering minions: they seemed to view the world with a simplicity that struck me as impossible for anyone whose faculties of reason were operative. As far as I could see, intelligent, thinking people were on one side of an unbridgeable divide, and easily manipulated, pious ones were on the other.

It probably didn't help that I had grown up in the eighties, as the religious right's influence was becoming increasingly apparent. Theological justifications were everywhere, from the NEA controversy about funding "obscene" artists, the 2 Live Crew censorship trial, and the new parental advisory sticker on music to homophobia and resistance to safer sex education in the wake of the AIDS crisis. Every Saturday morning my friends and I volunteered at abortion clinics, trying to help women past the screams and protests of scary people with fetus signs and New Testament verses about our ultimate fate in hell. These people all seemed so certain in their knowledge of God and the Bible. Their assertions seemed to me to be no more based in reality than the Tooth Fairy or the Easter Bunny, but they were a lot more damaging. As a result of their uncritical adherence to these ideas—and the arrogant certainty that caused Jerry Falwell to famously utter, "If you're not a born-again Christian, you're a failure as a human being"—I saw good people getting hurt and basic freedoms taken away.

Rev. Jim Wallis, head of the progressive, faith-based organization Sojourners, suggests that it doesn't have to be this way. He says,

> *Faith can cut in so many ways, . . . If [we are] penitent and not triumphal, it can move us to repentance and accountability and help us reach for something higher than ourselves. That can be a powerful thing, a thing that moves us beyond politics as usual, like Martin Luther King did. But when it's designed to certify our righteousness—that can be a dangerous thing. Then it pushes self-criticism aside. There's no reflection . . .*
>
> *Where people often get lost is on this very point . . . Real faith . . . leads us to deeper reflection and not—not ever—to the thing we as humans so very much want . . . Easy certainty.*[10]

In that sense, Nietzsche is right: there are dimensions of human existence that are, on some level, utterly unknowable, and we're best not getting too cocky about what we can understand. Blind adherence will make us stupid, dangerous, or both.

But Nietzsche's also wrong. The venom with which he attacks those who don't consider "love" to be a problem indicates his privileging of the left brain over any other faculty—a heart, say. If philosophy begins in wonder, it can all too quickly degenerate into cold list making, into enumerating proofs as though they were baseball statistics. And this hardened, calculated way of interacting with the world misses the point, belies the messy reality of human existence. Episcopal priest and New Testament scholar Rev. A.K.M. Adam, for example, both values and knows the limits of his research. He noted one day in his blog, "This morning I saw a new-born baby waving to his mother. I believe in that baby's wave more than in any bright idea, any plan or proposal of mine."[11] Or, as Keats put it, "Philosophy will clip an angel's wings / Conquer all myster-ies by rule and line / Empty the haunted air, and gnomed mine / Un-weave a rainbow..."[12]

Perhaps the mysteries of babies and rainbows aren't the domain of the philosopher, or perhaps a philosophy that does not allow for such things is distorted, incomplete. Perhaps the religious claim of understanding wisdom and love comes from experience walking through the haunted air, rather than pondering its meaning—which isn't to say that decisions about what to do with that expe-rience shouldn't be made, as Wallis suggests, in reflective humility.

But whatever philosophy's limitations, there was something that appealed to me in these systems—the quest to know, to grasp something of what it was to be human. That summer in Ithaca, I learned, and thought, and my horizons expanded tremendously. My intellectual world was bigger than it had ever been, and most ex-citing of all, I knew I was only hitting the iceberg's tip. I had a fan-tastic time living in the dorms, hanging around the courtyard with all the other kids from the high school program, walking into town and around the gorges with my friends, and, most of all, not being required to check in with anybody but myself at the end of each day. This little taste of college life and a marginal freedom was intoxi-cating. I returned home in August feeling ready to skip senior year entirely, wishing that I could just start right in at some university somewhere.

Then, two days later, my father came home from work and in-formed my mother that this time he was leaving for good.

My parents had dated on and off throughout college. There had always been a lot of fighting, a lot of breaking up, a lot of passion-ate and dramatic reunions. After they married, they separated once or twice; they both knew early on that this match was not ideal. Nei-ther of them was happy, but they eventually reached some sort of tacit agreement to stay together, for their own reasons or because of the kids—I'm not sure. But at a certain point my father had had enough. He wanted to flourish in a way that was simply not possible in an ill-fitting marriage. From my adult vantage now, this makes a great deal of sense, especially given how different they were—I had seen this even as a small child. It's probably too bad that my parents didn't part ways earlier, both for their own sakes and for ours. At seventeen, however, I was furious, and devastated—how dare he abandon us like that? And right when I had gotten home??

My father had had a four-day window between my coming home from summer school and my brother's return to college and he used it so that nobody would have to get a long-distance phone call. My brother went back to Boston two days later and my father moved to an apartment in town so that I could easily come to see him—which I did, eventually, after I started speaking to him again. However unstable the old order had been, it was at least the order with which I had grown up, and it had its own perverse predictability. My mother was seriously shaken; my last year of high school was colored much more by her depression and my increased household responsibility than the independence I was so craving.

I had already discovered feminism by this point. In addition to my Saturday morning abortion clinic volunteer shifts, I went to Women's Action Coalition meetings, attended important rallies downtown, and, with a friend, organized a fundraiser featuring five of our friends' bands, with profits going to a battered women's shelter. The need to do this work just seemed so *obvious*, and the reality with which we'd be left if we didn't seemed pretty scary. As much as anything, though, feminism was important to me because it gave me space to be who I needed to be; it, like punk, saved me from having to fear my intelligence or my strength, and it helped me to articulate why I was so repelled by what I perceived to be the pretty-girl aspirations of so many of my classmates. Simply put, I wanted more than that.

It would be a few more years, though, until I'd be able to understand how deeply ingrained these notions were. My mother had been a few years too early for the feminist explosion of the sixties and seventies; she was part of the last generation to get married before feminism hit the mainstream. As I was growing up, she would tell me to put off my own wedding until after I was thirty and make jokes about how I could enjoy this or that indulgence after I had finished medical school. By the time I was in junior high, she was speaking frankly with me about the pressure she felt to make the decisions that she had—she got married at twenty-four, which was quite old at the time, she said. She had wanted to be a painter, but her family hadn't thought that it was practical, so they sent her to a liberal arts school, where she studied art history instead. The message had long been loud and clear: my mother wanted me to have the career and independence that she hadn't felt able to choose. Now, she had a part-time job at the Art Institute of Chicago, which she loved, but it was limited both in remuneration and in the opportunities it offered for growth. In the months after my parents split up for good, it seemed that the full weight of everything that my mother had given up fell on her, hard. Our house was not the easiest place to be.

I spent a lot of senior year driving very fast through the ravines near my house, fantasizing about crashing, and listening to the Cure's *Disintegration*. The occasional Camel Light bummed off my friends when I was upset and drinking whenever somebody's parents went out of town helped sustain me during those first few painful months, and these supports would reappear for years when actually feeling proved to be too painful (until, somehow, one day my need for them suddenly disappeared). Weeknights I'd surround myself with candles and incense in my room and write poem after poem about betrayal and disillusionment in my notebook. When I think back to that time, I can remember things that I did, but very little about what I felt. It was like my emotions were muffled, like I was just holding my breath and waiting for the year to pass.

I tried to manipulate my situation, but my attempts were feeble and evinced a lack of natural talent for teen rebellion. The night of the 1992 presidential elections I told my mother that I was going to be at my father's, but I went out with my friends, instead. We didn't even do anything so exciting—we hung around the coffee shop du jour, waited for the election returns to come in, and had an impromptu dance party among the tables when it seemed clear that Clinton had won. I was busted, though—my mother had evidently spoken to my father, and was shaking with anger when I walked in the door. How dare I try to pull that? What if something had really happened to me? I knew that I could have just asked for permission to go out and that she would have granted it, but at the time, I preferred lying to my parents just because I could. I was sure that I hated them both.

I went reluctantly to my father's for dinner once a week. It was a musty brown place, "transitional" for both of us; he'd move into the city once I was off to college. For a while we would eat in silence as I glowered at him from across the spaghetti and store-bought tomato sauce. Slowly, though, I thawed, and after several months I found myself asking why he left. His answer didn't really satisfy me—nothing could have, at that point—but I suppose it was good enough, because after that I began (grudgingly at first) to share details about my own life with him. I didn't tell him anything meaningful, but little by little I began to report about school and grades, and that was, in and of itself, some sort of connection. I held on to my anger and resentment as tightly as I could, but my need for both of my parents was, it turned out, determined to emerge despite it all.

I applied to college. I spent my weekends loitering around the same old haunts with my friends, although I was becoming increasingly tired of the whole punk rock thing, of feeling like I was supposed to be so intense and hard. Sometimes I just wanted to sit in the grass with my shoes off. This was my life, though, so at this late stage of the game, with only months to go before I was going to leave town, it just seemed easier to let the tide carry me back to the scenes I knew so well.

Eventually, finally, mercifully, college admissions and graduation rolled around. After another summer working as a barista and hanging around crowded, noisy basements in my free time, I packed up my clothes and music and prepared myself for the next thing to come.

TWO

Three weeks after I got to college, my mother called to let me know that a malignant lump had been found in her breast. She'd waited until she had a full diagnosis and game plan before letting me know that anything was up; in retrospect, I suspect that she had driven me two days cross-country and moved me into the dorms with the knowledge that she might have cancer. I had been difficult on that trip, anxious, ready to leave the nest. I had no idea.

She asked if I had anybody I could tell, so I went to go find Beth, my closest new friend. Beth and I had bonded initially over the coolness of our respective shoes—mine were painted combat boots with plaid laces, and hers were those new platform raver sneakers. After my mom called, we wound up sitting outside on the lawn talking to Anish, a streetwise, preppy kid from the Bronx. I cried a little. Anish produced something he thought might make me feel better: an Indian cigarette called a bidi. It was legally bought at a mini-mart in his neighborhood, a combination of tobacco and herbs rolled in a leaf—it made everything tingly and high for just a few minutes. It was glorious. We lay in the green New England grass, looking up at the sky, feeling dizzy and detached. It was such a relief just to make jokes, to be far away, to allow myself to fall into the microcosm of friends and college and not feel like everything was about to fall apart, piece by piece.

After that, Anish and I became fast friends, and began a complex flirtation that dragged on for a couple of years. I'd wander into his room, sit on his lap, ruffle his hair, ask an obnoxious question or two. If his roommate wasn't around, we'd close the door and dance to the Cure. He and I and Beth and Lincoln, another kid from the dorms, would sit around his room watching cartoons and drinking beer. Beth and I walked miles into town for ska shows, crashed events at the art school, dyed each other's hair in the bathroom. Sometimes I dragged them to some party at one of the co-ops, sometimes we'd wander up and down Thayer Street in search of our friends. I went to class, read the assigned Aristotle, and didn't read the assigned anthropology. College proceeded apace.

My mother went through a series of treatments. First there was a lumpectomy, then chemo, then, as it turned out, she needed a mastectomy in February. Over the semester, things were mostly normal between us; we had lots of long, chatty conversations with a newfound sort of ease. The war we had had during my teenage years—the same unremarkable war that many mothers have with their teenage daughters—was coming to a slow truce as we entered the world of ideas together, as adults. She was genuinely interested in responding to my art history papers and hearing my reactions to the famous politicians and writers brought in to give talks on campus. I began to look forward increasingly to sharing the details of my intellectual life with her, and to hearing about the classes she had started taking in order to finally get her master's degree and become eligible for a more serious job at the museum.

I still didn't trust her not to act like an annoying mother when it came to my personal life, though, so I gave her as superficial a view as possible, mentioning friends' names but rarely interesting details, and always omitting the juicy stories. I knew that she was struggling with the chemo, but I didn't know what to say, how to fix it. I tried not to think about it too much, and my classes and friends, and the long, winding evenings of drifting from some party to someone's dorm room to some other party made that relatively easy. When I cried, Anish slipped me a bidi. I didn't cry that often, though.

Why would I have wanted to? Why would I have wanted to cry,

to feel afraid about my mother's health, to notice that I was still upset about my parents' divorce, to register all the shakiness and uncertainty that I felt in this new collegiate environment? Bidis made me feel smooth and calm, drinking made me feel free and unburdened. It was all too easy to check out, to disassociate from the quivering part of me that was certain that I couldn't manage any of it.

In a lot of ways, I *was* just trying to enjoy the first year of college, to experiment a little in the big world. As feminist writer Caroline Knapp so aptly wondered, "Where are the lines between satisfaction and excess, between restraint and indulgence, between pleasure and self-destruction? And why are they so difficult to find?"[1]

I didn't know where the lines were. Because however I may have understood my carousing at the time, drinking and smoking bidis those first couple of years of college helped to protect me from the fear and loneliness, the anger and uncertainty that seemed so unrelenting. In some ways, then, it was a relief, but there was also a price to pay for my disassociation. Determined to drown my sorrows, I didn't give myself the chance to hear what my sorrows really were. In silencing the subtle awareness of how I was feeling, I checked out of my intuition entirely. Writer Geneen Roth suggests that most of us are pretty sure that "if we let ourselves feel [pain], we will be overwhelmed, go insane, fall apart, be unable to function, turn into blobby messes."[2] I didn't want to be a blobby mess. I was terrified to engage the feelings I had buried. I decided not to go there, and I paid a price.

I paid in my refusal to face my mother's cancer, of course, but that wasn't the only way. It was difficult for me to connect with my new friends when I walled myself in with silence, too afraid to articulate to myself what I was really thinking or what I really wanted, let alone to share it with others. I lost touch with something important in myself during this time.

Years down the road, I would learn how hard it could be to follow my intuition, to feel whatever was buried deep within my fettered heart, to try to meet God without denial. But I would discover that fear and pain were a hundred thousand times better than this unconscious sleepwalking through parties and distraction—that even when it was harder, I would prefer to be awake, and alive. But that was all later. My freshman year, I was just trying my best to be eighteen, to try to enjoy my new life, and to not think too hard about the fact that my mother had cancer.

I flew home when she had the mastectomy. She seemed so thin and sad and helpless, but it was also a relief for everybody to have the cancer out of her body. By my brother's college graduation in May, her hair had grown back from the chemo, curly and chic, and she moved with the victorious posture of someone who had proven that she could survive anything (and had). When I remember her from that summery weekend in Boston, she was a woman who had proven that she could not be beaten.

A couple of days before sophomore year began, I stopped by a friend's house to say hi. A few people were over, and somebody had rented *The Last Temptation of Christ*. I was confused from the moment the title flashed on screen: Which guy was that one? Wait, in the Gospels does it say that Jesus had sex with Mary Magdalene?? Wasn't she, like, a hooker or something? It was a little embarrassing to realize that I didn't know enough about Christianity to even just watch a movie about it. My mother had always told me that college was the time to become an educated person, and I decided that part of getting there entailed knowing *something* about the faith that ran America.

I enrolled in a class on early Christianity. We studied the historical setting of the ancient Near East and where the first Christians fit, politically and culturally, among different factions of Jews. The professor cited Albert Schweitzer's idea that anyone who tries to describe the historical Jesus is probably going to be describing himself—hence the various pictures of Jesus as an angry homophobe, a communist, a mystical ascetic, and so forth. He explained that Matthew and Luke likely based their gospels partly on Mark's, which was earlier, and partly on another source that historians still haven't found.

This material was my kind of geek. I learned about the theory that the Torah had four different authors, identified in part by duplications in the text and various literary and linguistic inconsis-tencies. We talked about sociopolitical pressures that helped shape theology, and editorial maneuvers by later dogmatists who wanted to control religious history.

I had tried the philosophy department with great earnestness, but the squinty arrogance of my male classmates and the brittle texts themselves made it hard to bear. I found that I was perfectly capable of unpacking Hegel or Hobbes, but that it just wasn't all that much *fun* once the big ideas became too abstract, too disconnected from human lives. Camus had been rich and exciting. Locke was certainly manageable, but who wants to spend four years on "man-ageable"?

Religious studies, on the other hand, was philosophy and an-thropology and literature and history all rolled up in one. The boys in our department were also irritating at times, but I could take them down just fine in seminar. I wrote papers about Neo-Platonic themes in Dante and about eschatology in biblical apocrypha, about the use of the Ishmael story in early Islam, and about the implica-tions of Pascal's wager. Most of my friends wouldn't touch the dead white men; as usual, I couldn't get enough of them.

And better yet, the living white men from whom I was learning did a beautiful job of reinforcing my determinedly rationalist world-view. Religious history and textual criticism proved to be a candy store for a hungry atheist such as myself, and I was more than happy to share my newfound knowledge with anyone who asked— and a few that hadn't.

"This is what people believe," I would explain in a girlishly singsong tone, gesturing like Vanna White with my right hand.

"And this," I'd sweep with the left, "is what *really* happened."

Religion and I developed a comfortably distant relationship. I had a few friends who were on closer terms with their Judaism, like Jonah, a boisterous hippie who would tell me often that I just ab-solutely *needed* to come to Hillel, the Jewish center on campus, be-cause it was *soooo* great. Each time, I would smile politely and say, I don't think so, sweetie. I was content enough with my books and the chewy questions they offered, with walking around at night on campus with a copy of *Paradiso* in hand and its words fat on my lips: "You are in doubt; you want an explanation / in language that is open and expanded, / so clear that it contents your understanding."[3]

The spring of my sophomore year, my father had a conference to attend in Germany. He wanted to go early and spend a week traveling around Poland doing Jewish history tourism, and he didn't want to undertake this alone. I, of course, was happy to blow off school for a week and take a trip to Eastern Europe.

We landed in Warsaw and spent several days visiting the former Warsaw Ghetto and a lot of graveyards. It took a little time to absorb the strange remnants of Yiddish civilization, the grisly realities of the ghetto, the sense of the place as just a little bit haunted. Poland itself was a peculiar, squat little country, still quite obviously recuperating from Communism and the war before that. Warsaw seemed to be mostly uniform concrete boxes, built in a hurry over fresh rubble. There were a few swastikas spray-painted here and there on side streets. Everything felt heavy and gray.

Krakow was cheerier; it had the charm of old European plazas filled with music and pigeons. Our first night there, my father and I went out to eat in the "Jewish quarter." Like the ethnic neighborhoods of so many communities in the States, it offered a slightly exoticized experience for curious tourists. Our sense that this one was all just for show was made even more acute by the fact that it didn't seem to contain any actual Jews. We were about to check out one of the restaurants when its door opened and a girl about my age popped out, sporting dreads and a bright yellow *Thrasher* magazine sweatshirt. She was the first real peer I'd seen in a week, and I was thrilled by the chance for any brief interaction. She was equally happy to see me—she was traveling with her father and her grandfather, the latter a Holocaust survivor coming back to his old village for the first time in over fifty years. We both needed a brief respite from all the history and family dynamics, I think. Her name was Liz and she was from New York. I had already landed an internship in the city for the coming summer, so we exchanged numbers and hurriedly waved good-bye as our fathers dragged us in our respective directions.

The next day, as my dad and I were leaving the old Krakow synagogue, Liz and her family came in. They had nine men, one short of the quorum required to recite certain parts of the liturgy. My dad was drafted to be the tenth so that Liz's grandfather could say Kaddish, the mourner's prayer, for all the people he had lost. Liz's Yankees cap perched awkwardly on my father's head since he didn't have a yarmulke. Her family was so grateful, and they couldn't stop thanking my father: it had been so important for Liz's grandfather to be able to make this incantation. It was a deeply healing thing for him, Liz's father explained. A way to mourn properly, you know? Happy to help, my dad said. We all shook hands and went our separate ways.

Before I left for the trip, my mother had instructed me to leave stones at graves (Jews don't leave flowers, but rather these more permanent markers) and to say the Mourner's Kaddish when I got to the concentration camps.

"You know it, right?" she asked.

I had nodded, even though I didn't actually remember it by heart. I was embarrassed, I suppose—from the way she said it, it sounded like the sort of thing I was already supposed to have mastered. Now I was sorry that I hadn't told her the truth.

After Krakow but before Auschwitz, there was Bialystok, featuring more graveyards and the hunt for the town from which my great-grandmother had emigrated in 1907. All we had to go on was a sneeze of a name—Zubludov—plus the fact that it was on the outskirts of Bialystok, and that there had been a great wooden synagogue there. The guide we hired for the expedition drove into a near-empty ghost town; a couple of glowering older folks lurked, suspicious, in their doorways as we drove up. The first few people that the driver queried replied, "What Jewish quarter? There isn't a Jewish quarter here." Finally, someone pointed us toward the cemetery. It was a small patch of land out on the edge of town. The tombstones were crooked and fallen, overgrown with weeds, and only the vaguest traces of Yiddish and Hebrew were left on a few of them. Neglect had been hurled at our dead.

While we were at the graveyard, the guide had done some asking around and produced a wizened, tottering old man reputed to be the town historian. We visited him at his house and he gave us two photographs, one of Jews in the old Jewish quarter and one of the synagogue, once considered to be an architectural masterpiece. It had been written up in European architecture books as one of two wooden synagogues in Europe built entirely without nails. The Germans had come and taken all the Jews. Then the Russians had rolled in and burned down the synagogue.

Treblinka was train tracks and small, rough-hewn stone memorials, a whole forest of them. It was silence and stillness where people had once been alive. Some of the markers were carved with the names of towns and countries from which people had been taken. The place whistled with an empty sound, trembled under the weight of mass graves. We walked up to the central memorial full of death and suffering, and the words that came out, the only words that I had, were the ones my mother had asked me to say.

"Yitgadal, v'yitkadash," I said. I didn't know the rest.

My father broke down crying and finished the prayer for me.

About a week after the trip, I found myself knocking around on Thayer Street, killing some time between classes. I wandered into the New Age bookstore, generally a good source of incense and giggle-inducing curiosities. They had a jewelry counter with religious trinkets of many stripes, indiscriminating in its embrace of pentacles, Sanskrit Oms, and little Buddhist mandalas. I found myself, almost without thinking about it, handing over some money to the woman behind the counter and walking out with a silver chain from which dangled a very small Star of David.

It wasn't intended as a religious act. It was just that, somehow, after everything, however much I may have wanted to indict the opiate of the masses in a general, philosophical sense, I found that I could no longer bring myself to accuse Judaism. And even more than that, it seemed that in some small way, I felt a need to pick a side, even though I wasn't sure who or what I was defining as the opposition.

There was so much to learn, and I wasn't content to just passively absorb it from the back of the lecture hall. I wanted to understand the theological connection between Origen and Philo (less than I had thought), how much current theories about purity systems come from feminism (quite a bit), and whether there was a relationship between the Pauline understanding of *pneuma* and why Muslim women veil themselves (there isn't). And even that wasn't enough; I wanted the big picture, the whole forest instead of the leaves. I invented reasons to visit professors during office hours and called faculty that I didn't know for book recommendations. When the department put on a conference, I volunteered to do grunt work and stuffed envelopes with the resentful grad students, who, unlike me, didn't have much choice about being there. I loitered around the Religious Studies building, gossiping with the secretaries about who had just been offered a job at Harvard and why they were having so much trouble hiring for that Buddhist position.

I was, in short, a groupie.

I took class after class with one professor in particular, and we gradually developed a rapport. Eventually, I wound up being a TA for his survey course, and got to lead a weekly discussion section for bewildered freshmen, calmly explaining that though the material might not accord with what they had learned at church, it's the most historically accurate picture that we have so far. It seemed that I was finding my place in the discipline.

And yet, I wasn't sure. I was perfectly happy in my undergrad existence, but I found that I didn't want to focus on any one topic enough to suffer through learning Greek or any of the other rigors demanded of a Ph.D. The thought of having to ask small questions instead of big ones smelled a little bit like prison. Perplexed, I went to go visit my professor-mentor for advice. I plopped down on the chair in his office, all striped overalls and exuberance.

Folding my legs into a lotus position in the chair, I began, "You know...I love studying this stuff. I'm, like, passionate about it. But ...I'm not sure that I want to be an academic. What, um, other jobs are there out there in the field that I could do?"

This guy spent a significant amount of time shepherding undergrads through this process and he lived full time in the religious studies world, while I was a mere tourist with a limited visa. I figured that if there was anyone who knew, it would be him. My teacher paused and wrinkled his forehead in contemplation.

"Well, nothing really. But there are so many areas of research! It's simply astounding in how many directions you could go!"

Now, as a rabbinical student who has worked for a publisher of religion books, taught religion to both teenagers and adults outside academia, written journalistic articles and reviews on religion-related topics for a wide variety of magazines and journals, and become part of an extended network of professionals who think about religion for a living (and are mostly not academics), I could accuse this man of myopia. But in reality, his response merely spoke to his interests and priorities. If I wanted training in the academic life, he (and my other professors) would be more than happy to help guide me. But if I wanted training in thinking about religion in a broader sense—or even, on some level, in the quest for the meaning of life? Well, it became increasingly clear that I couldn't get that from the department. I wouldn't understand this fully until later, though, until after everything had begun to fall apart. When the bottom dropped out, theories about the social function of animal sacrifice and analyses of biblical poetry wouldn't, it turned out, be able to save me.

The summer between my sophomore and junior years, I went to New York to intern with an organization that helped museums teach about art. I spent my first few evenings paving downtown with my sneakers, agog at my good fortune at living so close to Pat Field's, Washington Square Park, and the pulsing urban energy I'd craved since I first found Belmont in Chicago. After a few days, though, I grew restless and lonely and I decided to dial the number scrawled in the corner of my journal: Liz, the girl with the dreads from Poland.

As it turned out, Liz was still in high school, just going into her senior year. We made plans to get together that, somehow, involved my taking the Long Island Rail Road and getting dragged to some sort of carnival at her local Jewish Community Center. (Liz's father, of course, remembered me and sent enthusiatic greetings to my dad.) Liz had a centripetal effect on people, drawing them irresistibly into whatever web of weird she had decided to weave that day. She would eventually go on to art school, work as a contortionist on Coney Island, and achieve renown as a tattoo artist. For us, that day, adventure involved making cotton candy at the Cedarhurst JCC and gossiping about our favorite bands in between serving fat cones to sticky children.

Partway through the afternoon, she exclaimed, suddenly and loudly, "Ohmigod! You are going to *have* to meet my sister Ariel! You are just so going to love her! I can just tell!" Ariel was my age, due back from Stanford in a week or so. What I gleaned from Liz that day was that Ariel was a lesbian (a *dyke,* Ariel would huffily correct her, later) and that Liz worshipped her. I didn't have any friends in New York. What did I have to lose?

Liz and Ariel arrived on my doorstep about a week later, on the evening before the gay pride march—in other words, prime time in the City. We hit the West Village, and it turned out that Ariel and I did have an awful lot to say to each other. She was short, with long, long hair, a tank top emblazoned with the words "Too Pretty to Burn in Hell," and seemingly boundless verbosity. Over the course of the evening she regaled me with stories of life in California, of the motorcycles on which she had ridden, the belly dance classes she was taking, the protests she had launched in the Castro district, and the crazy Cupid outfit she wore around campus to hand out condoms on Valentine's Day, all the while punctuating her narratives with snarky, self-deprecating remarks. I was immediately smitten. Ariel tended to get herself into the kind of purely harmless trouble that I loved, but never hunted down on my own.

The romance clicked easily. I had gone out with a couple of

women by this point, but neither of them had really made much of a lasting impression. I had real chemistry with Ariel, though, and after a bit too much on-and-off romantic drama with Anish, I discovered that there was something to be said for liking someone who was unabashed about liking me back—without the need for grand declarations or heavy conversations about what it all might mean.

Together, we crawled the city, from hipster bars to outdoor movie festivals, Cuban drumming concerts, and clubs where we danced until dawn. During the days I cataloged slides and wrote informational brochures, and at night Ariel and I terrorized Manhattan as only twenty-year-olds with fake IDs can.

One Sunday in late July, I returned home laden with packages after an afternoon bopping around downtown: a trendy new shirt from Avenue A, the good coffee from the place in SoHo, a dozen still-warm sesame bagels from Ess-a-Bagel on 21st. I hadn't even put down all of my packages when the phone rang. It was my mother. There was something funny in her voice. I sat down on the bed.

She told me, very slowly, that the cancer had come back. It had been a year and a half since the mastectomy and subsequent clean bill of health. She said something about tests in progress, something about having found a strange bump on her skin. She said she'd let me know when they had results, that she had at least wanted to let me know that this was going on.

The next few days passed, somehow, wobbly. Ariel came by and tried to cheer me up, but I wasn't feeling very cheerable. On the third evening after the phone call, my doorbell rang. It was Joan, my mother's cousin from New Jersey, and her teenage daughter, Reese. My mother had asked them to come tell me in person: the doctors had found cancer cells in her brain. Someone had already booked me a flight home to Chicago for the following morning. I don't have any concrete memories of getting from that apartment to my mother's house, but I'm pretty sure that Joan drove me to her house and then to Newark, that my mother's friend Cynthia picked me up from the airport on the other end. I think I cried. Somebody must have carried the luggage.

Cynthia and I got back to the house right as my mother was re-turning from her treatment. My mother hugged me, tight; she was glad to see me, she said. There were long hairs on her coat—she was already starting to shed from the radiation to her brain. My house was exactly as it had always been. The mauve kitchen had tan wall-paper trim with geese on it, there was a navy-and-burgundy carpet on the dark wood stairs, everything was both wide and stifling. But from that moment the house was holding something else, and later on, in my adult memories, I would never be able to quite fully get the stench out.

I spent what remained of the summer riding the train from our suburb to downtown Chicago and meeting my mother at her office. We would take a cab to the hospital and eat lunch, and then I would walk her down to radiation. While I waited, I read trashy magazines and tried not to stare at the bald children with pale, papery skin as they played with toys and acted as though they didn't have cancer. My mother and I would get a ride home each day from one of her friends. Then my mother would watch TV and I'd cook her dinner, usually scrambled eggs and a bagel or something else easily di-gestible.

One afternoon, despite the fact that my mother had a day off be-tween radiation cycles, she had me meet her at the Art Institute anyway. The guys at the dock entrance knew me by then, so they just issued me an ID tag without bothering to call my mom for confirmation. As usual, I wound my way through the offices in the back of the museum and then down the long hall of African art, on which my mother had worked for fifteen years—researching it, cat-aloging it, writing its wall labels, and teaching about it. A glance at any of it and I'd hear my mother's voice explaining why the Kuba had a mask combining different animal parts or why the Senufo made the base of a drum into the shape of a woman. The African gallery opened out to the main hall. From there I took the big stairs down to the education department, where she had begun to work just a year earlier.

When I came to collect her for radiation, she always took her time shutting down her computer and getting her coat, reluctant and dragging her feet. That day, though, she couldn't get out of the office quickly enough. The cumulative effect of the treatments had depleted her, but she was determined to enjoy as much of the evening as possible before she was too exhausted to continue.

The Chicago Historical Society had an exhibition of Jacob Lawrence paintings, and twentieth-century African American artists were one of my mother's passions—they were, among other things, the subject of the master's thesis she had begun researching. Though I generally preferred to walk through galleries in solitude, it was different with my mother—as usual, we linked arms and traversed the show together. I never tired of being with her in what I considered her natural habitat. I'd find myself lost in a picture-inspired reverie, musing about the historical context of the Underground Railroad and wondering about migration patterns to the North when my mother would whisper, with the glee of a delighted child incapable of restraint, that it was amazing the way the yellows danced on the canvas. "You can almost see them sweating on the blues, can't you?" she'd say, pointing to the upper-left corner with a look of pure joy on her face. "Those ladies defy the sharp angles all over the rest of the painting. It's almost like you can hear them singing."

My mother was the first person to teach me that the real action in life happened not in the recesses of my brain, but right out there in front of my eyes. I had to be willing to look, though.

It was clear that something was up. The women—Cynthia, my Aunt Susan, my mother, and her other friends—wouldn't answer some of my questions directly, and they wouldn't even touch some of the others. I asked to meet with my mother's doctor; everyone seemed visibly relieved by the suggestion. He was a very kind man, a family friend, and he explained very patiently what nobody else had wanted to. He told me that "metastasized" meant that the cancer had already entered her bloodstream. He said that she couldn't be operated on because the malignant cells were tiny and distributed throughout the brain. And, he told me, gently, that at best she had about two years to live. I don't remember any emotions that might have been connected to this meeting. I remember sensations—queasiness—and impressions: the table in his office was polished wood and very big, he was wearing a blue shirt.

Any other plans I might have had fell away as though they had never existed. There was, suddenly, only the house, and running errands, and my mother. And a slithering orange fear, inky and wet.

I spent the fall semester of my junior year flying back and forth between Providence and Chicago; I tried to be home every few weeks to be with my mother during chemo. Back at school, I poured my energy into work and shut out the people who didn't seem to know how to talk with me about the crisis. Ariel and I tried to keep things up long distance, but the combination of my mother's illness and three thousand miles proved too formidable for a six-week summer romance. We broke up amicably in October, and she continued to send me the occasional encouraging e-mail full of California platitudes. Other people did what they could, buying me dinner or tea and trying their best to listen attentively. Nobody really knew what to say, though. I chose to be alone more and more often. I cried a lot, and spent more time than could be recommended listening to a few miserable Ani DiFranco songs over and over again.

Early in September, I was invited to a new discussion group about hot issues in religion. A campus chaplain also attended, and he spoke at length about the nature of faith. It was such a funny word, so central to my academic life and yet—I wasn't sure how to parse it. Was it meaningless? A lifeline? I walked out of the meeting confused, beset by questions that hovered somewhere, barely visible, on the surface of my consciousness. Faith?

For the next few months I prowled the campus, a copy of *Fear and Trembling* in hand. Pretty much anyone who crossed my path found themselves being asked whether it was possible to take a leap of faith without believing in God. Kierkegaard argues that when God instructed Abraham to sacrifice his son in Genesis 22, Abraham "believed that God would not demand Isaac of him, while

33

still he was willing to offer him if that was indeed what was de-manded."[4] I wanted to get to that place of suspension, to the safety that comes with that level of trust—but I couldn't believe that there was a God looking out for me, involved or caring in any way, let alone one who would allow me to keep my mother in the end. I hoped urgently that someone would show me a way out.

My friends and classmates mostly told me I was crazy for ask-ing such questions. The chaplain looked at me with kind, sad eyes and told me that he was deeply sorry for what I was going through. My professorial mentor shrugged and said nope, sorry, that's not what Kierkegaard meant to include in the realm of the possible. I even went to go see the rabbi from Hillel; he told me that he didn't believe in God, either. Looking back, I'd guess that he actually tried to tell me he didn't believe that God was in the business of averting disaster or turning terminally ill mothers into healthy ones, but at the time, I didn't hear sophisticated theology. All I understood was that a rabbi had said that he didn't believe in God, which seemed like some kind of evil joke. Of course, if the rabbi had told me about a God who would let me jump the abyss and enter the expansive land of faith and saved mothers, I would have regarded him with just as much contempt. There was really no winning. I was terrified, I was angry, and I was desperate for an answer to pull me from the yawning darkness of my mother's illness, and at the same time I was pretty sure that there were no answers.

My mother's condition worsened rapidly. I went home for the week of Thanksgiving and found myself on another plane to Chicago four days later. Two days after coming home for winter break, I took her in for a doctor's appointment and the attending physician took me aside and told me she probably had about eight weeks, that perhaps it was time to think about hospice. My aunt Su-san set it up. Nurses and social workers stopped by every few days. Medical equipment slowly began appearing around the house. The symptom and pain management regimen was so complex that I de-vised an elaborate chart to keep track of what pills were to be taken when, and with what. My brother took a leave of absence from his job and came back from Boston, where he'd been living since graduation, and I got in touch with the registrar about going on leave for the spring semester.

My mother had long made it clear that she was not ready to acknowledge the fact that she was dying. She spoke with her boss about extending her work leave until she was better and able to return to the office. She talked about what a drag it was to be sick, how she couldn't wait to get back on her bike again and hit the woodsy trails, how it was annoying to be stuck at home when there weren't even baseball games on TV. Of course, on some level she already understood her prognosis, and had been trying since the summer to get her business affairs in order—but she never spoke explicitly to anybody about what she was really doing, or why. Rather, she communicated in many small ways that death was not a desired topic of discussion. As such, we invested exquisite amounts of energy in helping her to pretend that everything was okay. Health care workers came by, had a cheery conversation with her in her room, and then debriefed us in hushed whispers in the hallway. We told my mother about changes in the care plan, couched in the tentative language of "for now." The strain was unbearable.

At night I'd sit on my window ledge, staring out at the stars. Kierkegaard wrote, "Infinite resignation is the last stage before faith." I was not resigned in any way, limited or infinite. I had not accepted, I would not let go. I was numb. I was angry. I had never been more than a very casual smoker, but during the time that my mother was dying of cancer I spent hours on my ledge, window open, blowing smoke and more smoke out the window. The irony was not lost on me, of course, but this twisted little rebellion was all I had, a feeble protest against watching her die slowly, against this descent into drugs and pain and "adult diapers" and becoming my own parent's de facto parent. My brother ran the errands, so I almost never left the house. There was no reality outside of this hospice and its thick, heavy, dank air. At night I would stare out at the stars, exhale smoke, and think about taking a leap of faith—but I saw no God out there to catch me.

Years later, in rabbinical school, I'd stumble upon Abraham

Joshua Heschel's suggestion that Judaism demands "a leap of action rather than a leap of thought." And I'd remember my undergraduate self, so scared, fighting so hard. I'd wish that I could have whispered to her that the crucial leap of faith was not in believing that our mother wouldn't die, but, rather, in accepting the fact that she would—and in understanding that this, against all odds or apparent rationality, was okay. That the leap is in the fact that it's okay. I'd want to tell my younger self about the wave that sees the beach up ahead and starts to panic about crashing on sand, until it suddenly remembers with relief that it's been water the whole time. That there's only ever been water.[5]

I want to tell her that this metaphor applies both to death itself and to how she—I, we—will be after all this is over. Different, but not gone. I'd want to tell her that years later, I'd work as a hospital chaplain and see God's glowing presence hovering over the heads of those close to death, that I'd come to believe that dying is safe, utterly safe. Even when dying was painful, even when it was sudden, there was no danger in the precise moment of crossing over. In that split second, waves rolled back from the shore, an ice cube melted in a glass of water. I'd want to tell her that despite all my books and questions there was no way to grasp this intellectually, that faith had to come from a place deeper and harder to access, from the secret recesses of the heart—and though it could be chosen, it couldn't be forced. That both Heschel and Kierkegaard were right, both thought and action make faith, but that Kierkegaard was wrong about one important thing: there's no metaphysical abyss. Only waves.

I don't know if any of this would have given my younger self comfort. The only inspiration I had at the time was from someone at my summer job, a fiftysomething Buddhist. Remember, she said, that every emotion has a beginning, a middle, and an end. I clung to that. When I allowed myself to actually feel the sensations churning menacingly under the surface, they were unbearable. It was hard to believe that they would ever end.

Things got worse. My mother stopped walking. Symptoms multiplied, and multiplied again. There were a few horrifying episodes in which she howled at the top of her lungs for hours because the pain medication caused different kinds of pain, while my brother and I furiously tried to reach the nurse practitioner on duty or debated calling an ambulance.

Whether because of the strain and denial or because of the cancer creeping through her brain, my mother seemed, more and more of the time, not to be "all there." She was able to communicate, and we did things like watch movies or listen to books on tape together, but she was more often like a small child than a fifty-one-year-old woman, constantly astonished by questions like whether or not to drink broth or which pajamas might be the warmest. Then one day, at the end of January, she seemed to suddenly wake up, to suddenly be able to ask us the question and to hear its answer. She was dying. She sort of nodded. Yes, of course. She had known all along, but to engage the truth of her life out loud was very different from following the lifelong impulse toward denial—the impulse that kept her from pursuing her painting, that married her and kept her married to a man to whom she was not well suited, that kept her stuffed down and unhappy for decades and refusing to admit it. In this one moment of clarity and willingness to acknowledge where she actually was, I think she effected a sort of redemption for all of the times when she had refused to see or admit. She slipped into a coma about ten days later and died, finally, on an unnaturally warm day in early February.

I was there when it happened. Her breathing had been heavy and labored all day, and then, gradually, it shifted. I just knew. I sent my aunt downstairs to fetch my brother. The breaths got deeper and deeper, like the air was bullying its way out of her jaw. The space between them when there was no breathing grew longer. We three sat with her for some time. I don't know how long. I was sobbing, but the strange calmness surrounding her somehow steadied me. Her face was glowing, like a great light was trying to burst through. There was a thickness in the room; the air itself was pulsing, and it seemed as though the source of the power was my mother's body.

Finally, during a long, lingering exhale, she opened her eyes. They were light and clear and brighter than I'd ever seen them. Everything radiated in the slow place outside of time. And then, a moment after that, she was gone.

There's only ever been water.

We were just Jewish enough that the funeral and the rest of it were to be done according to Jewish practice. We—my aunts, my brother, my father, and I—flew to New Jersey within a day to inter my mother alongside her parents. Like most American Jews, we were concerned less with the mandates of Jewish law than with the fact that quick burials are what Jews "do." I don't know, at the end of the day, if there's always a difference.

We came back to Chicago, had a memorial service with the community and sat shiva, the weeklong process of formal mourning and receiving comforters. Shiva usually consists of a lot of people talking and eating in the mourner's house, with a brief break for prayer—but in nonreligious households like ours, that last bit was kept to an absolute minimum.

Of everyone in my family, I was the most interested in following the few aspects of the tradition with which I was familiar. I wore shoes that were made of canvas rather than leather, I didn't put on makeup, I covered the mirrors in the house. My need to go maximal was surprising in some ways, given my vociferous rejection of religious practice—but on the other hand, it wasn't strange at all. I'd spent the past two and a half years studying ritual and its uses and meanings, and though most of my work had been from the cool remove of academic distance, perhaps on some level I understood that rituals could be useful to people in real life. At the time, rituals performed a fairly basic service for me. I was so adrift that I couldn't quite manage anything for myself; I found it helpful to let a system tell me what to do. More than that, though, refusing to use makeup or leather gave me a concrete outlet, a way to scream: I was *not* okay. Everything was *not* normal. My life had just been slammed against a wall and I wanted everyone to know it.

Of course, "everyone" was actually the friends and family who came to pay a shiva call. They knew all too well what had happened and expressed deep caring and concern for my brother and me. But it wasn't enough. I needed more. There's a real logic in the traditional Jewish mourning practice of rending the garment; it's the only thing palpable enough to externalize anguish and visibly display its aftermath. I even understand why people in some ancient cultures used to cut themselves in mourning, though I wouldn't recommend it. The pain is so limitless. How would you know when to stop?

Shiva itself was really hard. The first couple of nights, the house was packed with people—my mother's friends, people from the community, parents of people my brother and I had known, colleagues from the Art Institute, my aunts, my paternal grandparents, my father and a few other people connected to him, and my mother's tight network of female confidants and their husbands. There were lots and lots of people, lots of noise. Shiva often provides equal parts comfort and distraction; for me, it was mostly the latter. Though it seemed tough at the time to make small talk with or even receive well-intentioned words of comfort from practically everyone in the greater outlying suburban district, I didn't much prefer the alternative. When everybody left, we were engulfed in the heavy quiet, the suffocation of grief, and the echo of everything that had just happened in this house.

There was never a moment when I deliberately and consciously decided to say the Mourner's Kaddish, as an adult child traditionally does for the first eleven months after a parent's burial. If I gave myself a reason, it was that my mother would have wanted me to— she had had a strong emotional connection to Judaism, even if she wasn't particularly religious in terms of actual practice. But I don't think I even articulated that to myself, not so early on. It was just that we all said it at the cemetery, at shiva, and when we all went to synagogue the Friday night of shiva week. So when I visited Providence right after shiva, it just seemed inevitable that I would follow Jonah to Hillel. I stood and recited the ancient Aramaic incantation, transliterated helpfully on the left side of the page. The rest of the service was a blur; people sang some things, chanted some other things, stood up and sat down, and generally seemed very energetic and enthusiastic about whatever it was that they were doing. I couldn't have cared less. The other students at Hillel knew why I had been gone and they saw the torn ribbon (a polite modern-day echo of garment rending) that I kept pinned to my sweater through the initial thirty-day period of mourning. They looked at me with polite, sympathetic faces and tried to engage me in their social activities. I didn't want sympathy. I didn't want to stay for the dinner afterward. I just wanted to say my Kaddish and leave.

A month or two after my mother died, I began clearing out the house, since it needed to be sold. It was one of the ways I filled my time, somehow, that spring. Cynthia and my Aunt Susan worked with me to clean out my mother's closets, to figure out what to do with her shoes and skirts and work papers, and the art and couches and kitchen stuff and linens and knickknacks and music collection and books and photographs and the old broken TV and the big good one. Cynthia, bless her heart, arranged to sell or give away almost everything but the stuff with which neither my brother nor I could bear to part—those things were eventually sent to my uncle's basement for storage.

After the shiva I moved into my father's apartment in Chicago. Realizing that he'd now need more room for his children to come stay, he got a new place later that spring. Soon thereafter there were summer sublets, a fall apartment, the postgraduation move. All in all, I would eventually move ten times in the year and a half between my mother's death and the month after college graduation. When I think back to that time, I remember having a perpetually dazed expression on my face, as though I had no idea where I had left my feet. I clung to the few mementos I had left—a pin I had given my mother one year as a gift, a necklace she had loved, a few of her sketches—and ascribed to them a talismanic potency. For years I would guard them jealously, taking them out only when I was trying to somehow invoke my mother, wearing the jewelry as though it contained some sort of fragile power. These little objects in some ways provided the only stability that I really had.

That year, I visited a great many synagogues to say my Kaddish— I sought one out wherever I was. Once the fall semester started, though, I just went to Hillel. Little by little, I became familiar with the service, the melodies, with some of the words (which I mostly didn't understand, but whose translation I could see on the other side of the page), and where people stood up and sat down. After so many books on ritual theory, I had developed some tools with which to analyze the liturgy, and as I sifted through the prayer book each week, I grudgingly found myself impressed. It seemed that the service was structured around several peak moments, the last being a "bigger" moment than the ones that came before. The other prayers appeared to help escalate or decrease the intensity of the service in relation those moments. There were certain things that signified the establishment of ceremonial space, and other things that uprooted it. The service rolled in cadences of openings and closings, of ascents and resting points up the mountain of worship and back again. The subject of the prayers moved from appreciation of nature's cycles to love; to hearing; to serving; to asking for protection; to a prayer so powerful that it could only be said in silence. This all made intellectual and intuitive sense, somehow. I still had no interest in the sky-god to whom everyone seemed to be praying, but at the very least I could acknowledge that, at least structurally, some parts of religious Judaism were not totally dumb.

Rituals do things. I began to realize this during the early days of mourning, as Jewish law steered me toward experiences I would have had trouble getting to on my own—being able to scream with the rent ribbon and not being distracted by vanities when I put cloth over the mirrors, not to mention actually having to stay in touch with the family and friends who came for shiva. And now, little by little, I was beginning to notice the various levels on which the Kaddish operated.

I could only say it among a quorum of Jews, which forced me to leave the hermitage of my grief. As a mourner, I stood to recite it—so other people knew immediately that I was hurting, that I might need some extra tenderness and care. The prayer itself is a praise of God, said by the liturgical leader many times in different forms throughout the service, only a couple of which are designated for grieving. As such, the mourner uses a prayer that is in some ways a mundane punctuation mark as an expression of her suffering—there's something ordinary and reassuring about that. At the same time, the words of praise in the prayer force the mourner to affirm magnificence and glory at the time when things seem bleakest. A medieval legend suggests that one should say the prayer to help the soul of the dead in the afterlife, thus giving the mourner one last way to help, to stay connected to the family member he or she has just lost.

Ritual works on multiple planes at once: emotional, physical, theological, familial, spiritual, social, communal, liturgical. The Kaddish's versatility is hardly unique, as I began to realize when I took a close look at the prayer book. Every rite worth its salt, every ritual built to last, has at least as many uses and understandings, operates in just as many different ways all at once, and is subject to just as many interpretations and reinterpretations and renewals of meaning. It's because, I think, there's an indescribable reality underneath the one for which we have words. Ritual, in part, helps to tap into that reality, helps us to work with it, and utilizes a network of actions and language and symbols to make things happen, to effect what is being signified. If it's ritual done right, it'll work no matter what explanations we offer for why this might be.

Rituals create change. People come to a ceremony unmarried and leave married because of the alchemy of the blessing and binding that happens under the wedding canopy. Lighting candles transforms ordinary time into sanctified Sabbath time. Conversion rituals enact the metamorphosis from non-Jew to Jew, from non-Catholic to Catholic, effecting an ontological shift in status. And, I was beginning to notice in my weekly forays to the synagogue as a twenty-one-year-old atheist, the order and nature of the prayers in the book, the way that it asks people to bow and stand and sing and whisper and cover their eyes and respond as one voice to the entreaty of the prayer leader—all of it does something. It would be years until I understood, really, what it does, and then only insofar as mystery can ever be understood.

As a college senior, the mystery slowly began to work on me, in me, on an almost imperceptible level. I reluctantly found myself actually enjoying the songs and the service—though when I managed to admit this fact to myself, it was always with the hasty disclaimer that, of course, this was more of an ethnic or cultural experience than a religious one. Whatever I might have felt about going to Hillel, it was explicitly only for Friday night services, and I certainly never stayed for dinner.

These Friday night excursions had accustomed me enough to prayer that I found myself choosing to spend the Day of Atonement in a gigantic lecture hall, converted slightly to accommodate a pulpit and the large cabinet in which the Torah was stored. The Yom Kippur service was long and relentless. I didn't try to keep up with the Hebrew—there was no way—so I studied the English on the left side of the page. I would not apologize to the sky-god and beg his forgiveness, but I did consent to reading through the long list of misdeeds in the prayer book: for the sin that we have committed before You by hardening our hearts, for the sin that we have committed before You through harsh speech, for the sin that we have committed before You by being scornful, for the sin that we have committed before You by wronging our neighbor. From an ethical or moral standpoint, I conceded, this thinking-over-what-kind-of-person-you-are business could be kind of useful. As the familiar tunes of my childhood Judaism swirled around me, I had conversations with myself about the connection between the liturgy and modern psychology, about using these ideas in a fuzzy attempt at self-improvement. Then I looked over at Jonah. He was wrapped in a big prayer shawl, eyes closed, rocking and swaying and singing to himself. I had no idea where he was. I couldn't quite decide if I wanted to know, or not.

THREE

About six months after my mother died, strange things began to happen. I would walk around Providence at night—wide, clean streets, rows of crumbling Victorians in candy pastels, the sort of humming quiet that can be found at night in sleepy towns—and I would talk to the moon. It wasn't really out loud, or even in words, but rather more like a sort of concentrated focus, a communion with this startling orb that seemed to be watching over me in a way that nobody else really was. I had never really *looked* at the moon, and now I was addicted. Some nights the sky was clear, and it would spread wide, clean light in all directions. On cloudy nights it would appear through a haze, swaddled in a muted rainbow. I began to connect to something long buried that only had permission to stir as I traversed the winding streets, more than a little lost.

I would listen to Tchaikovsky on my Walkman and weep at the moon. Not just the moon, though. I was equally moved by the shadows that were cast across the lawns by porch lights and the chunks of paint peeling off the old houses, or the weeds sprouting tenderly between sidewalk cracks. It was all too much for me to take. In the afternoons I'd walk home from class and suddenly everything seemed to take on a softness, an illumination of some sort. Colors seemed deeper, corners sharper. I would be walking down the street, and, abruptly, the only thing that seemed to exist in the world was the stop sign at the corner—its bold red flatness, the tinny gray of the post, the holes in the post and the silhouette it created. My mind would go still. It'd be absent of the clacking sound to which I was accustomed, with its endless running commentary about who I had seen and who I would see and what I had eaten that day and what I had to do and what had just happened in class and . . . Suddenly the only thing in the world was this stop sign. And, somehow, that was enough. In a life primarily defined by a sense of deprivation and anxiety, it was striking, for a moment or two, to feel as though things were exactly as they ought to be.

I didn't know what to call these experiences. I didn't think to label them at all, really. They just sort of happened. They captivated me for a time and then I moved on.

The sense of losing myself certainly echoed how I had felt sometimes at Medusa's or in the mosh pit, but these experiences against the Providence night sky were raw and unmediated; there was no music, no noise, no motion between me and this feeling of infinity. I had had smaller moments like this in years past, but I don't think it's a coincidence that they began to come fast and furious after my mother's death. My shell had been broken by grief, and perhaps for the first time in my life, I was unguarded enough to perceive a force that, for all of its power, is quite subtle in day-to-day existence.

I was empty, I was open. And I think it helped that I was also feeling alienated from the people and the routines from which I had expected solace as I mourned. It seemed that my friends were mainly interested in going to parties and riding the ups and downs of collegiate romance. My life had shifted radically while my friends' lives had remained fairly constant; I was grieving, while they were not. Eventually I would once again become preoccupied with the location for the next adventure and the merry-go-round of who I would be kissing next. But that first semester back, I was a college senior drenched in grief and loss and hurt and heartache and the horror of everything that I had witnessed. And that created a gap between my friends and me.

Gaps are powerful, potent entities. Inside a fissure, things can grow. In lag time, we can hear quieter impulses too long drowned out by a comfortable noise. In the spaces between our lives as we have known them and our lives as they are, our peripheral vision tends to expand. As Annie Dillard wrote, "The gaps are the thing. The gaps are the spirit's one home, the altitudes and latitudes so dazzlingly spare and clean that the spirit can discover itself for the first time... they are the fissures between mountains and cells the wind lances through, the icy narrowing fiords splitting the cliffs of mystery."[1] Stripped from my usual context, from the comforts of normalcy, I entered, unwittingly, another dimension.

It is inside the gaps that magic happens; an old defense is lowered, sensitivities are heightened, something calls in from the quiet. New questions flicker, and, whether or not we're aware of it at the time, a part of us follows after them. But it takes a long, long time to make sense of the clues we pick up along the way—usually years from the time we begin collecting them.

In our culture, spiritual change is often painted as quick, painless, and easy. Witness the language used to describe George W. Bush's conversion. According to the New York Times, the greater part of his religious journey took somewhat less than a week:

> George W., drunk at a party, crudely insulted a friend of his mother's. George senior and Barbara blew up. Words were exchanged along the lines of something having to be done. George senior, then the vice president, dialed up his friend, Billy Graham, who came to the compound and spent several days with George W. in probing exchanges and walks on the beach. George W. was soon born again. He stopped drinking, attended Bible study and wrestled with issues of fervent faith. A man who was lost was saved.[2]

Irrespective of what really happened—it could have been that quick, or it could have been more gradual and complex, I don't know—conversion here is painted as a drive-through affair. Bush asked Jesus to be his friend, quit drinking, and became a Christian, just like that. It's the thinner-thighs-in-six-weeks approach to religion, not uniquely American, to be sure, but matching perfectly the zeitgeist of instant gratification that reigns today. For some people, perhaps, change is that rapid, that dramatic—but even then, it tends to result in what Evangelical leader Shane Claiborne calls "spiritual bulimia." Of his initial experience becoming born again, Claiborne writes, "I did my devotions, read all the new Christian books and saw the Christian movies, and then vomited information up to friends, small groups, and pastors. But I never had the chance to digest."[3]

That's the thing with instant change—it's usually not change. Either that, or it's not actually instant. The real story of spiritual awakening tends to live beneath the surface for a long time. It's much more subtle and much less linear than it may appear; many of us absorb small changes in tiny doses over years before they even begin to flit up through the upper layers of consciousness. I remember biking in the woods outside Providence my sophomore year, gazing up at the leaves and feeling something within start to stir, almost to the edge of what Heschel has called "radical amazement." This, he argues, is the beginning of belief. But this feeling didn't assert itself, it didn't demand to be let out, and at the time I shrugged off the sensation. I didn't pay it much notice until years later when, open and wondrous, I combed my memory for help understanding how my life had seemed to shift so drastically. In truth, the veils in front of my heart had been lowering, slowly, for a long time—I just didn't notice until the day I found myself laid bare and expansive under the moon.

Transformation, if it's going to happen at all, is protracted, often imperceptible in the moment. Rabbi Zalman Schachter-Shalomi writes of his own experiece, "I did not experience *one* seismic and pivotal movement with its special theophany. The process was gradual. There was a long series of these ephiphanies, often unrelated to one another, and the effect was cumulative."[4] Few, if any, of us go to Damascus and have one experience that changes absolutely everything (though in hindsight, we might be tempted to try to identify some turning point or other this way). More often, certain events make us ripe to regard things with a different kind of lens—though it's never a foregone conclusion that we actually will. Maybe, regardless of a new experience, old ways of thinking will remain solidly in place. Maybe something within will shift slightly. And maybe, one day, we'll find ourselves sliding into one of the great, gorgeous, terrifying gaps of stillness and uncertainty, somewhere in the disquieting space between comfort and crisis.

Certainly, my mother's cancer didn't prompt any profound personal development during my freshman year—I managed to get by, immersing myself in college life and going to enough parties to avoid thinking difficult thoughts. But as a grieving twenty-one-year-old, the same strategy wasn't working. I found the same old conversations about dating and identity politics useless—they didn't address my situation, my new, broken perspective, my needs. When the usual routine doesn't click, there can be a space, a receptivity, to encounter something else that might. And I think that that's really why I was able to enter these curious nighttime experiences, and became even almost open to asking certain kinds of questions about them.

For, when I wandered around Providence and slipped into the place where the air vibrated, where rocks and leaves seemed to pulse with opalescent light, I didn't wonder why. I didn't really think at all. The experiences certainly didn't disturb me; they were gentle, sweet. Safe. What began to bother me, as time went on, was what to make of them.

One afternoon not long after these moonlit walks had begun, I had lunch with my friend Sabah at a café near campus. I don't remember what she asked me, but my response caused her to look up at me over the soup and say, "You *don't* consider yourself spiritual? I think of you as pretty much the most spiritual person I know."

Sabah did and still does identify as a secular humanist, with no interest in religion of any sort. She did, and still does, count on my short list of people whose observations are almost never off target.

The comment stayed with me, confounded me. What could she be talking about? What did she see in me to which this word could apply? I was confused and flattered at the same time, and then I wasn't sure why I felt flattered. Was it a good thing to be "spiritual"?

Wasn't it just silliness? I was embarrassed by even the thought of applying the word to myself. It had always struck me as one of those ways people tried to make sense of their own insanity, of their blanket refusal to accept the world as it already was. These experiences of pure, rushing, vibrant presence didn't inherently hamper my carefully constructed worldview. But a more objective attempt to give language to them, an attempt to explain *why* these deep connections with the night sky seemed to give me comfort when almost nothing else did . . . well, this direction of inquiry was philosophically devastating.

I had, at this point, spent several years studying religious phenomenology from the perspective of an academic trying to understand what people *thought* they were experiencing when they talked about God—even if, in reality, it was just a neurological reaction or something similar. And yet . . . I knew I couldn't entertain the possibility that my midnight excursions might be connected to the word *spiritual* without extending the word to what I regarded as its logical extreme. And opening even the question of the concept of God made me a little bit nervous, a little bit jittery, and rather nauseous.

Like a lot of people, the only image I had of God, or even of "spirituality," was this mythical, anthropomorphized God, the Guy in the Sky who sees you when you're sleeping and knows when you're awake. The Torah talks about a God who took the Jews out of Egypt with a strong hand and a mighty arm and whose nostrils flare when He (always He) gets angry. The artists of the Renaissance added a few Zeus-inspired touches: big beard, thunderbolt, menacing glare. The only archetypes that I encountered in my upbringing and in the wider culture were of God as fascist dictator or, maybe, God as the Big Buddy who makes everything okay. It was this latter God— the one who was going to somehow swoop down from the sky and save my mother from cancer—that I had so vociferously rejected the year before, and years before that. From my twenty-one-year-old perspective, it seemed ludicrous that I would throw away years of rational inquiry and historical-critical analysis, that I would give up my intellect and my power and go mooning after these problematic images in the naive belief that it would somehow help my life to do so.

Of course, I wasn't experiencing an angry, or even necessarily a personal, deity. And that was just the thing. There was a disparity between the language I felt pulled to use to describe these experiences and my belief in what that language signified. The experiences weren't wrong. The other possibility, then, was that these words—*spirituality*, or *God*, even—might refer to something much more powerful and primal, something much more fundamental than I had ever considered before.

The implications made my head spin. I had always believed that religious people were deluded, mistakenly transferring their need for a parent figure or for certainty in the world onto mythology. What could it mean if the devout had all long been citizens of the remarkable, translucent world that I was just discovering?

And, sure enough, I would eventually discover that a great many people, from the authors of the book of Deuteronomy onward, understood what I, at this time, did not: that all the business of God's flaring nostrils and mood swings was actually just metaphor, ways of describing the intangible force I began meeting more and more often. Judaism's ancient rabbinic texts make this point when they say that "the Torah speaks in the language of human beings,"[5] and the medieval philosopher Maimonides is adamant that anyone who takes literally either the emotional or physical descriptions of God's human attributes is committing idolatry.[6] But at the time, I didn't know this, any of it. I was like the people the twentieth-century Catholic theologian Thomas Merton described when he wrote

> *I know that many people are, or call themselves, "atheists" simply because they are repelled and offended by statements about God made in imaginary and metaphorical terms which they are not able to interpret and comprehend. They refuse these concepts of God, not because they despise God, but perhaps because they demand a notion of Him more perfect than they generally find: and because ordinary, figurative concepts of God could not satisfy them, they turn away and think that there are no other.[7]*

And here I was, suddenly, wondering if there were other concepts out there, if there were ways of understanding the world that I had never considered. Over the period of about a year, everything I had ever believed began to invert itself with a dizzying rapidity. As I hesitantly experimented with using the word *spirituality* to describe these strange luminous rushes—the sense of being outside time, the sense of stepping into eternity, the sense that my self as I understood it seemed to melt away into the moment—the rushes got bigger. And later, as I began first tentatively, and then more assertively, to use the word *God* to describe the experiences, they got bigger and bigger still. It was as though, like Anne Lamott, I "had discovered that if I said, Hello? to God, I could *feel* God say Hello, back."[8]

Eventually, my own belief in the Divine would echo that of Saint Catherine of Genoa, who wrote, "So clearly do I perceive Thy goodness that I do not seem to walk by faith, but by a true and heartfelt experience."[9] There was no need for a dramatic leap of faith, for a blind trek into darkened woods. My own lived experience was the guide here, and all I needed was a willingness to meet it, to allow myself to ask certain kinds of questions and be willing to hear the answers that might follow, no matter how disconcerting those answers might be. This, then, was the real test of faith—not whether I was willing to change my beliefs but, rather, whether I was willing to give language to that which I had already begun to experience as truth.

But that was all later. The present moment in Providence was asking enough of me as it was.

My father, sorry for the year I'd had, offered to bequeath me some frequent-flyer miles as a birthday gift, for use on my spring break in early April. He traveled often for business and had more than he could spend in a lifetime. I could go pretty much anywhere I wanted, though it was up to me to pick up the tab once there.

Italy, somehow, seemed like the obvious choice. The place had long captured my imagination: Dante, Caravaggio, Cimabue, Michelangelo. The Vatican. The pursuit of a very specific sort of sublime. And when I got to Florence, that first night, sure enough: walking along the Arno River, crossing the Ponte Vecchio, hearing someone's violin echoing in an almost empty piazza, sitting at a café with a glass of Chianti poured from a straw-wrapped bottle. I was besotted with how romantic it all felt.

I spent most of the four days I had allotted to Florence in its churches, the places where some of history's greatest visual imprints had been left and remained still. The Giottos and the Titians were genuinely breathtaking—they would be in any situation. But it was something else to see them on the wall right next to altarpieces that were far from historical; they were, rather, part of the city's living, thriving faith. Gazing at the paintings as the people came and went and lit candles and kneeled down and bowed and wept and shuddered, little by little I began to get the sense that these pictures were not just pictures.

My relationship to art had always been emotional. My childhood had been dotted with fond memories about that Grant Wood exhibit, this Yoruba sculpture, these Renoir slides that my mother needed to organize for a lecture. My young adult years were full of discovering new favorites, new friends made of oil paint that lived on the wall. Museums were places for intellectual, emotional, and aesthetic workouts, conversations with the fixed image, and opportunities to live more richly.

But here, in Florence, among the incense and the organ music, my experience of art and my understanding of what it might mean to look at it shifted and grew. I met Annunciation after Annunciation, watched as each artist told a different story inside the exact same scene. Sometimes when the angel Gabriel came to tell Mary of her pregnancy with Jesus and of his eventual fate, she glowed, serene and enlightened. Sometimes she looked startled, like she wanted to ask her visitor if he was sure he had the right address. Sometimes she cowered, terror spreading across her face as her life changed forever. Sometimes she seemed almost defiant, as though she were saying, "Fine! Bring it on! I can take it!"

I had seen Annunciations before. Here, though, as they appeared again and again, I began to become more invested in the story, in the variations and the details each painter offered, in the underlying meanings. And the Pietàs—they threw me against the wall. Every cool marble sculpture of the older Mary cradling her son's body after the Crucifixion was a variation on loss and sorrow, tenderness and lamentation. My own grief erupted in front of these sculptures, which expressed physically so many of the things I didn't know how to name or say. I knew that there was an inversion of sorts, that I had lost a parent and not a child, but it didn't matter. Those final months of caretaking had reversed our roles, and the aches I carried with me were saturated with the statues' parent–child intimacy.

Rabbi Arthur Green writes that "sacred myth describes a deep and ineffable reality, one so profound that it is not given to expression except through the veil of narration, through encapsulation in a story."[10] In cathedral after cathedral, I became more engaged in the mythic structures of Christianity. These foundational stories seemed to serve as archetypes for humanity and yet pointed at something beyond just human experience—this "deep and ineffable reality." The allegorical level and this other, more subterranean level did a powerful dance, one with the other, and they with me, the viewer.

There are several reasons that medieval and Renaissance churches were so richly decorated. One important one, however, was related to the fact of the general laity's illiteracy; the art on the walls taught the stories of the New Testament (and, sometimes, the Hebrew Bible). The best art, in doing so, distilled a lot of words and stories down to their principal mythic shapes, to the central themes at the heart of Christian faith.

The Pietà, as it turns out, didn't become a popular image until the Middle Ages. Then it emerged almost suddenly, for a few reasons. Europe had been devastated by plague, so the image of Jesus's death was especially powerful and relevant. While it wasn't safe for the grieving Europeans to embrace their contagious, dying loved ones, Mary could—and by doing so, she enacted their specific longing for closeness in mourning. At the same time, the Eucharist had begun to be reserved for priestly elites, so the image of a layperson

—Mary—literally receiving the Christ in her arms had an even more palpable, almost intoxicating, power.[11]

In religion, symbology is inescapable. The Divine, and the human relationship with the Divine, is vast, complex, and beyond language. There's no way to explain God in direct words. Rather, as a way of pointing at and expanding our notion of ultimate existence, symbols create a kind of shorthand. Jewish theologian Neil Gillman puts it this way: "We borrow aspects of familiar human experience to express a complex set of truths about a reality that transcends everyday experience."[12] How could it be any other way? We use what we have.

This, then, explains why there's so much anthropomorphism in the first place. Again: "The Torah speaks in the language of humans."[13] When Jews say *Avinu Malkeinu*, "Our Father, our King," it's not because we really believe that God is either literally a parent (stern, loving, or both) or king (benevolent, exacting, or both). Rather, we need some way to relate to the Divine—to the perfect unity, the transcendent power, the infinite expansiveness—that reflects our own feelings of smallness in comparison. Kabbalists might say that God's true nature contains aspects of both loving-kindness and justice—so these metaphors of father and king express something fundamental to the Divine nature. More rationalist theologians might say that God's nature transcends even those categories, but that this familiar metaphor helps to articulate our relationship to this mighty expansiveness, that it helps us situate ourselves in prayer and thus find God.

Critical to these metaphors is the fact that they're malleable, changable. As Mennonite pastor Shane Hipps explains, "the strength of metaphors is in their ability to anchor and explain ideas without defining hard or rigid boundaries."[14] There are many different depictions of Mary encountering the angel Gabriel when he comes to tell her that she will give birth to (according to Christian theology) the son of God, a messiah who will suffer and die young. What this encounter is and what it means might depend on how the artist painting her needs to enter this interaction. What it means that God is called *Avinu Malkeinu* in Jewish liturgy depends on the person with the prayer book in his or her hand. Certainly, the phrase can evoke the sort of patriarchal domination that sends many feminists reeling, that I found so off-putting even when I was finding my way back to services. But it can also evoke the feeling of a small child looking to a parent for comfort and safety, a feeling of submission to a greater force and liberation from self-importance, or a yearning for justice in the world. How these symbols and myths manage to be so powerful and lasting is that they both name something just outside the grasp of articulation, and that they are porous enough to name several things at once.

One lonely night after I had gotten to Rome, I sat in a pizza parlor with a margarita slice, a glass of red wine, and *Les Guérillères* by Monique Wittig. Using the lore of an ancient culture of her own invention, she explained how myths had the power to restructure human DNA, as it were. To become part of the person holding them.

> They say, like Esée you can steal power over life and death, like her become universal. They say, you advance with the sun's disc on your head, like Othar of the golden countenance who represents love and death.
> They say, in your anger you exhort Out, who upholds the sky and whose fingers touch the earth, to shatter its celestial vault. They say, conquered like Itaura, you readjust the two halves of your body, heaven and earth, you stand erect and go shrieking, creating monsters at every step.[15]

Imitatio Dei. Wittig makes it clear how strongly myths are to be inscribed upon the body, to sink under the skin. We become our myths. For Christians, the story of suffering can be found in the Crucifixion. It doesn't just reflect human pain, it changes it, shapes it, gives the religious Christian a way to reach out for and understand God in that pain, and a place to look for release from that pain. For us Jews, the central story of suffering is that of slavery in Egypt and redemption from it. We say that there are seventy faces of the Torah—there are an infinite number of ways to understand each event, each story, each mythic archetype, the lived experience of this Torah, and God's role in it. Myths are prisms that we can turn and turn and turn again, and the light refracts and reflects, brightly, into our hearts, each time a different color.

I spent the brief time I had in Italy intoxicated by gold leaf and silence. Altogether, I only had eight days for traveling in Florence and Rome. I preferred to explore fewer places with the chance of getting to know them, rather than jumping from city to city. As I traversed winding streets, returned to my hostel, sat in an open courtyard with gelato, waited in line at the Uffizi, prowled the Vatican museum, and sat in a café with my notebook, the questions that the great painters of Christian art asked about the human encounter with God followed after me. Standing before Crucifixions and Assumptions of the Virgin into heaven, in church after church, I started to feel something. I couldn't name it, but I began to notice a difference between the clean, cool feeling that I associated with museums and the subtle electricity that hummed in these buildings.

The dense lightness that I had begun to meet in my walks around Providence was here, and it was bigger. Through the Brunelleschi chapels and the Michelino frescoes, through being there at mass time and being there as the voices of the choirboys lilted, I felt some of what twentieth-century theologian Rudolf Otto called the *mysterium tremendum,* a feeling that comes "sweeping like a gentle tide, pervading the mind with a tranquil mood of deepest worship."[16] Here, though, unlike in Providence, it was clear to me that the mood of the churches was affecting my own inner states. Somehow, I could feel the church's purpose surrounding me. Most houses of worship have a certain kind of palpable vibe, perhaps the residue of so many prayers, or perhaps even of the sacred itself. The paintings inside these Italian churches felt like they had some sort of intention that animated the art, and the spaces themselves absolutely buzzed with it.

Here, for the first time, I began to suspect that those feelings of melting that I experienced on my Providence night walks might be related, somehow, to some sort of official religious mechanism—that tucked inside that feeling, there might be something for which somebody might use the word *God*. It made a certain kind of funny, illogical sense that I would be able to start asking these questions while visiting a faith center not of my own tradition. It may have been safer for me to notice magic within the strictures of organized religion in a completely alien context—there was never any danger that I'd become a practicing Catholic, after all. I was a Jew, and I knew that. But at the time my relationship to Judaism was weird, and uncertain. A familial relationship to my heritage was never in question, but attendence at a year's worth of Friday night services hadn't exactly made me an unquestioning believer. If anything, it made me less comfortable than ever, because I couldn't reject the religion outright as I once had. I had begun to enjoy services as a cultural thing, and I could get the ethical aspect of the Yom Kippur services, but when they said Avinu Malkeinu, I still pictured an angry daddy up in the sky with a crown on his head.

I was in the middle of a long, slow shift to belief. At the time, each incremental bit of receptivity to a new idea, to a new way of looking at the world, was so infinitesimal that I never considered myself in the middle of a sea change. I seemed to hold certain questions under my tongue, letting them dissolve slowly while I continued to espouse the beliefs I'd always held—each day, perhaps, just a little bit less loudly. In Italy I thought of myself as a secular Jew entranced by the power of one of the world's mythic structures. If something else was sneaking into my bloodstream at the time, I wasn't aware of it until it was far too late.

"Images and names of God enable us to approach the divine, but they can't quite get us there," observes Kabbalah scholar Daniel Matt. Rather. "They keep us at a safe distance."[17] And here, in Italy, I was willing to creep slightly closer than I ever had—but I very much needed the safe distance offered by the pictures and the stories of somebody else's religion. I certainly wasn't ready to be stripped of everything I had believed since I was thirteen years old.

After all, if I had understood at that time that these intimations of a larger presence could be connected to God, and that these experiences—and my faith—would only be strengthened and honed by religion and Torah and synagogue, I would have run screaming. The whiplash would have been too severe, the implications for my life too serious for me to be able to contemplate. It was much safer to start asking questions about religion's power on somebody else's turf. It was one thing to appreciate religious symbolism, another entirely to actually *be* religious. Becoming fascinated by the master stories of Christianity allowed me the more remote vantage I needed at the time, and made it possible for me to skittishly approach Judaism—and God—at my own gradual pace.

Merton writes of his own travels to Italy that he "was visiting the great shrines of Rome not for right reasons, but not for wrong either—shrines built for instruction of those who can't understand higher."[18] That may have been true for me as well. At the time I would have been neither willing nor able to understand anything more explicitly religious than art on a mythical and allegorical level, or to bring these insights closer to home. Meeting the sacred in the paintings of Florentine cathedrals would have to suffice.

As I moved further into senior year—having somehow banked enough credits to graduate on time—I became increasingly eager to return to the more social world that I had once inhabited. Writing and my ongoing midnight walks gave me a time and a place to enter into the grief that I still carried around, and still needed to express. More and more, though, I was able to spend the remainder of my day in class and working at the campus café and out with friends—some of whom had weathered my mother's death with me, and some of whom were new, with whom I was relieved not to have that reference point. I played darts and drank Guinness at the Grad Center Bar. I went dancing with Gabe, Pete, Chitra, Sarah, and Beth at the new club downtown. At night, old ghosts and the squeezing pressure in my chest would come to life, crawl around, demand attention. But most of the time, during the day, I managed to keep myself more or less together.

I started dating again. In February, after a semester or so of friendship, Gabe and I decided to see if we'd hit it off romantically. He was cultured and clever, with a mischievous streak. We had fun, spent a lot of time on the dance floor or cooking elaborate meals based on some exotic cheese or truffle that one of us had found at the market. Most importantly, Gabe was a very, very nice person, and gave me as much support and affection as he could as I navigated my way slowly back to life after mourning.

I couldn't explain to him what happened to me as I stood on the hill, a block from my house, somehow unable to move—but then again, I couldn't explain it to anybody. He noticed that I sometimes tuned in to some other channel when we were sitting in an empty park or listening to his friend's classical choir sing. Though he had no clue where I went at those times, it didn't particularly bother him, and he let me do whatever it was that I needed to do. It was okay.

Gabe had grown up in a religious family, and he invited me home to D.C. for Passover. I was a bit nervous about navigating a holiday among "real" Jews who did things like keep kosher and refrain from driving on holidays. Sure enough, I found myself (much to my later embarrassment) ranting about theories of biblical authorship and feminist critiques of Judaism to Gabe's bearded, pious father after the Seder. Fortunately, the man took my outbursts more or less in stride. He smiled, nodded politely, and managed, somehow, not to have any of the fundamentalist reactions that I expected of religious people. It still hadn't occurred to me that some of them might be a bit more sophisticated and well read than that.

The seven days between the end of finals and graduation were called Senior Week, a notorious time for last hurrahs. Philip, the art educator for whom I had interned in New York and freelanced a bit this last year, lived on Cape Cod, right on the beach. He was going to be out of town that week, he said, and offered to let me bring some friends to house sit—it was clearly a graduation gift, though he never framed it as such.

We—eight of us—loaded our cars with groceries, sunscreen, and books on which we would never be graded, and we set up camp in

Philip's country home. We took long walks in the woods and played a stripped-down version of softball in the sand, poked our toes in the water and confirmed that it was still too cold to swim. We cooked feasts for brunch and dinner and spent hours hunched over the Scrabble board. We dared one another to do silly things, took day trips to Provincetown, drank wine and danced to pop music in the living room until we were all too tired to continue. It was glorious peace.

One morning, not long after waking up, I walked out to Philip's wooden porch in my nightgown, fresh coffee in hand. The air was fragrant, the sun warm on my bare legs. It was nice just to sit. I took a deep, contented breath. Suddenly I noticed that, for the first time in as long as I could remember, there was no constricted feeling in my chest. I didn't want to cry. I didn't feel broken. There were just lungs, and quiet, and a lovely May morning.

Something had begun to heal itself, tentatively. Graduation was around the corner. Somehow, it seemed, I was ready to move into a new life—one not entirely defined by grief.

FOUR

Most of my friends began thinking about postgraduation plans sometime during the spring of senior year, March or April. I had started looking for a job in October. After so much instability and interruption and change, I was anxious to know what would happen next, and to have a little bit of control over my fate. I didn't entirely care where I ended up, so long as I ended up somewhere.

One of the people who had agreed to meet with me was at the San Francisco Museum of Modern Art; they had, I'd been told, some "exciting possibilities" coming up that would include creating jobs connecting art and new media. I arranged to visit my grandparents in Palm Springs over my winter break and to take a side trip up to San Francisco. I'd meet with my contact at this museum and with a few other people at different institutions, and stay with my one friend in northern California.

I had never been to the Bay Area before. In the shuttle from the airport, the hills rose up slowly in the distance. Everything felt pastel. The air was wide and clear. We drove onto the Stanford campus; it was sunny in the middle of January, and students were milling around in T-shirts and sandals. The buildings were red clay, Spanish-style adobe, which felt astonishingly relaxed next to the neat New England brick to which I was so accustomed.

I got to Ariel's co-op and she pounced on me like an excited four-year-old. We dropped my stuff in her room and she dragged me around the building, narrating and explaining and introducing me to people and telling stories and generally yammering away at an excitedly accelerated speed. Her roommate, Marcus, was a seven-foot-tall Viking in tie-dye who bounced up and down like a puppy and whose sense of humor could only be described as bawdy. "Liquor?" he'd bellow when someone mentioned the possibility of spirits. "I hardly know her!" People in Rhode Island did not talk like this. It wasn't that there weren't hippies or co-op types at my school, it was just that they were of a slightly different breed—more reserved, more apt to talk about environmental politics than the complexities of their dating life with a virtual stranger. I was shocked; I was enthralled.

Truth be told, I did go to California harboring a partly secret desire to see whether Ariel and I might get back together. As soon as we were in the same place again, though, it was evident that the stars had realigned over a year and a half of relatively minimal contact. Though many of the things that had made us click initially were still present, they were already taking different forms. Over the course of a few days, a lot of old stuff fell away and the foundation for a more solid friendship began to emerge. This freed me up in a lot of ways; perhaps it's no surprise that I began dating Gabe not long after getting back to the East Coast.

The second day of my visit to San Francisco, I had a meeting at a museum in the middle of Golden Gate Park. I took the bus for what felt like a very long time before finally arriving at my stop. Haze and fog from the ocean hung in the air. There was a little bit of sun peeking in through the trees. The place smelled dark and earthy—eucalyptus and cedar. There were plaster statues outside the museum. There were kids, dogs, roller bladers. The "informational interview" was fine—inconsequential—but when I walked back out into the park, it was dusk and the sky was poised between the bright blue of day and something deeper and more serious. In the Jerusalem Talmud, twilight is called "a drop of blood balanced on the edge of a sword."[1] That was the color of the sky. Standing in the middle of the city-forest, somehow in this moment, I knew that I was home.

It was dark when I got back to Stanford. The moon shimmered

under a layer of clouds; it was a good moon. I stood outside Ariel's dormitory for as long as I could take the overwhelming sky and the sensations, and then I unplugged and went in. I was still building up my tolerance for joy.

In New York, Ariel had rhapsodized about her people, about the *amaaazing* community waiting for her back in the Bay Area. I had friends from college too, but I didn't feel as compelled to talk and talk and talk about them. The idea of "chosen family," as she called it, sounded kind of silly and New Agey to me, but at the time I had just shrugged my shoulders; she likes her friends, I thought, that's nice. In any case, it was unthinkable to her that I wouldn't meet her people while I was in town, so she arranged for us all to go out the last night of my visit.

Jack and Rebecca showed up at Ariel's to pick us up. Jack was a wry, lanky, long-haired network engineer with a propensity for clever banter. Rebecca seemed to be all black curls and purple motorcycle jacket. She was expressive and immediately warm, and within about thirty seconds she was speaking with me as though I was already a loved and trusted old friend. We sat around chatting, and then there was a strange noise outside the window, like a whistle, except with undulating vocal cords. I jumped. Ariel, however, nonplused, lifted her hand to her mouth and made the same noise back, in return.

"Teresa's here," she said.

A tall, solidly built woman with long hair and torn jeans came in. Her face was stunningly beautiful, but it was the kind of beauty that takes a moment to register because she did not carry herself like A Beautiful Woman. Teresa, I learned later, had grown up on a farm and was a master of sword fighting. She plopped herself down, and the chitchat continued until it was time to go.

We drove up to the city, stopping at Jack's girlfriend Cass's apartment in the Lower Haight before dinner and dancing. I was wearing a black skirt and my vintage (that is to say, from Goodwill) Harley Davidson T-shirt. Cass—wiry, chatty, bubbly—announced that while a T-shirt was fine, she had the perfect top for me to borrow if we were going out on the town. She promptly produced something shiny, silver, and more daringly fun than I would ever have thought to buy for myself.

Where I came from, one did not lend one's clothing to people one had just met. One did not even lend one's clothing to friends, generally speaking. But according to the logic of this community, I was one of the People of Ariel. This not only meant that I wasn't a total stranger; by Cass's estimation, I was, in a way, already part of the clan.

Ariel had already changed into dancing clothes—a rainbow-striped tube top—as had Teresa. I shrugged my shoulders. I put on the shirt. We set out for the evening's adventure.

As we got to the restaurant, I was surprised at my own level of comfort. The idea that people could decide so quickly and effortlessly that they liked me seemed foreign, bizarre. Who, I wondered to myself, lends her clothes to someone she's just met? I had long been shy and hard to get to know, and after running my mother's hospice, after managing my grief and other people's reactions to it—after everything, I was more introverted than ever. The sort of easy trust with which these new people regarded me was unexpected.

They had an energy. With Ariel's friends, one had a sense that whatever we were doing—browsing in the kids' section of a bookstore, going out for Ethiopian food, cooking for thirty-five people in the co-op—was the most exciting and wonderful thing that could possibly be happening at the moment. Nobody was playing it cool. Nobody seemed compelled to act as though they'd seen it all before, whether or not they had. When someone was sad, he or she was very sad and all of the sadness came out. The feelings were there, unrestrained and uninhibited by the presence of others. There are a lot of ways I'd interpret the phrase "being present in the moment," and a lot of things that I'd suggest it might mean. This way of being, of interacting, is one of them.

The Buddhist writer Alan Watts describes Zen as "spontaneously intelligent living, without calculation, and without rigid conceptual distinctions."[2] There was an open impulsiveness to these people, a willingness to take in whatever might be in front of them and marvel at its wisdom and quirks, to not get too caught up in how or where it was supposed to fit into a bigger schema. The writer Geneen Roth talks about the need to celebrate "for no reason at all except that the sun is out and the color coral exists and the traffic light just turned green, and you are part of the ongoing wonder and the wonder is part of you."[3] These people were like that—they would notice a peony poking out of the cracks of a building, a guy across the street who looked like a TV show character from the eighties, or a restaurant sign misspelled just enough to be hysterically funny. On the East Coast, I often had the feeling that college was a gigantic cocktail party, with everyone looking over the shoulder of their conversation partner to see who else had just come into the room. Here, there was none of that pretension —just the sense that whatever experience we were in the middle of having, with whoever happened to be invited along, was plenty groovy on its own.

By the time I returned to Providence in January, my postgraduation move to San Francisco was a done deal; the feeling of contentment that I got walking around the city was incentive enough. The fact that Jack and Cass and I began trading goofy, friendly e-mails almost immediately after my return to the East Coast only augmented my sense that this was where I needed to go next. Gabe was supposed to come with me, but at the last minute he was offered his dream job in London, so we fondly parted ways. Both of us knew that the relationship wasn't serious enough to warrant changing course at this critical juncture in our young lives, and my sense of being pulled to the Bay Area was palpable. It was as though there were a string tied somewhere behind my navel, tugging me west.

Jack and his roommate, Davey, lived in a crumbling, rundown, bi-level in-law apartment that had the feeling of a renovated garage. The place was set back from the street, giving them something of a straggly front yard, which they littered with tiki lamps and, later, a small Jacuzzi. The lower level consisted of one room: a large, open space with shabby, moldy carpeting, a couple of couches dragged in from the street, a gigantic television and state-of-the-art entertainment system, and a wall of movies (on tape—within a year or two they would switch to DVD with zeal). There was also band equipment—drums, speakers, and a couple of basses—and the buzzing, humming rack on which their server system lived. Davey was also a network guy, so he and Jack had cobbled together a server of old computer parts, using bandwidth they had somehow pilfered from *Wired* magazine. They doled out free e-mail and website services to everyone within their rather extended circle of friends.

Outside, rickety wooden steps led up to two bedrooms, a dusty kitchen used mostly to store leftover takeout, and a back room piled high with unsorted books—tech manuals, sci-fi, and Taoist philosophy, mostly—as well as old monitors and hard drives that hadn't yet found a home or a use. There was a computer in every room, with a webcam attached. The stereo system could be managed from any terminal; any song selected would then be heard throughout the house. There were even speakers in the bathroom, as well as plenty of grime.

There was always beer in the fridge. There tended to be twenty-four-year-old guys milling around at all hours, playing video games or just hanging out. Despite the profusion of fancy tech stuff, the door wasn't usually locked. We were pretty much always welcome.

I had been in town about a week when Jack and Davey had one of their then frequent gatherings, so I got to meet the rest of the usual suspects. Everyone had already been friends for so long that the stories were complex and intertwined, initially somewhat hard to follow.

Ariel and Rebecca went to college together. They had met Teresa at some point along the way and adopted her immediately. Jack had joined Rebecca's band, Dublin Hills—that's how they found him. He and Cass had gone to the same high school in Arkansas, and they'd been together for about ten years by the time I met them. Ariel's new girlfriend, Kelly, had been one of Rebecca's first friends in college. Davey had been found by Jack through a roommate referral service some seven years earlier; even more than Jack and Cass, Jack and Davey were a bit like an old married couple.

Then there were Lida and Michael, though almost nobody referred to them this way. They were the kind of people who are prone to nicknames—she was Buttercup, Rabbit, Bunny, or La Grande Dame. He was Wolf, Coyote, or Maximillian. They were both heavily tattooed and intricately pierced, and Lida adorned herself with outrageousness the likes of which I had never seen. She tended to make a lot of her own clothes and jewelry, and even when she bought something retail she'd tend to improve it further, adding crystals or spiders or flowers or little plastic doll heads to the hem of a skirt, or running battery-operated electric wire through the bones of a corset so that it glowed red in the dark. Sometimes she modeled for tattoo magazines, but her day job was working—face piercings and all—as an administrator at a Fortune 500 company. Michael favored Hawaiian shirts and waxing philosophical about anything from ancient Egyptian society or contemporary Chinese politics to initiation rites and the Italian Mafia. He was pleased when I showed up, because someone, finally, could talk to him about Ugaritic and inconsistencies in the Bible. He, like almost everybody else in this group—save a couple of the kids from the Stanford end of things—had taught himself everything he knew about computers, and had managed to get himself a pretty good job as a tech guy. Bunny (Lida) and Coyote (Michael) had been married for about four years at this point. Coyote and Jack were friends from way back. Lida had dated Jack briefly about as long ago.

There were other people, like Davey's girlfriend, Ophelia, and Ophelia's ex-boyfriend (and Davey's best friend) Juan; there were Ophelia's friends and the people they dated; there was Cass's roommate, Amelia (also a friend from Arkansas), and all her friends; there were lots and lots of geekboys and of course everybody related in some way to Dublin Hills.

There were a lot of people.

Thomas Merton writes, "Love is our true destiny. We do not find the meaning of life by ourselves alone."[4] My own destiny had only just begun to unfold.

With my new California friends, spirituality wasn't this strange, hidden subject that it was—or felt like it was, anyway—in Providence. They talked about their inner lives and mystical experiences with the same casualness and frequency that they talked about everything else—there wasn't anything to hide, so why would you?

When I first met Ariel, she told me all about how she practiced something of a do-it-yourself spirituality with Rebecca and Teresa; Cass had a similar bent, but was more of a loner about it. As I understood it, this involved some combination of what Ariel called "energy channeling," trying to stay in tune with nature, and paying quite a bit of attention to the force that I had begun meeting in the Providence night.

My new friends talked about the great unity underlying and pervading all things, in a way that was similar to the writings of Rabbi Arthur Green:

> The essential truth of mysticism [is] that . . . the unity of being can be discovered by a disciplined training of the mind toward insight . . . The understanding that God is the innermost reality of all that is, and that God and the universe are related not primarily as Creator and creature, but as a deep structure and surface, is key.[5]

Little by little, I began to see that my new friends, and Green, were right about one thing: this force was everywhere when I tuned in to it, when I allowed myself to feel its presence. I never did become interested in doing things the way they did, though. Their eclectic practice was, like the Christianity of the Italian cathedrals, intriguing, but it didn't feel like my religious expression—not that I was totally sure what mine was.

But, nonetheless, with Ariel, Rebecca, Cass, and Teresa, I became gradually more comfortable sharing my own experiences, allowing my understanding of God to get bigger, more relaxed, more porous.

I began to use certain kinds of lingo much more freely—the Universe, the Divine, God—and to ask certain kinds of questions about what those words meant, how one accessed this Big Bigness, and what its implications might be for my life.

In her book *Enduring Grace*, religion scholar Carol Lee Flinders cites the historian Carolly Erickson, who "observes that when you live in a culture that accepts the authenticity of visions, you know roughly how to behave when the ground trembles and the room starts to glow."[6] Among people who accepted my "visions," such as they were, I felt a new permission to embrace them in a way that I never had. The experiences continued, bigger than ever—glowing as I stood on a walkway overlooking a park, transported by the smell of incense on my walk to work, dissolving, over and over again, as the cars rushed past and the noise of the city rose around me. Now, however, I regarded them as normal, and slowly began to to think of myself as a person full of longing and thirst for encounters with the Divine.

In the end, I didn't wind up working for SFMOMA; the mysterious jobs that they were going to create never materialized. It was probably for the best that I was forced to reevaluate my work ambitions, though, since I already had enough hangups about feeling like I was supposed to live the life that my mother hadn't been able to. It was just as well that I not fall into her career path out of inertia or nostalgia.

Almost by accident, I found something at a publisher of religion books. My job was quite entry level, but since they put out the kind of books I loved to read, it seemed like a good environment in which to learn something. And, probably even more important, the gig realigned me with my own passions and interests.

Somewhere during the job hunt, I had discovered a group for women in the tech industry to meet and network, called GrrrlGeeks. (This was back in the day when start-ups were looking to hire just about any young, intelligent person—actual computer savvy wasn't necessary.) Just as I got on the listserv, I discovered that some folks were splintering off to start a group specifically for the people focused on "content," as it was called back then, and I knew right away that I should follow them.

The GrrrlWordies' first real-life meeting was held at a tapas bar in the Mission District. About twenty women, many of whom were already friends, showed up for sangria and small bites decked out in vintage eyeglasses, Hello Kitty accessories, and unmitigated sass. The group was composed primarily of freelance writers, and a couple of them immediately began offering advice to me—the newbie—on how to pitch stories, get to know editors, and demand fair payment for work. They also invited me to come hang out the next night, since this swing band was playing up on the Haight, and it was guaranteed to be a swell time.

It didn't take long to realize that the chick scribes (and their assorted, nonwriterly boyfriends and girlfriends) were a never-ending source of decadent fun. We went to the Rhumba Bug on Tuesdays for New Wave night and Clementina Street Station on Thursdays for British Invasion pop. They took me to costume parties hosted by their Burning Man buddies with themes like "guests must use tin foil or duct tape as their outfit's organizing principle" or "guests must dress as a Muppet and stay in character the entire time." There were once-a-month feasts at rotating locations in which 1940s high glamour served as the benchmark for both dress code and restaurant selection.

This was San Francisco in the late nineties—money was everywhere, and the city was in a good mood. There were always parties. Some events were on regular rotation—Ophelia and her downstairs neighbors' two-story Heaven and Hell extravaganza every February; Jack and Davey's Big Kahuna barbeque in August; Lida and Michael's themed birthday parties every year; Halloween on the Castro; and half a dozen other citywide festivals at various points on the calendar. There were also, of course, plenty of one-off products of someone's genius whimsy. Many of the city's most intelligent and creative people invested untold time and energy into creating ways for other people to enjoy being alive. The results were, often, breathtaking in both madness of scope and precision of detail.

I wound up living with a friend from high school who had

started doing serious drag—he had been part of the Chicago club kid scene in college, but now he was buying wigs to go with his silver lamé sandals. Occasionally he let me borrow clothes; more often, he inspired me to comb thrift stores for outré treasures of my own. Sometimes he did my makeup before I went out, transforming me into an angel, a demon, or an old Hollywood screen siren just for the entertainment value.

The conventions with which I had been raised had little to no relevance in this culture. Everything was fair game. Gender roles, gender identity, choices about who to date, and physical appearance all seemed to be infinitely mutable, playgrounds to explore rather than assumptions to take for granted. All of us were exploring our imaginations without intimidation or fear. What was there to fear? There was much permission—even encouragement—for me to write my own map, to invent myself anew again and again. I could figure out where my own boundaries were, but there weren't going to be any imposed from without, that was for sure. This was the same open terrain I first sought out in punk and philosophy, but now there was no sign of the horizon.

Here, bigger was better, and costumes were always encouraged. Small, impish horns were great, but if one took the time to craft some gigantic ram's horns out of papier-mâché—well, that'd be even more wonderful. Store-bought fairy wings could be a starting point, but only after gluing large white feather boas to them and matching the wings with a white ball gown and white platform stacked shoes, bleaching one's hair blond, and then immersing oneself in a cosmic mother lode of rhinestones and glitter would a girl be fit to greet San Francisco properly.

Playing dress-up was a way to celebrate, to rejoice, to reinvent. It was a way to stretch the boundaries of self, to let go of fixed ideas about who we had to be. Silliness and fun were cardinal virtues. Refusing to play was the cardinal sin. There was always somewhere to go, some punk rock karaoke night, some performance piece acted by robots, some rave party in the offices of a promising start-up, some Dublin Hills gig, some impromptu cabaret with an alien invasion theme.

——

One of my coworkers at the publisher was into yoga. After a few conversations in which she enthused about how "totally incredible" it was, I agreed to join her one day after work. We walked over to the studio—just on the other side of Market Street—and she pointed me at the dressing room, where I could change into my stretchy pants and tank top. She helped me line up my mat at the back of the room (more advanced students practiced closer to the front). Then, without warning, the instructor was going at it with rapid-fire commands. Feet together, hands together, breathe in. Hands over your head now, breathe out, gaze at your thumbs. Bending slowly down, spine aligned, breathe in. Hands on the floor now: head up, breathe out. And so on, walking us through each breath and each pose, until we were holding poses for five breaths, then breathing out to change our weight and position again. I worked hard this first time, trying to follow the instructions, peeking up to see what other people were doing so that I could understand the posture, and trying at the same time to remember to keep my breaths in sync. I felt awkward and galumphing, like a chubby hippo, but in moments here and there, I caught my groove. And it felt so good! This alignment, this breathing, this pulling on muscles I hadn't noticed in years of using the Stairmaster at the gym.

As I breathed, I remembered techniques I had read about in books on Buddhist meditation or medieval mysticism—on the inhale, I pictured the air generating from a warm fireplace inside my solar plexus. On the exhale, I pictured it widening, swirling around the inside of my body, particularly through the muscles that I was pulling. On the inhale, I imagined that I was drawing down breath from the skies through a funnel on the top of my head. On the exhale, I felt it expand the recesses of my skin.

I became a yoga class regular. Over time, the poses melted one into another. I got deeper and deeper into the postures, twisting my spine around practically in a circle, resting my head on the floor, folded over from a standing or sitting position. Standing on the mat, palms together, I would look at my fingers. I had never paid much attention to my fingers before, and now, I often noticed them with surprise. There were capillaries, nerve endings, muscle and fat in there right at that moment! Connected to me! As I breathed in, a slow, clean ripening inhale, widening my lungs until I was full, I watched the blood in my fingertips dance. I exhaled, drop by drop, until I was empty. I inhaled again, expanding slow and wide like a human balloon. The blood in my heart pumped and surged, sent warm redness through my arms back to the fingers. I deflated again slowly, and the tide returned to the shore.

Toward the end of each class, the poses would become more concentrated and my breathing would get bigger, wider. Everything would begin to sparkle. Then we would all sit in lotus position for a moment, and the class would chant something in Sanskrit. My friend had explained that it was the famous mantra "the jewel in the lotus." Sometimes I just sat there as they chanted, sometimes I would try to imitate the sounds that they made. Unlike the rest of the class, this part never felt entirely comfortable to me.

In *Selling Spirituality: The Silent Takeover of Religion*, religion scholars Jeremy Carrette and Richard King observe that "generally speaking, popular yoga practice in the West has emphasized physical postures and breath control techniques, but tends to ignore the ethical and ascetic dimensions of yoga practice," thus "transforming yoga from a set of renunciatory practices for attaining liberation from the cycle of rebirths either into a psychologized 'spirituality of the self' on the one hand or into a secularized system of therapy, physical exercise and/or mood enhancement on the other."[7]

In traditional yoga practice, the Sanskrit chanting—and the meaning of the chanting, and its connection to all of the postures—would be key. At my after-work yoga class, it was treated as little more than a postscript. Years later, I would look up the meaning of "the jewel in the lotus" and discover that it was considered the mantra of the bodhisattva (enlightened being) of compassion and was meant to help the chanter perfect the practices of generosity, pure ethics, patience, tolerance, and altruism. I certainly never learned that at the studio on Folsom Street. Disconnected from its religious context, this Westernized yoga—much like the Westernized Buddhism and many other forms of "spirituality" often sold in the contemporary marketplace—lost yoga's underlying focus on giving to others.

Which is not to deny its power on me. Even if one accepts that the Western notion of spirituality hinges upon individual (rather than communal) transformation . . . well, little by little, I was watching myself become transformed. After class, I'd feel clear, like my mind was crystal, not bogged down with a parade of thoughts and chatter. It was not dissimilar from those moments in Providence when everything seemed to stop, but instead of being blissy-tingly, I was sharp, alert. The feeling never lasted long—the chattering monkeys of past and future, longing and fantasy were too persistent for that. But, more and more, I began to understand that "being in the present moment" was perhaps one of the goals of good living, and that watching my breath was one way to do it.

Later I would see that this "spirituality" stuff, if taken to its logical extreme, would require noticing more than the miracle of my own fingertips, and that it would demand my leaving those forms of practice that didn't encourage a more wide-ranging vision. It would require placing compassion, generosity, altruism, and ethics at the forefront, rather than my own ecstatic experiences. The spiritual pyrotechnics were amazingly cool, to be sure, but eventually I would begin to understand that they weren't enough.

At the time, of course, the changes happening within were magnificent—watching my breath swirl around my body, going deeper into the poses, visiting the present moment. Individual transformation is necessary, and it's miraculous to watch it happen, little by little, every day. These experiences offered important tools that would serve me in good stead for years to come. I'm grateful for everything that I learned on the yoga mat, although I would come to figure out that this practice, at least as it was being taught at my hipster downtown studio, wouldn't be able to take me as far as I needed to go.

A college friend who was working for a feminist newsmonthly in Boston called one day. One of their upcoming themes was religion, and while they had a pretty good handle on Judaism, Christianity, and Islam, they still needed somebody to do a story on nontradi-tional spirituality. I was in California, after all—could I help?

I was thrilled to get to write something for publication. I inter-viewed Ariel, Rebecca, Teresa, Cass, and a few of their friends about their beliefs. Jack (who wasn't into this stuff so much himself) sug-gested that I drop a line to his childhood friend Alex, in Savannah. I sent her an e-mail with a lot of the same questions that I had been asking everyone: How do you understand Deity? What does having a do-it-yourself spirituality mean to you? Does feminism factor in at all? She sent me back a reply the next day:

> For me, spirituality generates politics, slowly, insidiously. When you start to know that you are connected to all life, it rearranges a lot of the assumptions that make living in America comfortable. If you're trying to cultivate one kind of sensitivity—say, the kind that's needed to read Tarot or remember what phase of the moon it is, even in the city—eventually you run up against the heightened awareness that the person cleaning your office building is tired, is human, that somehow you are partly responsible for her being there since 4 a.m. Which is not a comfortable awareness. I think that feminism and poverty activism are inextricable at this point. Having standards for the quality of your life is a luxury. Having standards for the quality of everyone's life is radical, or insane. It's an absurdity that drinkable water is a class status marker... My feminism is becoming drastically refined away from "women should be able to be men if they want" to "everybody should get more time to have a life."

This, then, was the thing that I'd been struggling to articulate—the fact that beginning to pay attention to where I was, and the life I was living, might have implications for paying attention to the world around me. This idea had been churning under the surface of my understanding, but it hadn't yet managed to get up on the level of conscious thought.

Carol Lee Flinders talks about what happens when "you begin to recognize all the junctures in your daily life where you can either embrace [ethical] values or sidle on past." This is hard work, she says, and it "isn't completely pleasant, because going along on automatic is no longer an option . . . I no longer get to pretend I'm non-violent and still drive my car into town every time I feel like it."[8] I had slowly begun to realize that I might have to confront these issues someday, that I might have to start thinking about what I did and how it might reflect or contradict what I believed. The fact that Alex could articulate all this so strongly, and push me to think harder about it than I had yet, was certainly compelling. This was clearly someone with whom I needed to talk more.

She had included a note at the bottom of her e-mail asking what it was like to have studied religion in an academic setting. For, she said, she was thinking about doing a PhD in religious studies, or possibly looking into Unitarian seminary. She'd love some insights about what it's like to learn about this stuff at university.

And so we were off and running.

I had plenty of responses to her e-mail, and I answered her questions. She replied to my next e-mail, and then I to hers. She was working as a medical secretary. My job mostly involved data entry and mailing things. We both found that we had ample time to do more than was expected of us on the job and also to write long, thoughtful e-mails to each other every day. I sent her drafts of the short stories I was working on. She sent me long ruminations on what it was like to volunteer at her local old folks' home. We talked about feminism, spirituality, our communities; our questions about life and love; about God and how to live in a closer and more constant relationship with the Divine.

Jewish study is traditionally done in pairs: two people sitting over the Talmud, poring over the text, and batting back and forth what it might mean. It's understood that one person alone can't figure it all out—sparks fly only when two people challenge each other to think harder and more carefully about the issue at hand. Rabbinic texts are filled with aphorisms on the importance of study partners. "A knife can only be sharpened with another knife,"[9] they say. Or, "just as one piece of iron sharpens another, so two scholars sharpen each other's mind by discussion . . . Just as a fire does not ignite of itself, so words of Torah do not abide in him who studies by himself."[10]

Sometimes this kind of paired study feels a little bit like tennis. Sometimes it's like building something, slowly. Sometimes, as in the case of the informal partnering that Alex and I did through our in-boxes, it's an awful lot like jazz.

After leaving town to help a friend at her grandmother's funeral, Alex e-mailed,

It makes so much sense when you're there, in that between-space, whether it's moving day or the day after the funeral, Christmas or a christening, the moments when ordinary business is suspended and all your attention is supposed to go to this moment, this day, right here right now. To relationship and memory and objects. The wine goes in the chalice. The biscuit bowl goes in the car. It's such a relief to be reduced to seeing what's right in front of you. And to have everyone else stop talking in your ear about the Drachman report and the faxes to Tokyo and whatever noise people make all the time that isn't about anything you can put your hand on. You know?

I wrote back,

But in some ways, the between space is the proof that we're here, that we're doing things, we're living, building relationships, loving, gathering . . . The wine goes in the chalice. Because it's consecrating the rest of the moments in the day, the ordinary moments that aren't about wine and chalices, christening or death. I know it's hard to come back. But coming back to regular life is why going away from it was so important in the first place, no?

We jammed. We were pen pals, using the tools of new technology to kindle an ancient kind of relationship—without having ever met. It was a little weird, but it was also, in its own way, something of a miracle.

———

By the next January, Alex was in the midst of applying to Unitarian seminaries. There were three, one of which was in the Bay Area; she e-mailed to let me know that she'd be out to visit in a few weeks for her admissions interview, staying with Jack.

We met outside a small club where a friend of Cass's was singing. Alex was taller than I had imagined, quiet, with soft gray-blue eyes and fierce hugs. Nothing about her physical appearance particularly indicated that she was the person who had become one of my primary confidants over the last year and a half, except that she was.

"Oh, hey, it's you," she said, with a twinkle and a slightly impish grin. "Nice outfit." She meant the skin and bones that I had decided to put on for the occasion. I grinned back, and we went into the club.

A couple of days later, she met me at my place after her interview with the seminary in Berkeley.

"It was so much better than Harvard," she said. "Here, they asked me questions about things that matter—not, you know, church history." As we cooked and ate our chickpea curry, the conversation unfolded, as so many of our e-mails had unfolded, but looser, freer, more meandering.

After dinner, we walked up the hill from my house to the little café tucked away off the street. We sat in easy chairs by the roaring February fire, ate tiramisu, and raised our eyebrows knowingly as Alanis Morissette's "Thank U" came on the radio. At some point the conversation floated over to something that had come up a few times in recent e-mails, all this talk of "energy" and how it affected people. What *was* it? I had asked more than once—the first time after watching Cass put her hand on various points around a friend's torso, saying, "Hmm, it's warm over here, oh…yeah…a nice reddish-orange here, and…Oh! It's cold here, a bluish-green feeling…" and watching this woman start to cry, because she'd been having marital problems, and no wonder it was bluish and cold in the groin area.

I had consulted Alex for insight on this; she wrote and wrote and wrote about an electricity underlying everything, the way it rolls and connects, the way it affects and is affected by physical states in a lot of different ways. This all sounded lovely in theoretical form, but I still didn't totally get it.

Now, in person, she said, "Okay, one second."

She rubbed the palms of her hands together and closed her eyes, seemed to be breathing deeply and concentrating. She seemed to be holding the classic pose of hands in prayer; she pulled them slowly back from each other until her palms were about three inches apart.

"Gimme your hand," she said, nodding at the space between her palms.

I put my hand out, flat, and she put hers around mine, about an inch away from my skin on each side. She wasn't touching me. I felt something buzzing. It felt warm, like an invisible pressure. It wasn't just air; it was something else. Alex moved her hands, still parallel to one another, around in a small circle and I felt something like a small tornado on either side of my hand, with the point of the funnel—the most intense energy, pressure, heat—directly on my skin. I gave her a look that said, "What?"

She smiled and said, "Now, you do it." She took one hand away, so we just had two palms facing each other. I took a deep breath. I exhaled . . . out my palms. I felt something—the same thick, palpable something I had felt in the churches in Florence, the same warm pressure that Alex had just danced around my own hands. I felt a tremendous surge come out of my hands. Alex smiled a "See, I told you so" smile.

She took my hands and placed them in position, a few inches from each other. I breathed out my hands. A ball of energy swelled up between them. I breathed out again, a bigger exhale. The ball grew.

Over time, I'd figure out that if I breathed out my hands while my palm was resting on someone, I could move the energy—the qi, it's called in Chinese philosophy and medicine—from the palms of my hands into his or her body. Doing so is not radically dissimilar from the Hindu practice of Shaktipat or from the Japanese practice of Reiki—the latter of which, as the story goes, was discovered in ancient Buddhist texts by a Christian preacher trying to discover how Jesus healed by the laying on of hands.[11] There are also Jewish kabbalistic practices that involve energy transfer through touch, particularly in North African and Middle Eastern traditions.[12] Whatever it was that I was doing, I wasn't the first to have done it, evidently.

Alex watched me sit, entranced, with my new discovery for a couple of minutes, and then she put her hands over mine to get me to stop.

"This is a pretty dangerous toy, so be careful."

I looked at her quizzically. But it was so cool!

"No, really," she said. She was dead serious now. "You really don't want to poke around this stuff without a user's manual, and be careful if someone offers to do energy work on you. There are a lot of self-taught amateurs out there who think they know more than they do, and who think that knowing a few party tricks makes them spiritually *evolved*. You especially want to stay away from them."

Sure enough, Alex was right. Over the years, I've met plenty of people who were talented at shooting energy around a room or intuiting people's secrets, having or causing others to have ecstatic experiences, or even performing healings or the like, but who at the same time had an appalling lack of ethics, an inability to keep their desires in check, and/or the absolute arrogance to think that hurting others in the process of self-gratification was acceptable.

As Buddhist teacher Charlotte Joko Beck explains, "I meet all sorts of people who've had all sorts of experiences and they're still confused and not doing very well in their life. Experiences are not enough."[13] As entranced as I initially was with the fireworks, they cannot and should not be the yardstick by which we gauge spiritual maturity or power. Real power comes from doing painstaking work inside the dark, gnarly corners of the heart.

Spiritual pyrotechnics—these nifty, fantastical tricks and experiences—go down smooth, and for a lot of people, they're valuable as access into a different way of relating to the world. They're a shiny toy that entices us to ask new sorts of questions and lower our guard, that helps us to circle the perimeter of the Divine palace and (more important) to go looking for the keys to its inner chambers. These incidents are not the keys themselves, but they often lead us closer to them. That's not a bad thing.

But the danger lies in confusing these feel-good episodes with the path itself, as did the priest in a famous Zen story: "The founder of our sect," boasted the priest, "had such miraculous powers that he held a brush in his hand on one bank of the river, his attendant held up a paper on the other bank, and the teacher wrote the holy name of Amida [a Buddha] through the air. Can you do such a wonderful thing?"

The master Bankei replied lightly: "That is not the manner of Zen. My miracle is that when I feel hungry I eat, and when I feel thirsty, I drink."[14]

Spiritual pyrotechnics are fun, but at best, focusing only on this kind of encounter leaves us out of whack. At worst, it misses the point entirely.

Katrine, one of the GrrrlGeeks I had met at the tapas bar, had a boyfriend who was living in Spain. She traveled to Barcelona often to see him, sometimes smuggling a bottle of absinthe—the real stuff—back to the States.

She lived only a few blocks from me, and when we went out I usually stopped by her place to pick her up. Sometimes we'd decide to have a nip of the green dragon before, or in lieu of, cocktails. She would hunch over the glass, exuding mad scientist as she carefully dripped water onto a sugar-filled spoon, preparing the drink below for proper consumption. After some muttering and a careful stirring, she would pronounce the product worthy and we would toast whatever needed to be toasted. The absinthe—even with the sugar/water dilution—was bitter, but far from the taste itself, for me its allure was that it was romantic stuff, dangerous. And, besides, it gave me the pixies.

We would storm out into the night, dolled up for whatever party was on the docket. I would gaze lovingly at the streetlamps, captivated by the rainbows that glinted around the edges of the light. I would sweep my hand through the air and watch the imprint of my fingers linger against the black night sky. Everything twinkled—the glitter on my cheeks, the red beads in my necklace, the air, my friends, the music spilling idly from some passing window.

I was floating. It seemed that I was always floating in those days. Not on the absinthe, but on how beautiful and free it felt to be young, alive, twenty-three, and living in San Francisco. Watching my breath was beautiful, the rainbows on the lamps were beautiful, everything felt mystical and light, airy and full of limitless possibility.

Thomas Merton wrote,

> I remember how learnedly and enthusiastically I could talk for hours about mysticism and the experimental knowledge of God, and all the while I was stroking the fires of the argument with Scotch and soda . . . My internal contradictions were resolving themselves out, indeed, but still only on the plane of theory, not of practice.[15]

I was fascinated by everything I was learning, seemingly everywhere. The Sufi poetry and biographies of Catholic saints I devoured talked about immolation of the ego; the Buddhists spoke at length about the importance of seeing the world anew in every moment. I didn't really know what it all meant in reality, how to translate those concepts into practice, but I wasn't really concerned. Whether I was overtaken by strange experiences of energy and light or out surfing the city's music and frivolity until all hours, my life seemed characterized by a sort of glorious rapture.

Like Merton, I was full of enthusiasm. And certainly, on some level, I knew that someday, to go deeper, there might be some work. Augustine famously wrote, "Give me chastity, Lord, give me continence . . . but not yet!"[16] Whatever it was, I wasn't ready for it. And this? This living was just so delicious.

FIVE

Not long after moving to San Francisco, I decided to find a synagogue. I had grown to like Friday nights well enough in Providence, after all. I figured that in a new city, just as I had to know where I'd go to get my hair cut or in which cafés to sit with my laptop, so too I ought know where I'd go to services, in case I ever decided that I wanted to do such a thing.

I found a website with a listing of local synagogues and informal, lay-led prayer groups; there was nothing to do but check things out in person. Over the course of the next several months, I was offered an impressive survey of Bay Area Judaism: There were smelly drum circles punctuated by strange, off-key chants. There were services that substituted the names of ancient Near Eastern goddesses for the names of God and talked a lot about the "healing feminine essence." There were services that read modern poetry in lieu of the Psalms. There were mixed English/Hebrew services with a decidedly coercive approach to hugging—everyone was going to get thoroughly hugged, whether they liked it or not. There were quite a few different services led by charismatic gurus intent on building their followings. I felt a bit like Goldilocks, trying place after place and finding that not a single one fit—not one bit.

I was close to despairing when I decided to check out one last congregation. This one was called Beth Sholom and was located out in the relative boondocks of the Richmond district. I took the same

bus that had carried me to Golden Gate Park the previous, misty January and got off just a stop or two earlier. It certainly looked like a
synagogue—white stucco, big, imposing doors, flyers for community events in the foyer. The chapel was small. It had brown wood
pews, and the ark that housed the Torah scroll was covered by a
royal blue and gold velvet curtain. The carpet was ugly and patterned; I guessed that it had been selected sometime in the early
seventies. People filtered in and the room filled up. The service reminded me of the ones with which I had become so comfortable at
Hillel—slow but deliberate travel through the prayer book, no gimmicks. The singing—tight, shining, strong—left me nourished and
high. This, clearly, was my synagogue.

Then the rabbi gave a sermon. His basic argument was that
Moses' encounter with the burning bush was a model for the encounter between humans and the Divine. The bush itself was really
an external manifestation of Moses' inner spiritual states, the rabbi
explained, and it's only after he turns to examine it more closely
that he hears God calling his name—just as we hear God only when
we're ready to look with open curiosity at what might be flickering
within. He talked about how Moses was afraid, because meeting the
Divine stretches us way past our comfort zone. The rabbi also explained that when Moses asks what God's name is, God tells him
"Eheyeh asher Eheyeh," which may be translated as "I am that which
I am." That is, God's name is synonymous with absolute being, with
existence in its rawest form.[1]

In other words, he seemed to be saying, the story in the Torah
was a metaphor for the strange states I'd been experiencing for
some time—the feeling of light welling up, the softness that I met
when I let the noise in my head stop, the fear and uncertainty that
came with these encounters and my attempts to understand them.
As the rabbi—whose name was Alan Lew—put it in one of his books,
"the Torah is the record of the human encounter with God—the
transcendent, the absolute. Every page of the Torah either describes
this encounter or prepares us for it or discusses its implications."[2]

Paul Ricoeur talks about a "second naiveté," the ability to see God shining through the words of the Bible after immersion in potentially cynicism-inducing theories of biblical authorship. Many people become disillusioned when they hear the scholarly claim that the Torah is, historically speaking, not likely to be the direct word of God. Rather, academics tend to suggest, it's a compilation of fragmented manuscripts, written by different people at different times in the ancient world, and with a wide range of agendas. I've seen quite a number of people suffer from something of a crisis of faith in the face of this information. It can be pretty challenging, I suppose, to hear your seminary teacher tell you something that sounds an awful lot like "God didn't write the Torah." I wouldn't know personally, though, since I never really had much in the way of first naiveté; adolescent atheism and my undergraduate study of religion made sure of that.

But given my proclivity for manuscripts and fragments, it was startling to now discover that God was in this book, that God was of this book, that this book was of God—not of the Santa-esque Guy in the Sky but, rather, of the radiant expanse that made me feel so utterly safe and loved. I became less and less sure that the authorship questions mattered. Maybe the Torah literally came from God on Mount Sinai as described so breathtakingly in Exodus 19 and 20. Maybe it's the record of a group of people who experienced a tremendous, communal revelation of God (as the Sinai story would indicate). Maybe it's a collection of the various understandings of that revelation that those people or their descendents wrote down. Maybe it was authored by different groups of people at different times who were Divinely inspired, or who even had purely political motives when they wrote the words we have today. (I'm pretty sure I'll never know for sure.) Inside the vast world of the second naiveté, I found that my faith could permit questions without crisis. My former preoccupation with "what really happened" had fallen away; now, my concern was with what gleamed of truth, wisdom, and the holy.

The God of the Torah, I had begun to discover, was the luminous God that I had already met. The Torah already knew about this God, already knew how to live in service to and connection with Deity and had been trying to tell me all along. I was utterly dumbfounded. I had once thought that I was smarter than religion.

I was hooked; I began going to services every Friday night. I made sure to leave the office exactly at five so that I could get there on time. On Fridays, I tended to wear the most nightlife-friendly clothes that I could pull off in the cubicle—maybe a skirt with a wallet chain, perhaps a tank top with flaming dice, most likely motorcycle boots and a hoodie sweatshirt. Sitting in the chapel, I watched the well-heeled men and women in their mid-thirties to mid-fifties take their seats, chatting with each other. I would think to myself, "I don't need to dress up for services. God doesn't care if I dress up. It's not like God hasn't seen me in this outfit before." I would imagine that I was shaking up these people's perceptions of who might come to pray. It would be a few years before I understood that it was I myself who was affected when I made the effort to dress up for Shabbat, when I used my appearance as one of the ways that I set apart this time from other times, when I decided to honor the Sabbath by being ready for it. Despite my obsession with costuming, it took me a while to recognize that a subtle shift in ordinary clothing could have a powerful impact on my awareness. Back then, though, I needed to know that God would accept my prayers even if I came as I was.

The only people to whom I would talk were the old men who sat in the back. I didn't speak Yiddish, so mostly we smiled and nodded politely to each other, said, "*Gut Shabbos.*" (I didn't know at the time that seven or eight years later we would be having the same simple conversation, that by then we would be old friends.) The pews would fill up and the service would start.

Then I would find myself enrobed completely in the singing prayers, in the strange lilt of words whose meaning I didn't understand but whose melodies I did. Something connected as my throat opened.

I was learning how to pray. I'd sung these words many times at Hillel, but I had only just begun to believe them. At Beth Sholom, when we chanted the Shema—"Hear, Israel, God is our Deity, God is One"—I sang it from the place just below my solar plexus and I felt myself lifting somehow out of my seat, out of my body. The medieval Christian mystic Mechthild of Magdeburg described prayer as that which "drives the hungry soul up into the fullness of God, and draws the great God down into the little soul."[3] I'd always be surprised when I opened my eyes to find the concrete words in the book in my lap.

During the long, standing, silent prayer, I labored with my rudimentary Hebrew. After many months, I could make it to the end of the second paragraph (out of seven) before the rabbi moved to the next part of the service. I would peek at the English to see what I was saying, and discovered that the words lent themselves to all sorts of different ways of thinking. When praising God "who gives life to the dead," sometimes I'd feel flush with the cycles of nature, of winter and spring, death and rebirth, and atoms humming even as they decomposed into fertile soil. Sometimes I felt happy, as if for the first time after all that grief. Sometimes I felt my mother, somehow, vibrating inside me. Sometimes, as I prayed for the revival of the dead, I just felt God nurturing and enlivening me, and wondered vaguely how I could have ever lived without this.

These prayers, I realized, were real, deeper and more textured than I had given them credit for when I had coolly evaluated the prayer book at Hillel. They articulated things I hadn't known that I needed to say. They helped me to talk about praise, gratitude, awe, and wonder.

And then I finally made it to the third paragraph: holiness.

After the rabbi's sermon—often on the ways in which Judaism helps us meet God or how that meeting changes us—there would be more singing. The service would end and I would duck out into the busy night and catch the number 38 bus on the other side of the street, back toward the center of town. Sometimes I would meet friends for dinner, drinks, a movie, or a party. Sometimes there was some event at a bar or club. I'd pay my five-dollar cover, meet whomever it was I had arranged to meet, get a beer or a cocktail, and take in

the jukebox or thumping DJ and the frivolity, silly jokes, inconsequential chatter, snarky gossip, and calculated evaluations of "the
scene" around us.

For a long time I would go from services to the club or the party
and drink and laugh and flirt like the best of 'em. But over time, the
golden feeling that I got from Beth Sholom began to do its work on
me, and I would arrive at the club feeling as though my solar plexus
was still lit up. With my sense of being soft, open, light, I found the
noise, the rough laughter, and the flagrant excesses harsh and jar-
ring. Eventually it would make me feel jittery and out of place. But
I kept going out, despite the fact that it made me feel increasingly
off-kilter. I would grit my teeth and drink my beer and determine
not to notice the gnawing sense that this fun was not nearly as
much fun as it used to be.

My closest friends knew that I was going to synagogue, and most
of them understood my impulse to seek the holy. Many of them
were trying to do the same thing, in frameworks that just happened
to be very different from mine. In practice, this comparison worked
with varying levels of success. Cass joined me at services once, just
to see, and I spent a lot of the time sheepishly mumbling about how
that one bit in the liturgy about non-Jews wasn't as bad as it might
seem. Rebecca was intrigued to learn that the Jewish holidays with
which she'd grown up actually related to the agricultural calendar,
but she declined to join me in celebrating them. Jack's house was a
five-minute walk from synagogue; he was always happy to see me
when I stopped by all buzzing and prayed-up, but the geek guys
weren't exactly going to stop their video games to hear about the
weekly sermon, and I had trouble switching gears so quickly. Ariel
was supportive but twitchy. As a kid, she'd had some bad experiences with Judaism and she wasn't quite ready to hear me natter
on about the fragrance of prayer and the boundlessness of Torah.
My friends did their best, but, frankly, there wasn't a lot of interest.
And I was shy about sharing my experiences in great detail; a lot
of my questions felt intensely personal, were things I wanted to
work out on my own. I was still figuring out, even, what the questions were.

I didn't talk about my tentative new Judaism with the freelance chicks, my coworkers, or the gender benders, dot-communists, and political activists that I had begun to get to know. Naomi Wolf wrote of her own experience that "it felt embarrassing, a social liability, to admit an interest in God. It mattered to me that it would feel pathetic and nerdy to tell someone I was interested in spiritual issues in the progressive circles in which I spent my time; to confess that would be more uncool than to confess to various forms of vice or addiction."[4]

And it wasn't even just "spirituality" that I was seeking, it was God through organized religion. Whereas, according to the unwritten code of the Bay Area, it would have been acceptably experimental to dabble a little (but not too much) in Buddhism or Wicca, it was just downright strange to sign up for one of the Big Three monotheistic faiths. I didn't know anybody else who identified as religious in that way, except, maybe, for Alex, who was now ensconced in a Unitarian seminary in Chicago. She was a reassuring partner for theology talk, but far removed from my cultural and social milieu.

I knew a lot of people whose impressions of organized religion were either reflective of a repressive childhood or were similar to what mine had once been—that is to say, they regarded religion as a nice replacement for independent thinking. I think, in part, the strong fundamentalist presence in America has led a lot of folks to believe that there's no such thing as nuanced religious discourse. Wolf notes that "43 percent of Americans have had some sort of mystical experience in the past few years but have not been able to talk about it with people with whom they are otherwise intimate,"[5] because, in many circles, there's a taboo—or at least a fear—about sounding either too "woo-woo" or too brainwashed in enlightened company. Of course, my reticence was due at least in part to the fact that I was terrified of becoming one of those stupid sheep I had so long reviled. With two competing versions of sanity in operation . . . well, I wasn't confident enough in the one murmuring persistently, but quietly, under my skin to be sure it truly overrode the worldview I had held for most of my life as I could recall it.

But it wasn't just my own hang-up. When I did tell people where I was going after work on Friday or why I didn't want to taste the shrimp, I didn't always get an enthusiastic, Californian "right *on.*" Sometimes I got awkward silence, sometimes a too-sharp joke about being a good girl, and once or twice a mumble from some secular Jew about becoming, yes, "too Jewish." I think people were wary: Had I become a member of the morality police? Had I gone off the deep end? Was I going to start being sanctimonious and stop being fun? It wasn't always clear to them.

And it wasn't always clear to me, either, which was part of what was so scary. My glittery life was hard to beat, and I wasn't going to risk it lightly. I had a strong instinct to preserve what I had, and besides, I wasn't done. I still needed this—my friends, my work, the fun, all of it. If my life couldn't take the religion . . . well, I'd just have to work it out somehow.

One Friday night, I wound up sitting next to a middle-aged man wearing a mala (a set of Buddhist prayer beads) around his wrist. Making an exception to my general ban on talking to people at services, I asked him if he was a practicing Buddhist. My own turn to religion still surprised me so much that I was intently curious to know how other people had made their way to this particular chapel. The man told me that, indeed, he was a Buddhist, but that his father had died, and he felt a need to say Kaddish for him. He was enjoying services, though, he said—he thought he might keep coming back.

I can find a lot of different ways to explain why I was drawn to Judaism. There's a strong ethical tradition, but also a tremendous awe for the transcendent. It's a faith that is comfortable with debate and a diversity of opinion—of five thousand legal disagreements recorded in the Talmud, only fifty or so are settled on the page, leaving open the possibility that the "right" answer isn't so obvious.[6]

At the same time, as philosopher Yeshayahu Leibowitz suggests, "What Judaism created was a community that maintained the Torah and observed its Mitzvoth, a community that retained its identity despite extreme differences in theological opinion."[7] Judaism can embrace groups with radically different ideologies—kabbalists and rationalists, Hasidim and the opponents who had gone as far as to try to excommunicate them—because a unity of practice holds them together. In other words, to some degree it's less important how one understands what keeping Shabbat is all about than the fact that one does it. There's a tremendous freedom in that—not only wide berth in terms of how one makes sense of one's religious life, but room for those understandings to shift and change over time. I could write for days about why I came to God through Judaism, why I chose and fell in love with this particular religion. If I hadn't been born Jewish, though, would I have sought out Torah? I'm not sure.

When aspirants came to Gandhi and asked him to help them follow him into his righteous Hinduism, he would tell them to go back to their religion of birth. They would find everything that they needed there, he'd tell them. Most of the time, I think—a lot more of the time than, perhaps, people allow—this is true: one's religion of origin has everything necessary for complete spiritual fulfillment and service. Yet I also have dear friends who converted from the religion into which they were born to something else, and their stories are ones of real struggle, exhaustive searching, and, eventually, a clear recognition that their new faith was where they needed to be. I can't speak to their experiences, though, having never had them myself.

For most of us, I think, our roots have a primal pull. The man I met that Friday night had been a Buddhist for thirty years, but somehow, Buddhist mourning rituals weren't able to give him what he needed. Something was missing. He was a Jew, and Jews say Kaddish. In order to have his spiritual and emotional planes lined up, in order to get what he needed when he was neediest, he had to come home. Sometimes it's only in going somewhere exotic and far away that we can understand what Gandhi saw, that all along, everything we've needed was already contained in the religion with which we were raised.

Judaism is a powerful, rich system for living in service to and connection with the Divine. From what little I've glimpsed, Christianity, Hinduism, and Islam—to name just a few—are impressively complex religious systems as well. Like the grieving Buddhist, though, it was clear to me that if I looked for my spiritual gratification elsewhere, Judaism would be waiting there, patiently, for me to come reclaim it, and to be sustained by it in a way that I wouldn't be by anything else.

With the help and encouragement of the freelance grrrlies, I had been pitching and writing as many articles as I could and hitting the evening circuit of writer/editor networking events. I built up a portfolio, a decent set of contacts, a couple of marketing copy gigs to supplement my book review income, and, eventually, the nerve to quit my day job and strike out on my own.

In part out of concern about making rent, and in part out of excitement about my new writing career, I worked constantly. When I had a day job, knocking out articles over the weekend had been a fun, hobbylike break from the office. Now, however, my apartment (specifically, a large closet off to the side of the living room in which I crammed a desk) was my office. Whenever I was home, I was apt to be formulating story ideas or picking at one of my existing assignments—not reading for pleasure, not working on my long-suffering novel, not catching up with East Coast friends on the phone, not staring at the walls and decompressing. I began to realize that if I didn't make some time for myself, there wouldn't be any. After a flurry of e-mails with Alex, my perpetual sounding board for things of this nature, I decided that I needed to set aside one day in which I wouldn't work on freelance assignments. Journaling and working on my novel would be fair game, but nothing that could really be construed as "work for money" would be allowed. This way I'd have a little more time for pleasure, for the sweet slowness of my life.

There was, of course, no question: the day off would be Saturday.

The announcement handouts tucked into the prayer book every week indicated that there was a service each morning at 7, and that on Mondays, the rabbi held a Torah study class at 8. At some point I decided to check it out.

I set my alarm for 5:30 a.m. It was still mostly dark when I stumbled, sleepily, out the door. As I walked the three blocks down to the bus stop, the sky slowly illuminated; as I waited for the bus, it lit into a full, blazing sunrise. There was almost nobody on the street. Everything was so quiet, so still. Steam curled as it rose up from the potholes. The bus came and I took out my journal, tried to say something about how clear I felt on this morning.

I got to the chapel just in time. The Yiddish-speaking guys were there, as well as a few middle-aged men and women. The space felt different than it did on Friday nights—less anonymous, with only fifteen people instead of the sixty to whom I had grown accustomed. They zoomed through the liturgy.

This was not the languid prayer of people savoring the Sabbath; these were the crisp, efficient devotions of people who needed to get on with their day. Unlike the Friday night service, with which I had become so intimate over the past two or three years, this one was almost completely unfamiliar, pages and pages of psalms and tunes I'd never encountered before. I was totally lost; I flipped anxiously through the prayer book in an attempt to find my place and eventually gave up. It was like being back in that first week at Hillel, but this time without Jonah there as my guide.

Thomas Merton talks about the "tremendous, agonizing embarrassment and self-consciousness which [those new to religion] feel about praying publicly...The effort it takes to overcome all the strange imaginary fears that everyone is looking at you, and that they all think that you are crazy or ridiculous, is something that costs a tremendous effort."[8]

I hadn't been that self-conscious about my cluelessness when I began attending Friday night services at Hillel because I hadn't had a lot invested in the experience—then, Judaism was quite obviously not my sphere, and though it was a little humiliating to be so illiterate, I could drop the feeling as soon as I left the building. But now, here, I was trying to pray, to pray to God. And it was extremely daunting to do such a private, precious thing in public—especially when I was still learning what it was to pray at all. I still didn't know how to talk to God. And to let other people watch me try to do so?

This is part of why, when I came to Beth Sholom on Friday nights, I never spoke to anyone. I snuck in, kept my eyes closed for as much of the service as I could, and snuck out without so much as making eye contact with the other congregants (except the old men, who seemed to have come from an entirely other world). I wanted—needed—to pretend that I was somehow alone in this, that I was entering this prayer space on my own and experiencing it on my own, without the gaze of others upon me.

Here in the morning service, however, there was no pretending. I felt naked as my incompetence in talking to God was, I felt, exposed to all. I was still trying to develop what religion scholar Catherine Bell calls "ritual mastery," the second-nature knowledge of (in this case) when to sit, when to stand, which page we were on, what to sing, what it all meant—the Jewish liturgical baseline.

Much has been made about the relationship between the intention and the form—the words and mechanics—of Jewish prayer. There's praising God, who raises the dead, in the Hebrew in the right way at the right time, and then there's what one thinks about as these words are said, the meaning and feeling infused into the words. There's no prayer without letting God in, but Jewish worship is also very much about specific words and actions that hold the intention to pray, that give it a vehicle in which to fly. The mechanics are particularly hard, I think, for American Jews, since the prayers depend so heavily on knowledge of a tongue few know how to speak. I've seen accomplished lawyers and doctors fall apart in services when asked to recite a fairly simple blessing, because it's so nerve wracking and alienating to say—in public, no less—words that don't mean anything to you, because you literally don't know what they mean.

There are the two levels, then: learning the external form of the service, and finding the privacy in a room full of people to open your heart to God, figuring out what you might even be able to say. Merton was right—it's tremendously agonizing, and embarrassing.

Yet even so, this confusing, frustrating service still seemed to have some sort of effect on me. It reminded me of how my muscles were sore after that first yoga class, despite the fact that I didn't do any of the postures correctly. After prayer, I felt clean, like some deep part of me had been polished to gleaming. I would later experience this feeling often—when I prayed and was not in the mood to pray, or when I opened the book and said the words even though my mind was antsy, jumpy, inattentive, thinking of other things. I would nonetheless finish the set of prayers feeling . . . prayed. It was humbling to be such a beginner, to feel so vulnerable and discombobulated. But I had already learned from my forays into Friday night that there was only one way to ever become comfortable with the service: to take responsibility for my need to learn, and to keep coming back.

My freelance career rolled along. I pitched stories on religion as often as I could, reviewing books on Gen X faith and on the religious right, interviewing artists about their spiritual lives, analyzing the webcast liturgy offered by a particularly tech-savvy church. And yet, as intellectually pluralistic as I continued to be, my personal life—namely, my relationship to yoga—became increasingly fraught. I enjoyed moving through the postures, but something about the context, the chanting, and the statues of Hindu deities scattered around the studio began to irritate. I had begun falling in love with Judaism, and this other thing began to feel like a competitor for my attention.

The media, around this time, had gotten very interested in the phenomenon of "buffet-style" religion—picking and choosing aspects of different faiths and rituals as they resonated for the individual. Some of the writers and theologians weighing in on the issue shrugged their shoulders and said, hey, whatever gets people to the Source is cool, and it doesn't matter if they mix and match Native American, Sufi, Christian, and Buddhist practices in order to make it happen. But the opinions that seemed to resonate with me were against this pastiche of practices divorced from context, against choosing superficial breadth over committed depth. For example, Eastern Orthodox author Frederica Mathewes-Green wrote in the *Utne Reader*,

> One of the best pieces of spiritual advice I ever received was . . . that I should give up the project of assembling my own private faith out of the greatest hits of the ages . . . We are so indoctrinated by our culture that we can't trust our standards of evaluation. We can only gain wisdom that transcends time by exiting our time and entering an ancient path, and accepting it on its own terms; we only learn by submitting to something bigger than we are. The faith I was building out of my prejudices and preconceptions could never be bigger than I was. I was constructing a safe, tidy, unsurprising God who could never transform me, but would only confirm my residence in that familiar bog I called home. I had to have more than that.[9]

In other words, the religious traditions that have developed slowly, over thousands of years, are each a complete system. Each is designed to transform the practitioner into a servant of the Divine and to knock loose the imperfections, the pettiness and ego that get in the way. However, Mathewes-Green argued, in order for this to work, one must enter a single practice fully and let go of the attempt to control the terms on which this happens. There's a saying from the tradition of the monastic, early Christian Desert Fathers, "If you see a young man climbing up to the heavens by his own will, catch him by the foot and throw him down to the earth; it is not good for him." The Episcopal reverend Micah Jackson paraphrases the aphorism as follows: "The student does not know what he needs to be taught."[10] A novice practitioner picking and choosing from various disciplines will inevitably miss vital parts of the curriculum—most likely, the parts that she most sorely needs, that will require the most work from her.

Yoga and Judaism each seemed capable of taking me all the way somewhere, but it was clear that I'd have to choose one in order to do it properly. Judaism won because I was a Jew, and because it was speaking to me on a more fundamental level than anything else ever could. And because, in contrast to the superficial, yoga-flavored product offered at the South of Market studio, with Judaism, I was being given—sermon by sermon on Friday night—an education in its rigors and depths.

A year or two later, I'd find myself in Jerusalem scheduling a meeting with a rabbinical student around her need to get to yoga class. I'd be surprised by this—hadn't I just figured out that yoga was incompatible with taking Judaism seriously? But she wasn't approaching the practice as a competing religion. Stripped of context, perhaps the postures were "just movements," just as watching one's breath didn't necessitate devotions to Buddha. Certainly, whatever is taught from 7 to 8 p.m. at the Crunch gym is hardly the Hindu practice of self-annihilation. And yet, even in a neutral environment the postures still effected something—they were designed to, after all.

Eventually I stumbled onto a distinction made by a major interpreter of Jewish law that I found—and continue to find—very useful. Moses Isserles (known as the "Rema") writes in the law code the Shulchan Aruch that "the only thing that is forbidden in regards to customs of the [non-Jews] [are those customs] that are based on sexual immorality... or a statute of their religion that has no logical reason, in which case we suspect that it is tainted with [foreign worship] ... but other customs of [non-Jews] that have a [tangible physical] benefit are permitted."[11] Rabbinical student Yael Shor concludes: "From the Rema's opinion, one could derive that participating in meditative and yogic exercises is permitted for reasons of health, but to use Eastern mantras is prohibited for the reason that mantras do not have a benefit beyond their ritual significance."[12] In other words, there are ways to participate in certain kinds of practices without necessarily adopting them as part of some mishmash religious stew. One just needs to know how and where to draw the line.

I know a lot of people who have taken on complementary (but noncompeting) practices that enhance their physical well-being and/or inner life. The additions, however, don't cause them to practice Christianity, Judaism, or whatever else any less. They've already done exactly what Mathewes-Green talks about, immersing them-selves in a religious system and letting themselves be broken down and changed by it. For the rabbinical student in Jerusalem and many others, adding a yoga class or tai chi doesn't necessarily threaten that—because she, and they, don't regard the supplementary classes as religion per se, and don't participate in the aspects of a competing practice that have explicitly religious overtones.

If someone were to come to me now and ask for pastoral advice about whether or not he should give up yoga or meditation in or-der to become a more committed Jew, the first thing I would ask is what yoga meant to him. Is it exercise? Is it something that makes you feel good? Is it a path to truth? Is it taking you away from God and/or wherever you need to be right now? For me, this "secondary practice" was somehow holding me back from Judaism, and that was the problem. It was a bit like dating two people at once so that I didn't have to get close to either of them; once I had intuited that it was time to take my relationship with Judaism to a deeper level, I had to make space for that to happen.

Beth Sholom was offering an adult education series, so I signed up for eight Tuesdays of Introduction to Jewish Practice. The class covered a lot of the basics; whatever knowledge I may have had of Second Temple literature or Canaanite mythology didn't help me understand how to use all the different ritual objects, how to mark the end of the Sabbath, or what keeping kosher actually entailed. I wasn't sure that I was willing to *do* all this stuff, but I wanted, at least, to learn.

The teacher talked about the recitation of blessings before and after food. She suggested that, among other things, they were an antidote to the materialism of our culture—the way it tells us we always need more stuff, and feeds upon our feelings of lack. Bless-ings, she argued, help us remind ourselves of how much we already have. As it says in the rabbinic aphorisms of Pirke Avot, "Who is rich? The one who is happy with his portion."[13] But even more fundamentally, she said, these benedictions can be understood through the rabbinic statement, "A man steals from God when he makes use of this world without uttering a blessing."[14] That is to say, they're a way of asking permission to use something that belongs to God, or maybe a sort of mirror that reflects back in praise what God gives in bounty.

The teacher also brought in a quote from Rachel Naomi Remen, who wrote of moving to California and having the opportunity to garden for the first time:

> One evening, I had gone out to pick the salad as usual and ran a hand lightly over the crisp green square of lettuce leaves, marveling at its vitality, almost as if it were bubbling up out of the ground. Suddenly words from my childhood came back to me, words that I had heard countless times over the dinner table and knew by heart, words that I heard now for the first time: Blessed art Thou, O Lord, King of the Universe, who bringest forth bread from the earth. Far from being the usual meaningless mumble, these words suddenly were a potent description of something real, a statement about grace and the mystery of life itself.[15]

It didn't matter that she was using the blessing over bread rather than a more technically suitable blessing (I'd eventually learn that Judaism has benedictions for a staggering number of occasions on which a person could experience something—going to the ocean, meeting an old friend, seeing a rainbow, hearing either good or bad news, meeting a non-Jewish king, smelling a fragrant tree). What mattered was that these words expressed Remen's wonder, helped to give it a shape and a weight, transformed that wonder into an offering of thanks to the Divine. It was an articulation of mystery.

The video artist Bill Viola observes, "In the Middle Ages they painted the sky gold in the paintings. Today our photographs show a blue sky. We think the gold is an abstraction. To the medieval eye, the blue sky was the abstraction. It was realism they were after—the reality of the divine effused through everything in the physical world."[16] It was that reality—that feeling of radiance pulsing at all times—that I began to seek. I wanted that sense of Divinity catching me not just off guard at random moments when I least expected it, but infused, somehow, into every act. Alex and I joked that it was like trying to move from dial-up to DSL (this was before the wireless era), shifting from a slow connection for which you have to wait to something instant, fast, and reliably constant. I started to realize that blessings—in fact, all the doings of daily Judaism—were one way to get to DSL; that instead of waiting for moments of grace to hit me as I walked down the street, I could seek God out myself.

One beautiful spring day, I took a lunch break at one of the restaurants in my neighborhood, as I sometimes did. I ordered and settled into one of the plastic chairs outside. When the food arrived, I sat with it for a moment. It was hot, savory: couscous and chickpeas and onions and zucchini and carrots. It looked like a wonderful meal. I closed my eyes and said, very quietly, in Hebrew, "Blessed are You, God our Deity, Ruler of the Universe, Who has created various kinds of nourishment." As I took the first bite, I felt God's presence hovering, glistening like the sky in a Cimabue painting.

One Tuesday night, I took some downtime at Café Flore. I sat with a cappuccino and my just-purchased copy of Abraham Joshua Heschel's *The Sabbath*; all of my reading for pleasure seemed to be about Judaism at this point.

I had already begun to understand why, on the seventh day, Jews traditionally refrain from lighting fires or using telephones or cooking food or spending money or doing many other things understood to be either technically "work" or outside the spirit of rest that governs the day. It seemed clear that abstaining from this stuff would create long stretches of silence and a freedom from distraction that could help a person access the most silent, hidden parts of the self. Heschel, however, explained that there was even more to it than that. He wrote,

> To set apart one day a week for freedom, a day on which we would not use the instruments which have been so easily turned into weapons of destruction, a day for being with ourselves, a day of detachment from the vulgar, of independence from external obli-

gations, a day on which we stop worshipping the idols of technical civilization, a day on which we use no money, a day of armistice in the economic struggle with our fellow men and the forces of nature—is there any institution that holds out a greater hope for man's progress than the Sabbath?[17]

The irony is that human progress depends on saying no to technology and economic engagement, at least for a while. Heschel framed Shabbat as a way of returning to too-oft-neglected ways of being human—a way to help us remember what we have in common with the woman who got up at 4 a.m. to clean the office.

I sipped my drink and I chewed on Heschel. The idea of being free from commercial transactions on Shabbat was attractive. I thought through the implications: If I didn't spend money, I couldn't get the eggplant sandwich I loved from the deli up the street. I wouldn't be able to ride the bus, since I never had a monthly pass. I needed Friday-night money to tip bartenders, pay cover charges, pick up the tab on a date, get into a movie. The list seemed to be endless. No eggplant sandwich?

This, I realized later, connected to all that stuff about desire I found in countless books on spirituality. Carol Lee Flinders wrote, "as long as I believe in sex as a source of lasting happiness—or power or food or even long weekends in the mountains or *anything* finite—then no matter how much I want the mysterious something else that mystics speak of, I can't walk toward it because my consciousness is divided."[18] In Buddhism, desire—uncritical servitude to our finite cravings—is considered the root of all suffering. The Ten Commandments tell us not to covet, not to desire greedily. Attempting to rein in my impulses, however, sounded terrible. The mere prospect of not being able to do what I wanted, exactly how and when I wanted to do so, was causing me no small amount of my own suffering. There seemed to be no winning.

Up until now, dabbling in Judaism hadn't demanded very much of me. I had time in my schedule for both Friday night services and clubbing, I could spare an hour's sleep every week or two for morning prayer and Torah class. Avoiding nonkosher food wasn't so hard—I hadn't eaten meat in years, and I wasn't really a fan of seafood anyway. But as I contemplated Shabbat, and what it might entail to deepen my practice, I began to realize that this spiritual discipline stuff was . . . well, more work than shooting energy out of the palms of my hands. If I wanted to move past the "random cool experiences" phase and into something more like Divine DSL, I had to actually *do* things to make that happen. I just wasn't sure that I was ready.

I wasn't alone in my hesitation to take this next step. A lot of people hit their limit of spiritual experimentation, I think, when it comes to facing down desires. The happy glow, the rushing ecstasies, and the feelings of being understood are all amazing. A class here or a retreat there is sweet, inspiring. Doing more than that is harder for a lot of us.

It's not like we have a lot of help and encouragement from the culture in which we live, either. As Caroline Knapp noted, "some twelve billion display ads, three million radio commercials, and 200,000 TV commercials flood the nation on a daily basis—most of us see and hear about 3,000 of them a day, all of them lapping at appetite, promising satisfaction, pulling and tugging and yipping at desire like a terrier at a woman's hemline."[19] American culture today is the most consumer oriented in Western history, and the sytem depends upon our cravings. Buddhist environmentalist Stephanie Kaza suggests that "consumerism rests on the assumption that human desires are infinitely expandable; if there are an infinite number of ways to be dissatisfied, there are boundless opportunities to create products to meet those desires . . . How can [consumers] know what product will satisfy them when there are so many to try?"[20]

With a little practice not running after our cravings, we begin to realize that they, and the feeling of urgency to satiate them, might not be as endless as we had thought. If, one day a week, all of our needs can be met with prayer, slow walks in the park, reading, Torah study, sitting in silence, and long communal meals that allow conversation to unfold, what might that tell us about the things that seemed so urgent on the other six? What might that tell us about our culture's stories regarding what we can and can't live without?

It's not that there isn't a place for work, music, travel, and, yes, spending money—the world needs us to be creators and doers just as it needs us to take breaks from all that relentless creating and doing. As Heschel framed it, "in regard to external gifts, to outward possessions, there is only one proper attitude—to have them and to be able to do without them."[21]

This was what Frederica Mathewes-Green meant when she said that we should enter one religious system fully and allow it to change us. Judaism was beginning to ask things of me, to intimate that it might be in my own best interests to take on practices that were neither convenient nor comfortable. Me? I wasn't so certain. It wasn't that I didn't want a deeper relationship to God and my religious practice, but that—like many of us who grapple with desire—I was terrified of the implications.

I had created a tenuous balance, one hand grasped tight around my Judaism, another around my social life. It felt like any sudden movements in one direction or the other would cause everything to fall. I was terrified to think I might become so religious that I'd lose much of what I had in common with the artists, activists, and slackers cum Unix administrators who made up my world. If I said no to what I wanted, would I get things that I needed, instead? That piece of me that was always itching for more—more God, more connection, deeper encounters that lasted longer—would it be satisfied? How much of my life, my friendships, would I lose by seeking this out? Would oh-so-holy Friday nights without spending money be boring? Lonely? Feel like some sort of a punishment? If everyone went out without me...then where would I be?

Saint Teresa of Avila writes of her own experience,

> It is one of the most painful lives, I think, that one can imagine; for neither did I enjoy God nor did I find happiness in the world. When I was experiencing the enjoyments of the world, I felt sorrow when I recalled what I owed to God. When I was with God, my attach-

*ments to the world disturbed me. This is a war so troublesome that
I don't know how I was able to suffer it even a month, much less
for so many years.*[22]

I needed my friends. They had nourished and sustained me,
helped bring me back to life after my mother's death, given me a
sense of community the likes of which I had never experienced. I
loved them—Jack and Lida and Michael and Ariel and Rebecca and
Cass and everybody else. If saying yes to God meant endangering
these ties... well, I wasn't able to do that. And yet, it was clear that
my relationship to God had become fundamental to the point of
non-negotiability. Any attempts to run from it would just be denial
doomed to failure. God was calling me, but I wasn't sure to where.
God beckoned, but I couldn't face the price that I might have to pay
to follow.

The Catholic priest Henri Nouwen wrote,

*You have an idea of what the new country looks like. Still, you are
very much at home, although not truly at peace, in the old country.
You know the ways of the old country, its joys and pains, its happy
and sad moments. You have spent most of your days there. Even
though you know that you have not found there what your heart
most desires, you remain quite attached to it... you know that
what helped you and guided you in the old country no longer
works, but what else do you have to go by?... Trust is so hard,
because you have nothing to fall back on.*[23]

The feeling that I was living a double life began to wear. I still
wasn't ready to throw away the full, flourishing existence that I had
painstakingly built from scratch in a brand-new city, but inside the
so-called flourishing life, I was increasingly lonely. That I felt like I
couldn't talk about my desire for the sacred to become the organizing principle of my life meant that I had less and less to say.

My social life, like my freelance career, seemed to be far too
much about the quest for the fresh, the exciting, the new, the next
big thing. I, on the other hand, was yearning for the well tested, the

eternal, the timeless. I was getting too much candy and not enough protein. Even costuming—which had become one of my favorite activities—began to lose its sparkle. Though it had been delightful to reinvent myself over and over again, now I wanted to figure out who I was underneath all the artifice, underneath the makeup and the glitter and the thousand shifting guises. I still cherished the creativity demanded by the enterprise of getting dressed, but it began to be harder and harder to feel like I was "on" all the time. I started going out a little bit less, refusing invitations here and there. More often, though, I'd go out and simply not enjoy it.

All too frequently, it felt like there was something important missing from the conversation, something beyond romantic escapades, making rent, and the vicissitudes of pop culture. There just seemed to be a dearth of people with whom I could talk about this "something else," about not only my burgeoning religious life but all of the things that it might mean. My close friends' own spiritual lives allowed for some translation, but not enough. I needed people who were going through the same thing that I was, people who had also thought about keeping Shabbat or who were also afraid of their desire to become religious, and who might have some new ways for me to think about my private dilemmas. I needed those people, but I didn't see them anywhere in the life that I was already living.

Alex and I would later refer to this sense of longing as the search for the "party next door," for community and a life that felt cohesive, in which social and religious aspects integrated seamlessly. At this point, however, I didn't know that there *was* a party happening elsewhere, or what kind of fun that could possibly be.

I wouldn't give up one life or the other. I'd refuse to tip the balance. And, in fact, I didn't stop spending money on Shabbat at this point; I just couldn't bring myself to take that step and face its possible implications. I'd just live with the discord, I told myself, keep letting the feeling in my solar plexus get trampled by the loud music at the bar. I'd notice keenly every time the check came at a restaurant, feel guilty and far from God as I reached into my purse for my share of the bill. This wouldn't be a long-term solution, and I knew it. The problem was, I didn't know what else there might be.

———

It was a sunny, warm Rosh Hashanah. It *felt* like the "head of the year," the first day of a new cycle, the birthday of the world. I walked two miles to the bay with my bagel; the ritual casting off of sins is enacted by hurling pieces of bread into the water. Crumb by crumb, it started off easy: vanity, anger, lack of respect for others, selfishness. Slowly, it went further into who I was and who I had been, sometimes, over the course of the year. I named each thing I could think of that I had done to create distance between me and God, me and other people. It was a painful exercise. I used the entire bagel; the birds squawked and swooped down. Walking back from the edge of the pier, with the seagulls and the fishermen, I felt lighter, with glimmers of hope that I might do things better this next year.

Something I had heard two years earlier hit me, suddenly. When I had started at the book publisher, the executive editor mentioned that he had a daughter who was also called Danya. My mother had found the name in one of those baby books. She had loved that they translated it from Hebrew as "gift of God," and had reminded me about it often. I had always been embarassed by the meaning, found it stultifyingly corny. I made some comment to the editor about it, and he looked at me.

"It doesn't mean 'gift of God,' " he said. "It means 'God judges.' "

I thought for a second. In fact, a semester or two of college Hebrew was enough to remind me that the root word of "give" was *natan,* as in "Natanya" or "Tanya"—the suffix *ya* referred to one of the names of God, the giver. The root word of "Danya" was actually *din,* or "judgment," like the root of "Daniel"—which also means "God judges" (El is a different name for God).

At the time, I had shrugged this off as one of the funny quirks of my personal history: the baby book had been wrong. But now, on the precipice of a new year, by the water and the gulls, it hit me hard. I began to think about the fact that my mother had chosen to call me by this name, but with that meaning. I began to wonder how she had seen me, what role she thought I would play in her life, how she imagined that I would relate to the world and the people in it—or maybe she had been thinking of other things entirely, I don't know.

Throughout biblical history, name changes served as transformations of destiny, as initiations. Avram became Abraham. Jacob became Israel. And, I realized, in a very weird way, this is what I had been granted. I had gone from being a gift from God to being judged by God. It was a change from a passive past relationship to an active present one, an ongoing one, an unfolding one. I wrote in my journal at the time, "If it's true that I'm the sister of Daniel, I have work to do. There's an accountability implicit. I'm being watched—judged—and have an obligation to make good. Which is absolutely . . . well, it's daunting, but mostly it's invigorating. I am responsible to and for something, it's not just to myself."

Abraham and Sarah heard the news of their name changes from God, Jacob from an angel. Me, I got it from the executive editor at my first postcollege job. But the sense of metamorphosis was nonetheless palpable: whoever it was that I had been before, I was different now. And yet, the outer form remained the same—I was not going to drop out of my own life, to cut ties with those who had known me as Danya. I was still Danya. But what it meant to be Danya was something entirely different now.

Shortly after the inauguration of the holiday season of December, 1999, I began referring to it as the "Christmas of the Sixth Fat Cow." In the book of Genesis, Pharaoh had a dream in which seven emaciated bovines gobbled up seven plump ones. Joseph, as the story goes, interpreted this to mean that seven lean years were soon to follow the time of prosperity and wealth that Egypt had been enjoying.

San Francisco was on the verge. There was a freneticism in the air, a sense that these Egyptians knew their empire was not going to last forever. And just as this December seemed to be their attempt to hold on to something that they knew was slipping away, so too did it seem to be my own. Whether I understood it consciously or not, I wasn't going to let go of my life and its fun quietly.

I felt driven, somehow, to throw myself into the vortex of the city, to give it one last chance to enchant me the way it once had. I desperately wanted to rekindle my love affair with the town, even as I knew on some level that the passion had been fading for some time.

Katrine had been promoted to a new job every few months since starting at an electronic wedding registry start-up; she had gone from entry-level "content chick" to senior management in a few short years, after pioneering some subfield of Web design. She was well networked and her boyfriend was still in Spain, so she invited me to join her and some of our other friends on a serious tour of holiday parties, venture capital style.

There were lavish events with ice sculptures shaped like a company's "product," from which cocktails named after the CEO would flow. There were large halls featuring three different DJ areas, rows of private, enclosed glass booths with sprawling couches, and buffets snaking around immense ballrooms, offering every delicacy a mind could conjure. There was swag: more than just T-shirts with the company logo and a cheeky slogan ("hey, let's make some money!"), there were free tickets to events, ghoulish dolls designed by local cartoonists, messenger bags with specially tailored pockets for the gadget du jour. It was decadence, and madness.

By the night of Katrine's company's big party, we had been going out just about every night for several weeks: dancing, eating, socializing, cocktailing, and small-talking like it was what we were made for. It took a certain amount of effort to keep up the momentum, but I was dead set on doing it all, anxious to be once again bewitched by this brand of merriment. This next party was on the fancier side; I borrowed a purple dress from Lida and anchored a gigantic purple silk orchid behind my left ear for a tropical look. Katrine had decided to splurge on a shiny, ruched black gown with a floor-length fishtail skirt.

I got drunk, really drunk. I hadn't eaten enough beforehand, and what with the free alcohol flowing and the music flowing, and everything flowing, I sort of lost track of myself. The big fad that season was a tiny Polaroid camera; it was new and retro all at once. People were going mad, snapping everything possible, giggling deliriously as the tablespoon-sized photos emerged one after the other. Someone took my picture and when I looked at it the next day, feeling poisoned and utterly bereft of fun, I was embarrassed. It was me, all right—same girl, same dress, same haircut—but it wasn't me. Not the regular me, anyway. It wasn't that I was doing anything so incriminating; it was just that suddenly, it was clear that the slippery delirium of the party and the noise and the chitchat and the martinis had kicked out the part of me that was sensitive enough to feel the sweet, Divine shimmering goldenness most of the rest of the time. She simply wasn't there.

I decided at first to hang on to the photo, as a reminder of something—I wasn't sure what—that I didn't want to forget. Later, I would decide that this grinning, waving girl wasn't anybody I wanted to hang on to, and I would throw her into the garbage can. Nouwen's lament echoed in my ears: "To your dismay, you discover that the old country has lost its charm."[24]

Thomas Merton wrote, echoing the book of Deuteronomy, "The land to which God has brought you is not like the land of Egypt from which you came out. You can no longer live here as you lived there."[25] I knew that I had left this other place, already said good-bye to it even as I was still in San Francisco. Where I was going remained unknown, and uncertain.

When my mother was sick, I filled up a lot of the empty time by thinking about where I'd go—after, later. I worked it out as I washed towels and took out the trash: Spain to Morocco, across the Mediterranean somehow, ending up in Israel. Escape fantasies were obviously a way to disassociate from everything that was happening, but even so, the idea wasn't so outrageous. Most of my friends at the time were, after all, spending their junior year abroad in some far-flung place or other.

After my mother died I dropped the idea. I could barely function in my home environment, let alone handle schlepping around the world like that. Three or four years later, though, as my dissatisfaction and confusion slowly grew in San Francisco, the thoughts of travel returned. This time, though, there seemed to be no real reason not to take them seriously.

"My heart is in the East, and I am in the uttermost West,"[1] wrote Yehuda HaLevi from Spain, yearning for Jerusalem. I was at the edge of the Pacific Ocean, and I cried when I read this. Suddenly I felt very far away.

I was young, itching for adventure, and anxious to explore Judaism in more depth and rigor than I could with a few adult ed classes and whatever introductory-level reading I could dig up on my own. I had heard of a nondenominational yeshiva in Israel where a girl like me could study Talmud. I signed up for their summer program, hoping urgently that it would satisfy my need to understand more about how this religion worked—and give me some sort of insight about what to do next.

I had to figure out how far I wanted to take my religious dabblings, and it seemed clear that I probably couldn't do this from the safe confines of my California social circle, from a life of wacky theme parties and vaguely hipster downtown events. Even though I was risking the freelance career I had so painstakingly built, I knew that this was the right time to spend a little of the money I had inherited from my mom—while I was still young and unencumbered by a life partner or mortgage. I booked a flight to Madrid for early February, figuring that the scenic route to Jerusalem would undoubtedly be more interesting.

In chapter 12 of Genesis, God tells Abraham—then, a nice nobody from the land of Ur—"Lech lecha." Go, you, God says, "from your land and from your birthplace and from your father's house to the land that I will show you."[2] With no clue about where he was headed, Abraham walked away from everything that was secure and familiar. He trusted that God would get him a map when the time came, and, of course, God did. More than that, however, it was only after leaving that he entered into a relationship with the Divine. "Go" was the first thing that God ever said to Abraham, and from then on, the connection was practically constant; God appeared to Abraham, talked to him, came to him in visions and sent him messengers, negotiated with him, offered him advice, made a covenant with him, tested him, and performed miracles for him. But the story only began when Abraham took off, set out from the comfortable into the unknown.

This theme can be found in many biblical stories: Jacob was on the road when he had the famous dream about a ladder to heaven and learned that "God was in this place and I did not know it." Moses bumped into the burning bush after fleeing the Egyptian palace in which he was raised. Even the Israelites didn't personally meet God until they finally escaped from Egypt.

Granted, I was hardly in Egyptian slavery. And yet, I did feel like I was in an increasingly untenable situation, split painfully between my friends and my religion. I became increasingly convinced that the only way to find a new spiritual place was to seek it out physically. Was it Dorothy Gale syndrome? Maybe, but it seemed awfully clear that Rabbi Lew was right when he said in a sermon one Friday night, "when we leave home, when we leave our habitual relationship to the world, we see things freshly, we become flush with our lives."[3]

I knew that I needed to go, even though I had no idea what I was looking for, let alone whether or not I would find it. I put my stuff in storage, gave up my half of the apartment I shared, and threw a big party to celebrate going away and my twenty-fifth birthday. I cried a little. And then I got on the plane.

The Spain that I was chasing was an overly romanticized medieval one. I fantasized about Jews and Christians and Muslims all trading notes about poetic meter and techniques for inciting mystical states—this was, I was sure, the Spain of the kabbalist Nachmanides and linguist Ibn Ezra, of the Sufi Ibn 'Arabi and Islamic philosopher Ibn Rushd. My plans were made more on hunches, intuition, and a few survey-style history books than well-researched itineraries or meaningful knowledge.

Toledo—once called the city of three faiths—was my first stop, and disappointing. The eight hundred years since its heyday had not been kind. It was now a small, slightly rundown town with more traces of the Inquisition and the expulsion of the Jews in 1492 than its intellectual past glories. There was a Sinagoga de Santa Maria la Blanca—that is to say, a synagogue turned Church of the Virgin Mary—and a museum displaying Jewish ritual objects as the cultural curiosities of (so it seemed) a primitive people. I had a long afternoon and evening on my hands before I'd be able to skip town, so I amused myself by playing with the inside of my brain.

I had begun meditating as soon as I got off the plane in Madrid. I was determined to get myself onto the Divine DSL, and though I had dropped the specific practice of yoga, I didn't see anything wrong with watching my breath. While I was waiting in a long line to have my passport stamped, a huge tour group of young Christians swarmed around me and I began to breathe in radiance and light. It flowed into my lungs and out my hands. Waiting is a primary component of travel, and in odd moments those first days—sitting at a café, pausing in a cobblestone alley or on a castle turret—I would stop, and I would breathe.

As a going-away present, Ariel had given me *Pure Heart, Enlightened Mind*, the journals of a twenty-four-year-old American named Maura who had entered a Japanese monastery. Maura wrote about trying to understand the notion that everything is nothing and everything, all at once—something like what the kabbalists call *Ein Sof*, the limitless aspect of God that encompasses all of existence, including the material world. Moshe Cordovero wrote,

> *The essence of divinity is found in every single thing—nothing but It exists. Since It causes every thing to be, no thing can live by anything else. It enlivens them. Ein Sof exists in each existent. Do not say, 'This is a stone and not God.' God forbid! Rather, all existence is God, and the stone is a thing pervaded by divinity.*[4]

If everything is interconnected as part of the underlying Divine, if the seemingly differentiated waves of this world are all really water in the big sea, then in some respect even our ideas of selfhood, of being a separate self, are illusory—we are part of this great everythingness as well. This idea is found, somewhere, in just about every world religion.

And yet, it's gotten lost in America. Religion scholars Jeremy Carette and Richard King suggest that the integration of modern psychology into religion has had a significant impact on how we regard the bigger questions. For, they argue, the advent of the late-nineteenth-century interest in the contents of the individual's mind created a "history... where the religious 'experience' has become an individual event and where the boundaries of the self have been reinforced."[5] Instead of focusing on how our small selves are part of the larger picture, we've become consumed by interest in the machinations of the smallness.

Maura wrote in her journal that one day she "stood in the garden and was the garden, really was it."[6] She experienced the hard lines of her self fading away, until the distinction between Maura and the garden was irrelevant.

It's not just about meeting the flowers, though. If I could transcend the understanding of myself as a discrete individual, if I could see the "me" that I call "myself" as part of the Big Bigness—if I could become the garden or the waves on the water, I could, necessarily, also become starving children, wartorn cities, and polluted oceans. And if I could understand that I am not so separate from the suffering and injustice in the world—well, how might that affect how I prioritized what I do with my time? Talk about uncomfortable. Small wonder that books about identifying with starving babies aren't flying off the shelves at chain bookstores in the same way that books about improving the self—the separate, discrete, disconnected self—are. If we could make the connection between ourselves and everything else happening around us, what might that change?

When I first read about Maura's garden moment, though, I wasn't thinking about that. I was just impressed. Like a lot of people, I thought that wide-angle insight could only come from a big mystical experience. I was convinced that the meaning of life, the key to the Kingdom, was found in the place where another dimension of reality is revealed. I wanted to be, well... enlightened, or as enlightened as a person like me could get, and it seemed to me that the way to get there was to chase enlightenment experiences. I'd hear stories of people suddenly, sometimes unexpectedly, encountering the Nothingness of the universe, and I was desperately curious to know what that meant. What had they perceived? How had it changed them? I was certain that once I was allowed into the secret club of deep spiritual wisdom, once I ascended to the next plane, all of the fear and confusion and uncertainty about my life and what to do with it would vanish in the glare of illumination. Also, I just wanted to be close to God. This perpetual feeling of longing and distance was just so painful.

"Oh, please show me Your glory!" cried Moses to God. He wanted to see the Divine not just shrouded behind clouds or pillars of

smoke, but revealed in fullness, without guessing, without hidden-
ness. In this, the most intimate exchange in the Bible, God acqui-
esced to his ardent servant's demands—but only to a degree. "You
will not be able to see My face; for no human shall see Me and live,"
Moses is told. Rather, God would shield Moses until after the Divine
Presence has passed by him.

Even the greatest prophet of all times—as my tradition understands it—experiences the Divine with a hand over his eyes, his
vision blocked, protected from a blinding light he is not capable
of surviving, let alone understanding. He can hope to perceive, at
most, traces of God's presence, the imprints of the effulgence left
behind, lingering in the air, before disappearing. That's all any of us
have, really. Not the opportunity to behold God's glory in its full, unmitigated splendor, but rather just the chance to catch a few traces,
the moment that they began to vanish.

My experiences of God have taken many different forms over
the years—and thus my understandings have, as well. Of course we
all make sense of the traces we've been lucky enough to glimpse,
try to derive from them what we can, even though, at times, we
receive contradictory information from them, or have difficulty
squaring them with our faculties of reason. There's no pithy quote,
no single story that can succinctly tie up a theology of the One who
is, necessarily, greater and more expansive than the human attempting to understand. How do we describe that which transcends
language? And yet, who would we be if we experienced moments
in which the veil was, however briefly, lifted for us and we didn't try
to learn from them?

In Toledo, I stood on the cobblestone street and tried to become
the wall of a yellow house, to breathe away separations between
myself and everything else. I wanted so badly to know what happened on the other side of the divide.

My third morning in Spain I arrived at the bus station early, eager
to leave the letdown that was Toledo. Too eager, in fact; it turned out
that the station didn't open until eight. I sat at the café next door

and tried to pay attention to the coffee, the cup. I took my backpack outside and watched as the sunrise pushed forward, pink.

I returned to the café with thirty or so minutes yet to kill before my bus. The guy sitting next to me was reading a book about meditation in Spanish, and somehow we started talking. Raul had trouble understanding my spoken English (too fast) and I his (his accent was too thick), so we took to communicating by writing. As such, the conversation had a strange, otherworldly quality, the intimacy of human contact with the brevity of instant messaging, and silence.

At some point, he began to insist that I travel next to El Escorial, a town north of Madrid. There was much I didn't catch in the course of our strange, choppy conversation, but I surmised that there was some sort of magnetic field there, or some similar groovy-type attraction. It sounded like they had something like the Mystery Spot, a site in Santa Cruz, California, rumored to be beyond the laws of physics and gravity (it's actually just an optical illusion). Adamant as he was that I go to this place, he didn't seem to benefit from my doing so—he was headed home, to Madrid. I didn't have anywhere else, particularly, to be; I had time for a day trip. I said okay, why not? He paid for my ticket.

The main attraction in El Escorial was a large palace-monastery built by a sixteenth-century king. It was, frankly, not very interesting. I asked around—was there anything else to see in this town? Oh! Someone said. You must be looking for the Sitte Filipe II! This, it seemed, was the magical location Raul had mentioned. It's over there, I was informed, by someone gesturing toward a very imposing mountain.

I began to walk, my big backpack buckled firmly onto my back. I met some Germans along the way, and we hiked together in the warm spring sun. Eventually they forged on. The path was steep and hard to climb, but I climbed. I felt like a woman on a mission. Finally, I reached the top.

Evidently, many other people had, as well. The park at the mountain's peak featured several snack shops, families picnicking, and a ground littered with beer cans and ice-cream wrappers. There was a parking lot where people had left their cars after driving up. Later, I figured out that the word I had thought was *sitte* (which, evidently, doesn't actually mean "site" or anything else; that's what I get for not knowing Spanish) was actually *silla*, or "chair"—that is to say, this place was nothing more than the lovely view from which King Philip II had sat to watch his palace's construction. No Mystery Spot, not even any mystery.

I had been looking for a profound experience. Instead, I found a second-rate set of park benches and picnic trash. Crushed and cranky, I ducked around the side to have a little quiet before beginning my the trip back down. There were some large boulders behind which I could hide, to separate myself from the crowd.

I was on a decent-sized mountain. The hillside view *was* gorgeous. I sat down, and began to breathe. I focused my gaze on the tree branch not far off. I breathed in, I breathed out. I tried to breathe with the tree.

I find it difficult to explain what happened next. I breathed deeper and deeper into the tree, and suddenly I could absolutely, completely see my consciousness in the tree, and then see the tree's consciousness—whatever that means—somehow in my own mind and body. I looked at a bird. Just as I was the tree, I was the bird. There was only one consciousness, and it was mine and the tree's and the bird's and bigger than all of us and it was God's. Everything really was nothing; I could see it. Just as the atoms in my legs were in motion and of fundamentally the same stuff as the ground, the ground was in motion and of the same stuff as the tree, and the same was true of the bird and the branch. It was creation and destruction, but it was really neither because it was all one thing, constantly changing form. Blessed are You, God, who resurrects the dead.

Dazed, I hitched a ride down the mountain with a couple of nice women from Madrid. The transcendent feeling that had overtaken me began to flicker on the bus to Cordoba; I found myself next to a very persistently chatty man, and irritation began to win out over euphoria. I didn't make it to the youth hostel until late, after the main door had been locked, and I leaned against its doorbell, exhausted and frustrated. But I was still feeling the meditation's effects to some degree: Over the next day or two, I giggled, delighted, at oranges rolling around the Cordoba streets. I studied the ripples of a fountain. I was convinced that I finally *really* understood Japanese poetry. I'm sure I was quite a sight.

Gradually, though, my old restlessness came back. I started to feel lonely wandering around the city on my own, and the feeling of blissful serenity ebbed away as an increasingly loud clatter of memories and fantasies reclaimed my brain. I trekked to the other side of town to find an Internet café for the same reasons I always did: because I was bored, because I was convinced that something hugely exciting—more exciting than the day I was already having—would be waiting for me in my in-box. Two nights after arriving to Cordoba I met a boy from the hostel, and we had dinner, made lame conversation, walked around the city together. It was nothing romantic—I don't think there was any interest on either side—but we both found each other's company a welcome respite from all the relentless solitude.

The day after that, it was as though the El Escorial thing had never happened. After a day or two of rhapsodizing in my journal about the wonders of haiku, I now wrote snarky entries about the local who had clumsily tried to pick me up and ranted about the selective information on historical plaques. I was aware that the enchanted way I had regarded the world right after the meditation was gone, and I felt sad about it, but I didn't know how to make it come back. I was stuck back in my old, usual, neurotic brain, and there didn't seem to be much to do about it.

By the time I got to Seville—where I rented a bike for zooming around town, contemplated buying overpriced but adorable shoes, and stayed out at a dance club until 4 a.m. with some random people I had met at the hostel there—the world had most decidedly returned to its separate forms.

This, I learned later, was par for the course. As Buddhist teacher Jack Kornfield notes, "our realizations and awakenings show us the reality of the world, and they bring transformation, but they pass," and, even more than that, "for almost everyone who practices, cycles of awakening and openness are followed by periods of fear and contraction."[7] Six months after Maura O'Halloran had her *kensho* [initial enlightenment] and was said to have "seen into her Buddha nature" she found that she had not become the perfect angel she had hoped to be. She wrote in her diary, "I hated [a fellow monk] for a thousand little, trivial, insignificant things. The fact that they were trivial and insignificant made me hate myself. One year of ascetic practice and I seem to have got nowhere...I felt vaguely hysterical."[8] Her teacher reassured her that this only meant that she was still human, but her reaction is a common one.

Unfortunately, fancy experiences do not hit some magical reset button with which all of our anxieties and dramas are suddenly erased. They're not the thing that determines whether a person is nice, loving, generous, moral, or kind—there are plenty of people who have had some remarkable episode who are not nice people, and many more who have not encountered spiritual fireworks, but who are. Certain kinds of encounters can open the door for us to see the world in a different way, to be sure. But, as I had yet to learn, it takes the grunt work of an ongoing religious discipline to put those insights into a framework, to nurture fragile sprouts into something strong and hearty. Mystical happenings or not, it's the daily work that helps us become who we're supposed to be, moment by moment.

The sexy thing about chasing big experiences is that they can be pursued and, if one is lucky, had. It's not nearly as difficult as confronting the hurt, the pettiness, the bad moods, the hazy feelings of panic, and the treachery of the day to day, which don't necessarily offer a definitive end-point. Eventually, though, we all have to go back to our regular lives, to face the pain and fear and boredom and magic within them.

Of course we all long for some kind of immolation. This yearning for union is perhaps the greatest pain of the human condition. Even when we mask this yearning with unsatisfied hunger of other kinds—for the mythical perfect job or relationship that will rescue us from any and all feelings of discontentment—what's really underlying, for most of us, is the desire to feel the distance between ourselves and the great Everythingness melt away. The psalmist cries, "My father and mother abandon me, but God will gather me in."⁹ Not even a parent's love ultimately suffices; only God's love will satiate. Yet paradoxically, the experience of union can make day-to-day living even harder. As the writer Martha Beck puts it,

> *I know this sounds strange. I always used to think that if I just Knew there was Someone Out There, if I had some evidence of Higher Power... life would be a bowl of cherries. Nope... after tasting that kind of love, that kind of belonging, it is almost unbearable to feel separated from it again.*¹⁰

It is our lot as human beings to live in the world of separation and form, and to face the grief that comes with that. It is in a daily practice, a series of deliberate gestures aimed at reminding us of the infinite and God's never-ceasing presence, that we remember the love of which Beck spoke, and in which we feel intimations of the return home.

My Jewish practice was a little bumpy on the road. I had brought a prayer book with the intention of using it every morning, but I barely touched it. Eating in Spain was particularly tricky because everything, everywhere, seemed to be made of pork. I tracked down the sole Friday night service in Seville, but didn't quite get around to it the next week, in Barcelona; there were too many other things to discover. Gibraltar was small and British; I tagged along to Shabbat lunch with some geriatric tourists and spent the afternoon, lonely, walking along the water with my journal.

When I sailed into Tangiers and traveled through Morocco, I sought out Jewish communities on most Friday nights. Religion hung in the air; calls to prayer ricocheted through the streets five times daily, bus stations and restaurants had special rooms for patrons to worship as needed. Here, I saw more acutely the holes and inconsistencies in my own behavior: the neglected prayer book, the blessings I sometimes forgot to say, the intercity buses I caught on Saturday mornings (sometimes passing up Shabbat lunch invitations to do so). I had missed the holiday of Purim entirely.

But there were so many other kinds of experiences. I sat for hours on a musty rooftop on the Moroccan coast, watching the Atlantic roll in. In Marrakech, a couple of local girls that I met took me to a Bollywood movie and the *hammam* baths, and gifted me by painting elaborate henna designs on my hands and feet—"for luck," though I was the rich American who needed luck much less than them. I took a few spontaneous detours to countries that I hadn't intended to visit at all, each time becoming culture-shocked all over again after having, finally, adjusted to the pace of the last location. I found myself in so many different contexts, reacting to so many different kinds of stimuli, that I barely knew who I was after a certain point.

This is, in part, why leave-taking looms so large in the Bible. When we venture out of our usual lives, who we are is up for grabs. Rather than holding on to the same identity in every context—as is easy to do amidst the comforts of home—we shift and change and become new in every moment, in every new situation. In travel, practically every situation is new. Like the great golden everythingness I met in El Escorial, we rise and fall away, and our sense of self melts and melts again.

There's a lot of talk about "annulling the ego" in spiritual literature. For example, Rumi writes, "If you could get rid of yourself just once / The secret of secrets / Would open to you."[11] The idea isn't that we should permanently give up being ourselves—there's no way to do that, really. Rather, our task is to understand how much we are connected to the Divine and the great everythingness, to really internalize the fact that we are not just individual, discrete entities. As Rabbi Zalman Schacter-Shalomi puts it, "The ego says, 'it's all me.' But we need to own that everything in us is God."[12]

Sometimes, as our ideas about ourselves become less fixed, the walls we use to separate ourselves from others, and from God, begin to lower. Climbing the steps to the great Alhambra, getting lost in the Fez medina, finding common ground with the full spectrum of people that I met in cafés, bars, and bus stations, carrying only the barest minimum of belongings with me, I became someone more expansive and multidimensional than I had been traipsing up and down Sixteenth Street in my motorcycle boots—not only because I could be, but because I had to be.

Travel—even to one town over—is one of the most classic ways to effect this kind of shift. But although I didn't understand this before I left San Francisco, it's not the only way. Ironically, it was Rabbi Lew who would later help me see this: He talks about a trick he learned from the Indian philosopher Krishnamurti, who suggests that the immediate answer to any question—no matter how basic—should be "I don't know." What's your favorite color? Dunno. Who are you voting for? No clue. How do you like your eggs cooked? Haven't the faintest. This buys a person a moment or two to get off autopilot. Lew writes, "We have to say, 'I don't know,' and spend a moment or two in the void, having let go of our old, habitual, secure response, and having no idea what will arise in its place."[13] The crucial piece is not that we leave where we've been geographically—it's that we allow ourselves, no matter where we're situated, to leave who we've been.

I think that for a lot of us, it's easier to go away physically and readjust ourselves as the circumstances dictate than to do all the work ourselves. It's not easy to break out of the comfortable roles we inhabit in our relationships, to interrogate the set ways in which we think about ourselves. Given how invested I was in my fabulous San Francisco life, I would have been very afraid to answer "I don't know" to seemingly easy questions—to risk coming up with answers that didn't mesh with the life I had been living. Rather than willingly enter the void from a place of security, I forced myself to meet the void head on, to put myself in situations in which "I don't know" was really the only answer I had. But just because this is what I chose doesn't mean that it's the only way.

——

Finally, in May, I arrived in Israel. Jerusalem was much more disorienting than many of the other places to which I'd traveled, because my expectations were so much higher. The language of the Torah was splashed all over street signs and advertisements, vendors at the bus stations sold Jewish religious objects, eighteen-year-old boys strutted around with M-16s hanging off their hips, everything hustled and bustled. There were ultra-Orthodox men in big beards and black hats, jean-clad guys with colorful yarmulkes, women in headscarfs with babies hanging on their backs, and frosted, blow-dried secular peacocks in low-cut shirts. Everyone was talking a million miles an hour in a language I recognized but didn't understand.

More than that, though, it was bizarre to discover that Jerusalem was a place that actually *existed,* that all of those history books, Bible stories, and CNN clips reflected something taking place in real time, something more than an Atlantis above ground. I wandered, baffled, on the cool white limestone of the Old City, through the market to the Western Wall, all that remains of the Second Temple. It was big, built of large, pale, rough-hewn stones that gleamed like compressed clouds. Green plants poked out between the bricks here and there. There was a divider in the middle of the Western Wall plaza separating men and women. The men's droning chants filled the space like smoke; the women were quiet, long-skirted, whispering their prayers pressed up to the stones.

And the stones. I approached the wall slowly, hesitantly. Everything seemed to vibrate with a strange density. Though I didn't and don't believe that God is in any one location more than in any other location, it was clear that this place had something. I'll never know whether the ancient holy Temple was built here for some reason inherent to the space itself, or whether this site is so powerful because of the ways that we have sanctified it, again and again, by designating it as the spot for our most exalted worship and by directing our prayers to this place for two thousand years. Either way, the wall burned, like fire.

I put my hand on the stones, felt them sizzle. I began to pray—

not anything from the liturgy, though. I just poured out my heart to God, weeping and whispering and feeling like I had come home and like I didn't belong anywhere, and like the volume of my life had just been turned up and I wasn't sure if I could handle it.

I didn't know what I was supposed to find in Jerusalem. I was hoping that the sense of gravitas that I felt had been missing in San Francisco would be here, that somehow all of the turmoil I was feeling about who I was and what kind of life I should live would somehow be resolved. I wanted answers to all of my questions about how Judaism might fit in with everything else I needed so badly. I wanted certainty. I wanted to stop feeling like I was torn in two. Leaning against the old white limestone, I prayed and prayed that somehow this place would give me the peace that I was so desperately seeking.

A college friend living in Tel Aviv invited me to come stay for Shabbat—my first Shabbat in Israel—with the apologetic disclaimer that she had an obligation Saturday afternoon and would have to leave me to my own devices then.

We went to services Friday night, had a nice dinner with her boyfriend and some of their friends that evening, and I crashed on the couch. We decided to sleep in rather than go to services in the morning; she asked what I wanted to do with the afternoon. Perhaps a museum?

I never really had a conscious conversation with myself about how I would handle Shabbat in Israel. There wasn't necessarily a reason why my practice in this country would have been any different than it had been elsewhere. But now, suddenly, I declined. Museums require admission fees. Maybe, I asked my host, we can just take a walk instead?

We took a nice stroll along her neighborhood's side streets. All too soon, however, it was time for my friend to attend to her other business. I could have gone back to her apartment, but her boyfriend was there and I didn't want to be in the way. I decided to head back after Shabbat ended to collect my stuff, and to spend the three or four hours in the interim on my own.

Tel Aviv is a secular city. Long stretches of beach hug the Mediterranean, and that day they were (as they often are) crammed with girls in bikinis and guys doing capoeira, boom boxes blaring techno, seaside bars dispensing beer, and fat men hawking ice cream from Styrofoam coolers. I walked up and down the promenade—the only street on which I could be sure I wouldn't get lost—and tried to carry the sacred feeling of Shabbat with me. It was hard. Everything grated: all the pop music, all the selling, all the hubbub. I kept walking.

I was very, very lonely. I longed for my close friends. After so many months on my own, I really missed their warmth and love. (My host was little more than a friendly acquaintance, and our conversations had been a bit stilted.) I had been keeping a running list of observations about this strange, ancient, modern, Jewish, Middle Eastern, sometimes religious country that I was anxious to share with Ariel and Jack and Rebecca and Cass and Alex. Mostly, though, I just wanted to hear the voice of someone who knew me well.

I walked along the beach, tried to drown out the noise, and yearned to pick up the phone. It was, by this point, morning in California, midmorning already in Chicago. I had already memorized my international calling card number; I certainly could just stop at any one of the pay phones by the restrooms along the beach, to just say hi. To ask how folks were doing. To... connect. It was Shabbat, and this wasn't a thing a person did on Shabbat. But I wanted to call. I experienced a strong magnetic draw to the phones as I passed them, one after the other. A few times I stopped in front of one and told myself that I could pick up the receiver.

I wanted consolation in this faraway place filled with strangeness and expectations. God was supposed to be here? Why did I sometimes feel embraced by a feeling of the Divine presence, and other times so far away from everything? I thought I might explode if I didn't pick up the phone and hear Ariel twittering on about this thing or that or Alex's supple words rippling over me, telling me that I was okay, that I was safe, that I wouldn't feel this lonely forever, that yes, really, this part is hard. I stood in front of the pay phone in contemplation. It was Shabbat. I kept walking. All of my willpower was focused on keeping myself on track. It was exhausting, this day of rest.

In the years since then, I have had many similar moments, but none so acute. I've wanted to do all kinds of things that are either explicitly forbidden by Jewish law or more generally outside of the traditional understanding of "rest." Each time, I've had to fight the temptation.

In the year or so following this day in Tel Aviv I experimented a bit, tried to figure out where the perimeters of my own practice would be, within the boundaries of mainstream Jewish law. Was it okay to go to a secular event (say, a music concert) if I walked there and got in for free? Was it okay to sit in a bar or restaurant and visit with people if I didn't order anything? What about window-shopping, or watching a DVD that non-Jewish friends already had on when I get to their house?

Alex (who has always had a good sense for ritual) once likened keeping Shabbat to living in delicate soap bubble. She observed that ERRATA certain kinds of activities seemed to cause the fragile tranquility of the sacred to pop for me. Picking up the phone? Makes the bubble pop. Spending money? Makes it pop. Being around all that techno, really? Makes it pop. There's very little in life that can't wait until the sun goes down on Saturday night, and for the few things that really can't—like, say, a medical emergency—Jewish law has created provisions.

Once all of these fences are built around the day, once the thin wall of soap is erected between myself and the world, the richness of the silence is unbelievable. With no obligation to the telephone, with no invasion from the Internet, with the return to the slowness of walking on foot and talking with people only face to face, something long buried becomes free. The Talmud suggests that Shabbat is one-sixtieth of the World to Come,[14] the taste of a future paradise. In the World to Come, I suppose, we are more fully ourselves than we are able to be in the current world, where all we seem to do is go and make and rush to achieve.

I walked along the shore of Tel Aviv until I got to Yafo, the town on the city's Southern border. A big garden overlooked the sea. Finally, there was some relief. The only noise, now, was the cooing of pigeons and the swishing of the waves, back and forth to the shore. I was hungry, but there wasn't much I could do about that. I sat, birds flapped and circled, the sun glinted off the surface of the water, families played with their kids. I thought about calling my friends and wondered what I was doing in this insane country. Watched the birds some more. Listened to my breath.

I walked back to my host's house as the sun slowly set. The beachfront was still loud and secular, but things had settled down a little. I tried to see God everywhere, to perceive the great glowing everythingness emanating from the sand to the people and back again. I itched to pick up the phone and call my friends.

I got back to my host's part of town just as three stars—the traditional signal that night has fallen and that Shabbat has ended—snuck out from their hiding places. I bolted to the nearest pay phone and dialed a flurry of numbers. Alex answered right away. Hi, I said. This is really hard. But I kept Shabbat, and it was correct, even when I wanted so badly to break it. Oh, honey, I'm so glad, her velvety voice came through the receiver. I'm so glad. And yes. This part is hard.

My first two weeks in Jerusalem were filled with ambivalence, with crazy highs and lows—visiting the Dead Sea Scrolls at the Israel Museum, being shaken by some ugly harassment on the Mount of Olives, sitting for hours in a bookstore coffee shop, gobbling falafel from a street kiosk, stumbling inadvertently into a part of town that had posted big signs blaring, "Women and girls! You must dress modestly!" There seemed to be no moderation, no middle path.

Four cities in the region are, according to Jewish tradition, thought to have a special, holy status, and each is said to correspond to a different element. The cave in which most of the biblical matriarchs and patriarchs are believed to have been buried is in Hebron: earth. Tiberias, on the shores of the Galilee, is water. Jerusalem is fire, and not just because burnt sacrifices were offered from the Temple and because Romans later set the city aflame—there's an intensity to the place, a sense that if you're not careful, it might engulf you completely. I was starting to feel a little crispy around the edges, so I decided to skip town for the weekend.

Tzfat, where sixteenth-century Kabbalah had flowered, is the fourth holy city—air.

The bus let me off in the lush green of the Galilee. There really was something in the air there, something sweet and decadent, like an intoxicant that made you dizzy as you breathed. I could feel the difference right away.

I had heard of a "spiritual" hostel offering a full Shabbat program and classes on mysticism for the price of a Friday night bed. We—all of us staying that Friday night—lit candles to mark the beginning of Shabbat, and walked as a group to synagogue. Something changed as we entered holy time; now the magical Tzfat air was electric, shimmering. The old part of town was full of narrow, winding streets and houses of prayer or study. Every building, it seemed, had some connection to a different giant of Jewish thought; the souls of Isaac Luria, Yosef Karo, Moshe Cordovero, and Shlomo Alkabetz, all dead for centuries, seemed to illuminate the cobblestone path.

The synagogues were divided by gender, as they had been in Spain and Morocco. The women sat in the balcony and peered down as the prayers rolled along. The men's section surged with an enthusiasm that was maddeningly far away from where I was sitting. Everywhere I went, the women's section seemed to be flatter, less vibrant, too far removed from the action. Nobody in the upper gallery here was singing. I thought wistfully of the small chapel back at Beth Sholom and the feeling of being surrounded by music on all sides.

After services we were escorted, in pairs, to the families with whom the hostel had arranged for us to have dinner. I was sent to a Hasidic couple in their thirties who had nine children. The mother was extremely pregnant, and she served us dinner on paper plates with some clear physical effort. The kids swarmed around in age-appropriate groups. My assigned "buddy" from the hostel, an Australian woman about my age, asked the woman when she was due.

"In about a month," she said, shrugging.

"Oh wow!" the Aussie burbled with perky enthusiasm. "You must be, like, so excited!"

The tired-looking woman slowly raised her head. "Excited?" she asked, with a sour tinge in her voice. "Why should I be excited?"

That first month in Israel, I had a lot of experiences with people who seemed to share my passion for this religion and who, like me, understood their relationship to the Divine as a central concern—but who understood what Judaism meant to say, what it is to serve God, in an altogether different way. The fact that a woman would believe God wanted her to have more children than she seemed to desire—to the point where she couldn't get excited about bringing a new life into the world—confounded me, and made me a little bit sad, because my understanding of Judaism and life was so radically different.

There was a piece of me that wanted to tell my hostess that there are a lot of different ways to read our religion's texts. That wanted to tell her that, at least according to my own understanding of Divine love, and of the principle of *kavod ha-briot* (honoring God's creations), the path to God didn't have to come at her own personal expense. Maybe nobody had ever told her that the world could be anything but black and white, with one living either in this specific version of holiness or mired in sin. Maybe there were a thousand locked doors in her heart that she'd never felt safe to open.

On the other hand, maybe a liberal feminist attempt at "enlightenment" would have been arrogant and out of place. It's possible that she had lived several lives before becoming a Tzfat hasid, that she chose her life knowing about all the alternatives, and that this is the one in which she feels the most whole, the most nourished by God. Honestly? I don't know.

Rabbi Elliot Dorff observes that

> Theology makes sense only in the context of the person believing it ... [It is] neither [the case] that people are all the same and see the world through transparent lenses ... nor that they are so bound to their views that no new thinking or experience can change them.[15]

I don't know what God intended. Nobody does. Those who believe that God doesn't want to give women access to Talmud study, or that God loves and reveres Jews more than any other group—they, like I, are doing their best to understand what God is saying in the Torah and in other Jewish texts. I may understand those texts differently, but my perspective, like theirs, is highly subjective and exquisitely flawed.

There's a tension that we all walk between pluralism and integrity. On the one hand, there's a tremendous need for humility, for the understanding that none of us has complete access to the Divine mind—that our ideas of what God wants could be just as faulty as other folks' ideas, or even more so. We need to remember that we might learn something from views that seem radically different from our own. Yet, we have to be careful not to confuse our intuitive sense of what's right with other people's ideas of who we should be or how we should behave.

We must endeavor to relate to folks who understand the world, and God, differently than we do, and help them to serve the Divine as they want to—as long as they don't hurt anyone else in the process, and as long as all adults consent to the situation at hand. I may personally find the fact that women aren't allowed to study Talmud in some communities to be morally problematic, but as long as the women in a community freely consent to this worldview, I don't have the right to impose my perspective. (Of course, issues of consent can get murky if a person doesn't believe that she has any other options or, in some cases, actually doesn't have other options. This is why many of us work to make alternatives available to those who might want them, and to fight institutional violations of human rights—for example, finding ways to address the fact that Judaism's highly unequal divorce laws have hurt many women along the way.)

Sometimes we even need to take pains to help others fulfill their religious obligations, to generously go out of our way to make sure that they're comfortable in our environment. That's about creating an ethic of caring, about loving our neighbor as ourselves. There are limits, however—just as we need to make space for other people,

it's fair as well to ask them to make space for us, and we're not required to violate our own sense of justice or integrity just because
someone might like us to. Sometimes groups with very different
understandings can find ways to come together—and sometimes
we must respectfully part ways so that each can do as he or she
sees fit.

Close to the end of that Shabbat in Tzfat, the hostel people called
us together for afternoon prayers. We—the tourist kids—were ush-
ered into a room to the side of the lounge area and handed prayer
books. I was distinctly relieved to notice that there was no divider
up to separate men and women. It had been too much, all this gender segregation. I wanted to be a person, not a temptation to male
concentration who had to be banished to the sidelines. And then
the rabbi who'd been running the program came in with...a divider. Not even a lacy curtain or latticed screen, as I'd encountered
in some places, but a heavy, nine-foot-tall wooden wall. This particular barracade was not intended to divide the room into even,
side-by-side halves as one finds in some synagogues. We women
were to stand behind it, squashed against the back wall of the room,
unable to see anything that was happening up in the front, where
the Torah was being read—and, frankly, barely able to breathe.

I walked out.

Somebody called for me to come back, but I kept walking. I ex-
ited the hostel and stood with my prayer book on the edge of the
hill overlooking green valleys. The sky was aflame, rose and peach
and bright, bright orange. I sobbed and shook and begged to be
sanctified in the Divine commandments, given a portion in God's
Torah, satisfied in God's goodness, for my heart to be purified in order to serve God in truth. I didn't know where I belonged. It wasn't
anyplace where people wanted to crush me behind a divider lest I
come too close to the Torah scroll or the men reading from it. But it
wasn't in the Friday night bars of San Francisco, either. Outside,
against the variegated fire of sunset—this was where God was. I
didn't know where I belonged, but I knew that wherever it was, God
was there, with me.

After returning to Jerusalem, I decided that I had to get a set of tefillin. The boxes holding special verses from the Torah, attached by leather straps to the head and arm and worn during prayer, are typically worn only by men (though, according to Jewish law, women are also permitted to adopt this practice). I was nervous. As far as I knew, the only place to buy them was in an ultra-Orthodox neighborhood. I just had to hope that nobody would ask if they were a gift for my brother or father. I dressed in my modest, nice-girl best, a long skirt and a long-sleeved shirt, awash in fear and resentment that shopping had to be such a production. As it turns out, I didn't wind up buying tefillin that day. I did buy something else, though.

About a block from the hostel in which I was staying, I passed a man with a small storefront crammed with *kippot* (yarmulkes) of every conceivable variety, color, pattern, and design. I knew some women at Beth Sholom who wore yarmulkes when praying, or even all day on Shabbat. In Judaism, this kind of head covering is considered a sign of respect for God, an acknowledgement that God is always above (higher than) us. Though it's unusual to see women wearing yarmulkes outside of very specific denominational contexts, there are certainly fair legal arguments to be made in support of their adopting the practice.

I had never thought of myself as a yarmulke-wearer, but on impulse I stopped into the store. For some reason, I was comfortable rifling through the stacks and stacks of knitted discs, letting the store owner pull out larger and smaller ones, hand and machine made, even trying them on in front of him. He didn't seem to want me to pretend that I was buying them for my brother or to shove me behind a big wooden wall. (If nothing else, he was probably used to American tourists and their strange ideas about *kippot*.) He offered his advice on styles, laughed as I cracked a joke or two about his wares.

I walked out with a blue hand-knitted *kippah* with a light-blue and green border. He threw in a couple of yarmulke clips for free. I put it on immediately, but something still didn't feel right. I dashed back to the hostel and dug out a dress that Katrine had given me, a short-sleeved black cotton thing that fell just below my knee. I threw it on, shoving my long batik skirt and modest shirt to the bottom of the backpack. I grabbed the red lipstick I had also brought traveling, applied it in two swift strokes, and hurried back out of the hostel.

Looking back on all of this now, I can only shake my head and smile at the image of this young woman strutting around Jerusalem in a yarmulke, a sundress, and bright red lipstick. It was such a childish rebellion, this insistence on combining as many unexpected elements as possible—a woman in a yarmulke! A woman in a secular-looking sundress and religious garb! A woman in lipstick and male religious garb!—and walking around the place where it would be likely to shock.

But these first few weeks in Israel, I had fallen prey to a common syndrome. Even as I struggled with ultra-Orthodox expectations about my behavior, on some level I believed that the folks with the most stringent attitudes were the "real" Jews, the ones enacting some true, pure version of what Judaism was supposed to be. And it chafed. (I'd later learn that the weight of Jewish legal tradition wasn't necessarily on the side of stringency, but that's another story.) Pressed hard in one uncomfortable direction, I felt the need to fight back with equal force, even to exert myself to the degree that I became a caricature of myself. Years later, I lived in Jerusalem for some time, and it's not that I've never walked around town wearing a yarmulke—I certainly have. It's more that my choice to do so came, later, out of the calm, balanced decision to do my thing sometimes and take the heat for it, rather than as an angry reaction and out of the need to prove something. (There have been just as many times when the desire to connect with other people was paramount, so I would choose a more innocuous bandanna as my way of both showing respect to God and sidestepping people's surprised reactions.)

But at the time, I badly needed that one experience in order to release some of the tension I'd been feeling, to officially mark the end of a certain chapter in my travels. Transparent as the act may have been, wearing the yarmulke and sundress together served as an important signal to myself that, from now on, I had to take Jerusalem, and Judaism, on my own terms.

Over the next few weeks, I began to find equilibrium. I began attending services at one of the Conservative synagogues in town; it was gratifying to return to an environment in which men and women both counted in a prayer quorum and could sit next to each other. I sublet an apartment with a couple of students from the pluralistic yeshiva program in which I had enrolled. I met people who pointed me toward communities, prayer groups, and events in Jerusalem where folks were both passionately committed to Judaism *and* interested in grappling with hard questions about the Israeli–Palestinian conflict, the role of women in Judaism, the relationship between religion and the state. I attended some of the most inspired services of my life in places where Shabbat mornings ran twice as long as the norm because the congregation sang every single word in the prayer book, jammed like jazz musicians, and danced in a whirling frenzy at the end of this or that psalm. Shabbat became a time of full rest; there were almost no cars on the street, just about no music streaming from people's apartments, almost nobody jabbering on their cell phones. I began to meet the ecstasy that is Jerusalem, the fiery rapture that can overtake a person there.

Daily life was, as always, daily life—groceries and bad moods, uncertainty and fear and all too frequent phone calls back to the States as I constantly questioned what I was doing, who I was, and who I might become if I let the tidal wave of religion fully wash over me. As thrilled as I was in some ways to finally be in a place where I was able to enter religious practice uninhibited, I was also totally overwhelmed. It was so much Judaism, so much piety and purity, and part of me wanted to color outside and all over the neat lines that defined this total religiousness, to bring the brash secular world crashing into my life here.

The yeshiva program began. I took classes on Jewish liturgy, philosophy, the weekly Torah portion, the Mishnah, and the Talmud.

We studied the rituals that a community undertook if God was slow to answer prayers for rain, and the procedure for determining whether the citron required for the holiday of Sukkot was kosher or unfit for use. We compared different commentators' takes on a single verse in the Torah, and examined the meanings behind the Grace After Meals. In the study hall I glimpsed the outermost corner of an entire world, saw how more serious learning might give me access to Judaism's source code. All the minute legal details showed me how holiness could be expressed with every small act, with every choice to do or not do something, with every endeavor to understand God's will.

We studied a range of theologies in the philosophy class. I had encountered a couple of these texts in college, but here, the lens was entirely different. Instead of asking, "How can we understand the sociocultural context in which this was written?" we talked about whether or not a theology was...true. We talked about whether it reflected human experience and our limited understandings of the Divine, whether it was conducive to the kind of Judaism that we were trying to build. These, at long last, were the questions I had been seeking.

And yet, it was all too much, too quickly. I didn't feel at home that summer, nor remotely at peace. The gap between who I had been (the girl of grimy dive bars and lavish costumes for citywide dance parties) and where I was then (adrift in a sea of religion in Israel) was too great to jump in a couple of months. Everyone in Jerusalem—or so it seemed—came from a religious background, already had a full, robust observance, and was utterly unconflicted about any of it. I know now that this is in some ways the opposite of the truth, but that's how it looked to me at the time.

Judaism was all-encompassing, and I wasn't sure that I wanted to be fully encompassed. Was I going to become one of those people who had to check with their rabbi every time they made any little decision? Who couldn't travel because kosher food was hard to find in places like Thailand or Denmark? Who had no gentile friends or secular interests? I had gentile friends and secular interests, and I had no intention of giving them up. In some ways, this

Jerusalem was the vitamin I had been craving, the corrective to all those San Francisco nights when I had felt isolated, even in a crowded room. But it seemed to be so much of this one thing, without other parts of me along for the ride.

I had already begun letting go, allowing the markers of my identity to recede somewhat. I no longer thought of myself as, say, someone up on all of the latest indie bands and art events—it didn't seem relevant here, and I found that I cared less and less about those things. Gender was certainly front and center in much of my Jewish struggle, but I didn't imagine that my friends who worked at a women's shelter or ran a feminist zine would regard my conversations on liturgical language as interesting or relevant. I had thought of myself as a freelance writer, but here I was, sitting on a million fantastic stories, and I didn't notice any of them. Who was I now?

Leave-taking had done its work on me, but not completely. I was open to new versions of myself, but unwilling to throw away one entire identity in exchange for another. I hadn't stopped being the person who had loved what I used to love, even though it was clear that both the "I" and my loves were now going to exist in a very different configuration. I was permeable, but not infinitely so—I wasn't going to suddenly become a Hasidic housewife in Tzfat, after all. But I didn't know what I would become. Even though I knew I was no longer this, I was not yet that, not yet sure how I needed to push myself, how I should grow. I was here, there, confused, a mess. What did God want from me? What was I supposed to do?

I felt like the Nachman of Breslov that Arthur Green described:

> Even the journey to Eretz Israel [the land of Israel], an attempt
> at radical self-transcendence, had not succeeded in liberating him
> from cycles of presence and absence of God, of personal fullness
> and utter emptiness.[16]

I wasn't comfortable in this religiously saturated environment, and I wasn't comfortable giving it up. I loved being in a Jewish community, loved discovering that for most people, Shabbat was a series of traveling dinner parties rather than a day of purist solitude, loved talking about my spiritual life without embarrassment, loved being around people who shared my questions and marked the holidays with me.

But I couldn't stay in Jerusalem. To do so would be to give myself over to one side of myself at the expense of other sides. At the same time, I wasn't sure that I could go back to San Francisco, where my Jewish life had been so impoverished. What I needed was some sort of balance. Something wasn't gelling for me internally, so of course I couldn't figure out how to line up external reality. Before I'd be able to feel like my Judaism, my friends, and the rest of my world all lived in one place, I'd have to make that space available within. I began to see that geography wasn't the issue at hand, not really.

I was exhausted. After all this time on the road, there had been a lot of change, a lot of the new, and, despite my anxieties about what lay waiting for me there, I longed for the familiar comforts of home. I clicked my ruby slippers. It was time to return—physically, anyway—whence I came.

By the time I got back to San Francisco, something had been broken down and something else, tender and new, was tentatively taking its place. I was still me, but I was different. Like a foal emerging on wet, wobbly legs, not even sure what color it might be.

SEVEN

Rebecca and Ariel let me stay with them until I found an apartment. Rather than looking for something in my old Tenderloin Heights neighborhood or the "cooler" (despite the recent influx of yuppies) Mission District, I restricted my search to the Richmond District— far away from just about everything but Beth Sholom. I didn't travel on Shabbat anymore, so I had to prioritize the synagogue's proximity over other geographic comforts. The rest of the week, I'd be spending a lot of time on the 38 bus.

It was only in coming back that I began to see how many things had changed along the way. My willingness to live so far from my old social stomping grounds was only a symptom of some other process that seemed to be happening. I realized with a bit of a start that it had been six or eight months since I'd ordered anything but a soda when I met friends at a bar—it was, simply, what I had felt like ordering. I hadn't eaten beef or chicken since my freshman year of college, but somewhere during my travels—I had no idea where— fish had stopped looking like food. It wasn't that I consciously decided one day to go totally vegetarian, but at some point I just no longer regarded salmon as something I wanted to put in my mouth. I couldn't remember the last time I had bummed a cigarette off of someone.

But it wasn't just about what I was putting into my body. My tolerance for forms of "entertainment" with violent or excessively sexual content had plummeted—I'd go to visit Jack or Lida and Michael, and if some explosive action movie or shoot-'em-up video game was on, the images would hit me so hard that I'd feel like I wasn't wearing skin. Bedtime had, just as inexplicably, jumped to a few hours earlier; I was ready to crash by 10 p.m. instead of midnight or later. And when I did manage to stay up late enough to go out, well, the parties based on the never-ending quest for novelties and the so-retro-it's-new-again club nights struck me as trite and boring. I found that now I had relatively little to say to my former barhopping comrades and their self-consciously ironic friends. What had we discussed before, all those hours together? Had we really had so much in common?

When I first moved to San Francisco after college, these scenes had felt exciting, refreshingly outré. Now, however, far too much felt like rebellion for the sake of rebellion, like rather than being free from the norms of the dominant culture, some proponents of this supposedly unorthodox dogma were locked in eternal reaction to it. It's not that there wasn't plenty in this world that was valuable, brave, and full of beauty, and plenty that I had learned from it—but it began to seem that some of the sweet candy had a bitter aftertaste.

Some years later, I was invited to take part in a trendy reading series at a local bar; I ran into old acquaintances I hadn't seen for quite a while. The host of the series had invited me, advertised me as one of the featured readers, and given me carte blanche on my selection of material. I suppose she did so based on some stuff I had published not long before on Judaism and transgender issues— variations on gender, sex, and sexuality were standard fare in this particular forum. Nonetheless, I took her open invitation to heart and decided to use the opportunity to try out some new work. As soon as the host realized that I was reading a fairly straightforward piece about my experience of prayer—about a quarter of the way through my allotted ten minutes—she began to give me very public signals to wrap up, effectively kicking me off the stage. The whole thing was pretty dramatic. Evidently my inability to live up to her (sorely mistaken) impressions of my "subversive" potential meant that drastic measures needed to be taken.

The issue wasn't even the host's narrow range of vision, but rather the militant imposition of this narrowness. What was at stake if one of the evening's five performers read material with content that diverged from the usual tales of sex, drugs, and government conspiracy? My piece wasn't advocating for any particular position; it was telling a decidedly first-person story about my own life. And even if it weren't... What's so threatening about hearing another point of view, even one with which you don't agree? The host's need to censor one of her invited guests said more, it seemed to me, about fear of her peers' reactions or her (unresolved) issues about religion than it did about me personally. Ultimately, though, it didn't really matter why; her behavior was rude, whatever the reason.

Even if the reading series story was an extreme example, it was of a piece with an attitude that I began to see was, at times, all too pervasive in the circles I had once frequented. When I got back from my travels, this zealous enforcement of the radical and the edgy became increasingly apparent, and it wasn't entirely comfortable for me. More and more, I began to let myself acknowledge that there were some real problems with the scenes I had once happily haunted.

Martin Buber makes the distinction between what he terms an "I-It" relationship and one that is "I-Thou." In an I-It relationship, he explains, the other person is little more than an object at your disposal: the waitress is the object that brings you your food, the cab driver is the object who brings you from one location to another. An I-Thou relationship is one in which the other person is regarded as a whole being, full of hopes and dreams and selfhood, as created in the Divine Image. The relationship is not bounded by a more utilitarian, you-do-for-me-I-do-for-you attitude. I-Thou relationships have no preset boundaries. I-Thou is the model of the relationship that we have with the Divine.

Certainly, not everyone that I knew in hipster San Francisco treated others in an I-It, utilitarian sort of way, but plenty of people did. I occasionally suspected that someone had been invited out with the group because she had useful work connections, or was able to offer access to some party or event—and was dropped just as fast when she was no longer able to provide such services. I'd see people treat those with whom they were romantically involved with such casualness and disdain that it made my stomach churn, as though the other person's feelings were of little or no consequence. I had a friend who, though engaged to be married, wrote off an evening making out with some other guy as "something that just happened," as though she had had no agency and her fiancé had nothing invested in her behavior. I was once stood up by a date who never bothered to e-mail or call and explain what happened. When I ran into him several weeks later, he just shrugged, as if to say "stuff happens," as though I were . . . well, an object to be blown off for a more interesting invitation. I knew plenty of people who thought that it was funny to refer to someone who might be good for a brief affair, rather than a serious relationship, as a "snack." A small bite to be consumed and then discarded. Nobody ever seemed to wonder what the "snacks" themselves might think of this, let alone what would happen if interpersonal ethics were placed front and center in one's life and thinking.

It's not that everyone who acted this way was a bad person, or mean—plenty of them were just regular folk trying to do the best they could, making some loathsome mistakes along the way. In this culture, though, a blasé approach to other people's feelings had somehow become a sort of white noise: inevitable, par for the course, not something to stress about or interrogate too deeply. Before I left town, I had found this attitude annoying and problematic. Now it struck me as toxic.

Moreover, the more I learned about Judaism, the more it became evident that there wasn't a lot of room for ambiguity regarding how one treats one's fellow humans in a life striving toward the holy. The late-nineteenth-century legal decisor Yisrael Meir Kagan (also known as the Chofetz Chaim) wrote multiple volumes on the importance of regulating careless gossip. Maimonedes made it clear that true modesty demanded everything from taking care not to show off one's money to not shouting in conversation and behaving discreetly in a public bathroom.[1] Care and concern for others is placed above self-aggrandizement. The rabbinic text Pirke Avot suggests that a wise person "does not interrupt his friend's words, and does not reply in haste, and asks what is relevant, and answers to the point ... Of what he has not heard, he says, 'I have not heard,' and he admits the truth."[2] Though I knew and still know folks in the secular world who are able to live with this kind of awareness and humility, the posturing and posing I used to see sometimes in the old scenes certainly didn't hold up well in the face of this kind of careful wisdom.

That I would willingly spend time with people with whom I couldn't share my full self, to whom I had been afraid to reveal my earnest faith—lest I be deemed "uncool"—seemed preposterous now. And, sure enough, as the host of the writing series made all too clear, my religiosity sometimes did prove to be a real liability when I dared to speak of it as though it weren't a dirty secret or some sort of involved joke. After I got back to San Francisco, I didn't bother calling the people who, I suspected, didn't really care to have an I-Thou relationship with me. So much for all the parties.

It was as if the things that had kept me from being in a more consistent relationship with the Divine or from really taking care of myself had just somehow fallen away of their own accord. "The more deeply you live your spiritual life," wrote Henri Nouwen, "the easier it will be to discern the difference between living with God and living without God, and the easier it will be to move away from the places where God is no longer with you."[3] It wasn't that I decided one day never again to drink scotch, it's just that it began looking less like a golden elixir and more like bad juice that would make me feel fuzzy and sick. (Interestingly, my refraining from alcohol generally meant that the wine that I'd drink for ritual purposes had more of the effect that it was probably meant to.) If I stayed out until 2 a.m., the next morning I'd be too depleted to offer anything of myself to God, or even to tune in to my own spiritual and emotional states. It was becoming less and less worth the price, and not even really so much fun anymore.

This heightened sensitivity wasn't always comfortable; sometimes hiding under my bed sounded a lot better than trying to face the big, scary world outside. This shift was kind of confusing, not to mention irritating, frustrating, and annoying. After all, I had already done so much letting go of my old life and ways of thinking about myself. Now I couldn't even watch a stupid Bruce Willis movie?

Shortly after entering a convent at age sixteen, Saint Catherine of Siena—who had taken a vow of perpetual virginity at age seven— was tormented by a vision. Demonic voices called to her, and she saw a painful image of naked men and women copulating wildly and beseeching her to take part in the frenzy. After it was over, she somewhat grumpily asked Christ, "And where were you when all of that was happening?" Her lord insisted that he had been in her heart the whole time—after all, he said, "if I hadn't been there, you would have found [these visions to be] most pleasurable."[4]

The more I found God with me, the more I found that things I had once found "most pleasurable" had ceased to be. As Carol Lee Flinders suggests,

> every great undertaking begins with some form of asceticism, including political resistance work . . . it looks to me as if all forms of mysticism share the understanding that "prayer and sacrifice" or "meditation and renunciation" are of the essence. Training the mind, and redirecting desires. Simplifying thought processes and life at the same time—the two efforts requiring one another.[5]

In order to do anything of significance, Flinders suggests, we must pare away anything in our lives and thinking that's not absolutely crucial. It is only then that we can give ourselves over completely to the task at hand.

This process of simplification may be harder than it once was. About 1.7 billion people now belong to what's considered the "consumer class"—"the group of people characterized by diets of highly processed food, desire for bigger houses, more and bigger cars, higher levels of debt, and lifestyles devoted to the accumulation of non-essential goods."[6] More than $120 billion a year is spent on advertising in America[7]—advertising that is, of course, highly effective. The richest fifth of the world's citizens account for more than four-fifths of private consumption expenditures,[8] spending $18 billion a year just on cosmetics.[9] New products are constantly being created—more than twenty thousand new products are sold each year at the supermarket alone[10]—and the combined effect of both the products and the ads that sell them has had a profound impact on our understanding of what we can and can't live without.

Researchers Susan Fournier and Michael Guiry discovered that only 15 percent of their survey respondants said that they'd be satisfied "living a comfortable life." The other 85 percent claimed that they would only be happy when their income and lifestyle reflected that of the richest 18 percent of American households.[11] The mind boggles: living a comfortable life is no longer enough. Rather than finding joy in being alive and connecting to others, now, more than ever, we're seeking gratification through external means.

How does one break free of all of this endless wanting? The answer is not, of course, in indulging the constant and never-ceasing craving for more. Still, as Teresa of Avila discovered, "one cannot break attachments by force . . . [for] they are the expression of an inner hunger." It is only "when that hunger is assuaged [that] attachments will fall away with almost no effort on our part."[12] It seemed that I had begun to attend to the demands of my inner life more adequately, because, almost suddenly, things that seemed to impede my physical, emotional, or spiritual self-care had begun to vanish of their own accord. This left me feeling oddly unprotected, but I also found that the force welling up from within caused me to feel stronger than I ever had before.

Spiritual self-care demands constant attention to the small voice that murmurs barely comprehensible information about what one needs from moment to moment. Sometimes that voice says, "This is dangerous." Sometimes it says, "not this, now." It's no coincidence that the mystical sects of many religious traditions

weigh in on the consumption of meat and alcohol, and that countless contemporary teachers have suggested taking breaks from the
mass media; certain things really do affect one's spiritual state. In
the days after the writer Kathy Acker had a particularly profound
experience during meditation, she found that she was rather discombobulated, clumsily bumping into cars and the like. She asked
her Zen master how to come down off the high, and he said, "You're
supposed to enjoy it! Oh—go get drunk!"[13] So she did. The foreign
substance served as the antidote to her elevated condition. If Acker
had wanted more of the blissy feeling, she should have stayed away
from anything known to bring a person "down"—but for her, it was
time to get back to her regular state of mind.

Sometimes our internal compass might tell us to stay off the
sauce, sometimes it might say (a week, a month, ten years down
the road), "oh, have a beer." There isn't necessarily an absolute or a
constant. A few years after my disorienting return to San Francisco,
I discovered that the occasional glass of wine didn't feel destructive
anymore. Something's shifted from within, and I can handle a little
alcohol now, whereas I couldn't tolerate any for a long time. Is it because something that was, then, just starting to develop has had
some time to settle in, take root inside me, and it's not endangered
by the periodic indulgence in the way that it once was? Am I living
more of my life now in a "regular state of mind"? I don't know.

I do know that my experience was not unusual. Alex stopped
eating chicken during her first couple of years in seminary, and
other friends have gone celibate or stayed away from news head-
lines while they were deep into a certain stage of some great internal undertaking. Sometimes you need to strip down to the barest
essences. Sometimes you discover that, later, you can bring back
some of the things you had left behind. Sometimes you find that
you don't need them anymore, after all. Only time and attention to
the subtle shifts of the deepest, quietest part of the self will tell.

Those first few weeks back in town, I would wake up in Rebecca's
apartment and discover that I wanted to pray, that I wanted to
spend time with the morning service on my own. Just doing the ba-

sics—the bits considered most obligatory—could keep me enter-
tained for up to an hour, even when I did a lot of it in the English
translation on the other side of the page of my bilingual prayer
book. It was wonderful to greet God in this way every morning.

After a couple of weeks of this—waking up, putting on my prayer
shawl, working my way through the service—it happened that I met
Gabe, my ex from college, for lunch. We'd remained friends; he'd
been in town for a couple of years, and we'd hung out now and then
before I had left to travel. While I was gone, though, the dot-com
bubble had burst and he had been one of its many casualties. As always, it was nice to see him and catch up. After lunch, I put in a couple of hours helping him pack up to move back to the East Coast. At
some point he looked up from a pile of books and CDs and eyed me,
almost quizzically.

"Danya," he said. "Do you want my tefillin?"

The phylacteries had been a bar mitzvah gift, and he had barely
touched them since. He wouldn't be willing to give them to me outright, he explained, but if I wanted to use them for a while, I could
consider him my own personal Judaica lending library.

I was thrilled, of course. I went to Beth Sholom the next morning so that Herb, the sixtysomething guy who organized the
service, could show me how to put them on. He and the old Yiddish-
speaking guys spent some time bickering about which customs I
should use as I wrapped them around my arm and hand. (They
were, at least, in agreement about how I should don the head
tefillin.) It was a little awkward getting everything to sit right, but
when I finally had them on—oh, the feeling. I was tucked in, bound,
secure. The straps and boxes heightened my awareness, made me
feel like some portal in my body had just opened for easier connection heavenward. It was a strange, delicious sensation. I wondered how I'd been able to live without it for so long.

While I'd been traipsing around the world, a meditation center
called Makor Or had started up in conjunction with the synagogue.
The idea was this: basic awareness meditation—sitting and watching one's breath—was a way to bring a practitioner to prayer and

Torah study with a deeper level of attentiveness. There were hour-long sittings every day before Beth Sholom's morning and evening services. There were also classes: The group would meditate for twenty or so minutes before discussing some aspect of the Torah or Jewish theological writings. People could attend on any sort of basis, but the highest-octane option was a yearlong practice period: participants were expected to attend daily sittings, weekly classes, and monthly Shabbat retreats. More than all-night zombie- or pirate-themed extravaganzas, this now sounded like my idea of a good time, not to mention the rigorous training I'd been hoping to find. It was a bit daunting, though—a whole new ballgame in terms of the formality, duration, and frequency of sittings. I wasn't sure I could handle it, but I knew that if I could, it would do me good.

Carol Lee Flinders suggests that, to some degree, paring down and turning inward requires a physical and metaphysical withdrawal from the vicissitudes of daily life. She writes,

> The literature of mysticism is shot through with images of enclosure. Of walled gardens, interior castles, cocoons, and beehives. There is no great mystery here. Meditation . . . requires that we withdraw attention from everything around us. It is all but impossible to do if we have reason to feel self-conscious or vulnerable or apprehensive . . . "A sapling must be fenced about carefully," goes a Hindu proverb, "if it is to grow into a sturdy tree."[14]

The synagogue had bought the rickety blue Victorian next door for Makor Or. Both buildings were a short ten-block walk from my studio apartment; I could roll out of bed, pull on some clothes, stumble up Clement Street, and usually make it on time for the 6 a.m. sitting. I did get out that year—I saw friends and had fun and worked in several synagogues around the Bay Area to supplement my freelance income—but my strongest memories of that time are of the carpeted meditation hall at Makor Or, and of the walk back to my apartment. Makor Or was a refuge, a place of safety in which I could be vulnerable without actually having to hide under my bed. Traveling had, paradoxically, created one kind of cocoon, splitting me off from my social context—but it hadn't offered me the chance to really let my guard down. There had been too much external stimulation, too much new information to digest. Now, it was time to enclose myself more intentionally, to see what might happen if my only stimulation came from within.

At first the sittings were hard. I'd sit on the pillow, fidgety and antsy, surreptitiously scratching my leg (we weren't supposed to move, even for that) and lost in the millions of thoughts that zoomed through my brain at an accelerated rate. I'd think about the work that I had just gotten and the guy on whom I had a crush. I'd think about people that I had met on my travels, people from the fourth grade, and what I needed to get at the hardware store. Then I'd hear Rabbi Lew's voice reminding me to readjust my posture and I'd remember with a start that I was supposed to be watching my breath, and I'd return to that for a few brief minutes—until the rowdy imps in my brain took over again.

When I was able to focus on my breath, the difference was striking. I'd feel the inhale pouring through my body, not unlike how it did on the yoga mat. As I exhaled, sometimes I would experience a sense of brightness, or feel somehow connected to the other people in the room. Sometimes my eyes seemed to open in a new clarity, and I'd be positive that I'd never before seen the wall or the carpet the way I was seeing it then. This was similar to what had happened to me those long-ago nights in Providence, but here it was more directed, deeper, less encumbered. Mostly it was a revelation just to see that I could choose to make the prattle in my mind die for a moment, to understand that perhaps I wasn't really so beholden to the ticker tape of thoughts that tromped by.

More often, though, the sittings were long and kind of boring. I would sit, my brain would chatter, and I'd try to remember to watch my breath instead. And then my mind would start to wander—rinse, repeat.

Alex had become increasingly weary of the sense that she wasn't getting what she had wanted out of her graduate training. This was mostly due, she said, to a Unitarian reticence to impose theological language and beliefs on the students. She needed God to be the default setting, and she didn't much enjoy feeling like she was being un-PC by talking about the Divine at seminary. She was thinking of transferring to the Episcopalian school, or at least doing some of her coursework there. In the meantime, she needed some space to relax, and think. So she came to spend the summer in San Francisco.

She alternated her time between my cramped apartment and Jack's drafty one, spending untold hours walking the twenty blocks via Geary or Clement. We spent a lot of time sitting in Golden Gate Park, where our conversations folded over themselves like complex origami. We sharpened our changing perspectives one upon the other, confirmed that neither of us was nuts, debated living in the world versus running away to the proverbial monastery, extracted lessons from our misspent youths, crafted theories mashing up theology and pop culture, and complained often that God didn't seem to be interested in offering any easy answers. We also cooked garlicky dinners and drank massive quantities of tea.

I came back one day after a particularly good meditation at Makor Or. She wrinkled up her nose in delight.

"Oooh," she said. "You're all shiny. I can see that *that*'s working for you."

Practice period members were, in addition to the sittings, classes, and retreats, expected to sign up for monthly meetings, one each with Rabbi Lew and his co-teacher at the center, Zoketsu Norman Fischer. In these meetings, I talked about everything from my relationship with God and my fears about staying "in the present moment" to the distressing character traits I was beginning to notice in myself—the moments of clarity sometimes shone all too bright a light on my selfishness, my pettiness, my constant need for attention. Far from allowing me to feel comfortable and "spiritual," a regular meditation practice began to show me just how far I hadn't yet come. Norman and the rabbi helped me to make sense of what was happening in the way that only people who have been doing this work for a long time, who have seen many people through the process of spiritual adolescence, can.

Most established religious systems have figured out that you don't want to drop a novice into the deep end of practice without a lifeguard nearby. It's not that prayer and meditation aren't beneficial even without a teacher, but there's a limit to how far a person can go while still trapped in his or her own brain and perspective. Sometimes it takes an observer—an observer who's had serious experience both in the doing and in the teaching of the practice—to illuminate the issues at hand. It's the difference between trying to find one's way through a dense forest alone and periodically asking someone with a map which way is north. I was long overdue for guidance—I'd met with Rabbi Lew a couple of times since I'd started attending Beth Sholom, but not enough to keep from feeling like I was constantly lost in some woodsy thicket.

I don't know if it was intentional, but Rabbi Lew and Norman had something of a good cop/bad cop thing going on. The Hasidic rabbi Simcha Bunam of Peshischa used to say, "Keep two truths in your pocket, and take them out according to the needs of the moment. Let one be, 'For my sake the world was created,' and let the other one be, 'I am but dust and ashes.' "[15] I would often leave my sessions with Rabbi Lew feeling as though I was the most Divinely connected, most powerful creature in the universe. ("You see that? You did that. Your problem is that you don't give yourself permission to do everything that you are capable of.") With Norman, however, I'd often feel humbled for my arrogance—never shamed, just lovingly pulled back down to Earth where I belonged.

Norman is a tall, thin, quiet man with a shaved head and, often, an austere expression. He's one of those people who doesn't speak unless he has something worthwhile to say. I was a clumsy, impulsive extrovert with more than a few delusions of grandeur. Needless to say, he intimidated me a bit—but I trusted him, as well.

During one of our meetings, I found myself telling him about my experience in El Escorial; I think that I was secretly hoping he would tell me that I had crossed over to some higher level of spiritual attainment. As I spoke, his face remained impassive. I finished, and there was a long pause. Finally, he said, slowly, "You know that those experiences don't mean anything, right? They might be pleasurable, and even compelling, but there's no real meaning in them."

Norman's attitude about meditation could be summed up by something he once wrote in an essay: "Every day I have new problems, nothing is solved. But I am willing for that to be the case, possibly forever, which I suppose is my main achievement."[16] At a retreat once, he said that the quality he most admired in others was perseverance. This man, of all people, was not going to be terribly impressed by the fact that my brain went "pop!" one time and it was nice.

Though I didn't understand it until later, the fact that Norman didn't validate me for this experience was tremendously instructive. As Thomas Merton—himself a longtime spiritual director—put it, "We should certainly be serious in our search for God—nothing is more serious than that. But we ought not to be constantly observing our own efforts at progress and paying exaggerated attention to 'our spiritual life.'" Not only that, but "the mere effort to admit that we are not as unselfish or as zealous as we pretend to be is a great source of grace."[17] I liked pretending that I was zealous, liked thinking of myself as something other than the true novice that I was. Norman's refusal to mirror back to me my own illusions about my experiences and their meanings burst a balloon that I'd been carrying around inside—it hurt a little, but it ultimately created more room for me to see, potentially, what might really be.

My meditations shifted over time. Sometimes I'd sit down on the cushion, start watching my breath, and become aware, astoundingly, that I was in extreme physical pain. I had never found a solution to the tendinitis I had developed a couple of years earlier, and it had flared up pretty badly with all the hauling of boxes entailed by my move back to town. Even so, most of the time I didn't really notice it; I had figured out how to make a few adjustments to my life here and there so that it didn't slow me down too much. On the meditation cushion, however, I'd close my eyes and my arms would throb and burn. I began to wonder how I could not have noticed just how bad they'd gotten. When the brain weasels were in charge, nattering on about to-do lists and falling into some elaborate fantasy scenario, it seemed that I was much less aware of what was happening to me physically. I could practically become a disembodied head. Watching my breath brought me back to the fact that my breath was coming from, and returning to, a body. And this particular body, it turns out, had been in pain for a while without my really noticing.

It turned out that there were other things I hadn't noticed, as well. Sometimes when I sat down on the cushion and got into the rhythm of my breath, I would become aware not of throbbing tendons, but of strong, strong emotions: Anger. Fear. Hurt. Sadness. Occasionally I'd find myself flooded by images, as though watching a movie: I'd see myself at age five, cowering in the hall closet under my parents' coats as screaming raged outside. At age twelve, running through the family room, wailing and beating everything in sight with a baseball bat, setting things on fire. I know for a fact that the latter scene never happened, and I'm not sure if the former ever did. Nonetheless, the images were clearly reflective of feelings I'd had at the time—probably about my parents' turbulent marriage—but had never felt safe or comfortable expressing. If I wasn't even aware of physical pain during day-to-day activity and brain chatter, how much more was I removed from latent emotional states?

Norman and Rabbi Lew taught us that the point of awareness meditation was not to keep our minds perfectly blank to the point where we forced away the thoughts that popped up. Rather, we were to work at not grabbing on to the thoughts. In other words, if the words "shopping list" came into my head, I wasn't supposed to indulge their presence by saying to myself, "Oh, gee, what about the shopping list?" and saunter off into a reverie about yogurt and tomatoes—but, rather, to keep breathing and know that the grocery interest would soon fall away of its own accord. But, though I slowly became a bit more able to let go of mundane, everyday thoughts, I found that emotions didn't vanish immediately, even when I actually stayed focused on my breath (as opposed to wandering off into the emotional equivalent of yogurt land). Rumi famously wrote,

"This being human is a guest house / Every morning a new arrival. / A joy, a depression, a meanness . . . / Welcome and entertain them all!"[18] Sometimes the feelings rose up strongly and ran around for a while before they'd get bored and go somewhere else, leaving me with my breathing. My job was to not try to persuade the feelings either to stay or to vanish before they were ready, but rather to let them come and go without getting tangled up in them.

And so on the meditation cushion, long-buried emotions, finally given space, began to rise up and burn through me. I would spend entire sessions shaking in anger (hands still carefully arranged in the formal sitting position) or crying, as silently as I could so as not to disturb the other folks in the room. Sometimes I didn't understand what was going on in any intellectual way and other times the feelings would be connected to some painful insight. As the months progressed, I began to articulate things about the nature of my parents' marriage, about the ways I'd been hurt by them or other people, about why I had chosen or avoided certain romantic relationships, about the more difficult aspects of my relationship with my mother. After she had died, I had tried not to think about the ways in which she had been, by turns, critical, withdrawn, demanding, and impenetrable. It was much easier to grieve for a saint than for someone with whom I had unfinished business, and hard to accept that, on some level, I'd never find the kind of closure with her that I so wanted. Now, however, there was nothing to do but face the truths and the unsettled issues as they were. Everything I'd never wanted to acknowledge about my life began asserting itself, unfurling in rapid succession on the meditation cushion. It was a little difficult to bear.

Facing unpleasant emotions is one of the most important and underrated facets of spiritual (to say nothing of human) growth. As the Muslim writer Kabir asks, "When deep inside you there is a loaded gun, how can you have God?"[19] We hit a limit past which there's no possible way to progress without emptying out some of the unresolved stuff we've been carrying around—the grief, the anger, the sense of abandonment, the feelings of inadequacy. At some point, we have to face the worldviews and coping mechanisms that we've constructed either to avoid those feelings or in response to them. "You have to weep over your lost pains so that they can gradually leave you," writes Henri Nowen, "and you can become free to live fully in the new place without melancholy or homesickness."[20] In order for Dante to move from hell to paradise, he had to pass through purgatory. Thomas Merton likens the healing soul to a bone that is broken and reset.[21]

Of course it's not fun. Nobody wants to remember that they were once a terrified five-year-old or to think about the ways in which avoidance has shaped a life. Plus, we may be culturally hardwired to resist the sort of letting go that's necessary to make ourselves so vulnerable. As environmentalist Joanna Macy notes,

> The model of the self that predominates in Western culture is, "I am master of my fate and the captain of my soul." It makes us reluctant to engage in issues that remind us that we do not exert ultimate control over our lives. We feel somehow that we ought to be in charge of our existence and emotions, to have all the answers. And so we tend to shrink the sphere of our attention to those areas in which we feel we can be in charge.[22]

Every discomfort—any sensation that might suggest that we're not in total control of our situation—is, in American culture, meant to be fixed and hurriedly soothed with the right cream, pill, or technological gadget. There's not a lot of allowing for the possibility that a person might just feel sad, or lonely, or grumpy because, sometimes, people are sad, lonely, or grumpy.

But, as Macy writes, "repression...take[s] a mammoth toll... [with this kind of] anesthetization...loves and losses are less intense, the sky is less vivid—for if we are not going to let ourselves feel pain, we will not feel much else either."[23] And if we can't feel much, how are we going to perceive the subtle murmurs of the Divine, which requires at least as much sensitivity, if not more, than what it takes just to know what we're feeling? The price isn't just living numbly or even that we shortchange personal relationships by letting our unconscious goo get in the way, as it inevitably does.

At the end of the day, trying to avoid uncomfortable emotions might be worse than actually just experiencing them. Buddhist teacher Sylvia Boorstein says,

> If I say to myself, "This is painful, but it's O.K.," and I stay there, then it's just what it is and then it changes. But when I run away from it or I push it away or pretend that it's something else, that is the suffering. All those maneuvers that we do to avoid saying, "This is true. This is what's happening"—the maneuvers themselves are the suffering.[24]

Perhaps ironically, God is often found precisely when we let go of the maneuvers, when we surrender to the emotions that are already there. The Talmud teaches in the name of Rabbi Elezar, "From the day on which the Temple was destroyed, the gates of prayer have been closed... But though the gates of prayer are closed, the gates of weeping are not closed"[25] and the Hasidic master the Baal Shem Tov is quoted as saying, "There are many halls in the King's palace, and intricate keys to all the doors, but the master key is the broken heart."

Once, in a meeting with Rabbi Lew, I revealed how terrified and uncertain I was feeling about some big work-related issues. He asked me a few questions, and then concluded, "So you feel like a failure, in other words."

Uh, yeah. I guess so. Thanks, I feel better now.

Then he softened. "Of course you feel like a failure. Everybody does, deep down." He instructed me to embrace those feelings until I got to the place where my failures merged with everybody else's failures, with all the failures of the entire world. The next day was Tisha B'Av—the anniversary of the destruction of the Jerusalem Temple, a holiday about confronting suffering and disintegration. So after Tisha B'Av services I went home, and I sat. I watched my breath, and I allowed this dark, nasty, voracious fear to rise up and overtake me. As it came up I descended to meet it, like a swimmer pushing toward the ocean's floor. Eventually, somehow, I got down into a place where my own loss and grief and fear and disappointment merged into Loss and Grief and Fear and Disappointment, into fundamental facts of the human condition. Deep in that place, I felt, somehow, connected with all those millions of people out there feeling these things—not because of the specifics of these emotions, but because of our shared sweet, vulnerable, messy humanity as a whole.

The feelings of failure didn't just merge into something more beautiful, fragile, and neutral—though they did do that. The meditation also enabled me to plug into a picture much bigger and much more important than my isolated, solitary woes. Suddenly, I was only a bit player in a much grander drama. I was all the more normal because I felt like a failure—not special, or weird. And that, in itself, was strangely empowering.

This realization also gave me a sense of responsibility and obligation, not unlike the feeling I had in El Escorial and have had many times since. It's not that I had forgotten the things I had apprehended before, but certain kinds of lessons must be learned over and over and over again, reexperienced anew from many different angles. That's how they stick, how we begin to internalize them. That Tisha B'Av, I realized once again that if I was, in fact, linked to all of these other people, it would be harder to pretend that their needs mattered less than mine. And my actions, speech, and attitude might have to change as a result.

Neither the inner work nor the willingess to do it is linear. One day I was on my way to a meeting with Norman and I was hit with a blast of anguish—yet another insight about one of my family relationships had worked its way up to the surface of my consciousness. I stopped, doubled over in the middle of Clement Street, overcome by waves of suffering that I couldn't name, let alone control. I leaned on a parking meter for support and, as usual, I cried.

By the time I got to Makor Or, I was drained and cranky. I tried to summon up a serene equilibrium before I spoke. It didn't work. Instead, I whined.

"This isn't any fun. I feel terrible and nothing's getting any better—it's getting worse. I don't feel like a better person for seeing so clearly just how messed up my life is. I don't want to be a spiritual aspirant anymore. Forget the present moment. I just want to go back to drinking and watching TV."

I sounded like a petulant eight-year-old, positively dripping in self-pity.

Sitting in lotus position on a pillow across from me, Norman raised his sleepy, half-closed eyes and said, in a cool, even tone, "Going back to drinking and TV won't work. Believe me, I've tried."

The more intense my meditations got, the more I relied on my teachers for guidance through the brambles of my own brain. I took eager notes in the classes. I hung on every word they said during retreats. Before each meeting with one of them, I'd try to distill down my neuroses and crazinesses of the previous few weeks in order to understand as precisely as I could where I was stuck or struggling with the practice. Following procedure, I'd show up for the regular meditation during my meeting time slot and sit with the others until someone tapped me on my shoulder to let me know that it was my turn. (When I was done, I'd be told whose shoulder to tap when I returned to the cushions.) I'd climb up the creaky stairs and walk, as contemplatively as my galumphing self could manage, toward the room in which the practice interviews were held. I'd sit down, and there would be a silence. Sometimes the rabbi or Norman would ask me what I wanted to discuss, sometimes they just waited for me to begin. Our meetings never went in a direction that I anticipated. Even after the worst feelings of burnout, these conversations would always leave me surprised and strangely invigorated to return both to the cushion and to my life.

Religion scholar James Carse writes,

We know we have met . . . a teacher when we come away amazed not at what the teacher was thinking but at what we are thinking. We will forget what the teacher is saying because we are listening to a source deeper than the teachings themselves. A great teacher

exposes the source, then steps back. Great teachings . . . pass away.
As soon as we hear them they are gone and we are listening to
what follows.[26]

Rabbi Lew and Norman were my teachers—the rabbi most of all. I
learned a lot from Norman, but it had been years, at this point, that
I had been following Rabbi Lew's sermons and attending his services at Beth Sholom, dropping in on his Monday morning Torah
classes and going to talk with him in his office. He was my guide to
building a Jewish observance, and I looked to him for cues and insight about keeping Shabbat, learning how to pray, taking on new
mitzvot, and understanding what Jewish law was all about. Plus, I
felt more of an affinity for his style than I did for Norman's—he was
outgoing, funny, and occasionally self-deprecating in a way that
I recognized all too well. Fundamentally, though, he became my
teacher because he said things that I needed to hear. I knew this
from the first sermon I had heard at Beth Sholom, some three-plus
years earlier.

Teachers are especially important early on in the game, when
the woods seem darkest and the path the most thorny—which is
not to say that we don't always need other people to help us move
past our own limited view of things. But a first teacher is kind of like
a first love, possessed of a bizarrely comparable ability to affect how
we think and how we see the world. And, by nature of its power, this
kind of relationship is simlarly fraught with dangers and risks.

The intensity of the work done within a spiritual discipline can
create a strong bond between aspirant and advisor. Sometimes
these connections become lifelong, though they rarely evolve into
a friendship between equals. The teacher–student relationship
is, by definition, an unequal one, with one party requesting help,
insight, and guidance, and the other (hopefully) providing it, sometimes dramatically shaking up the novice's inner world in the
process.

The seventeenth-century Benedictine monk Augustine Baker
said, "[A spiritual] director is not to teach his own way, . . . but to in-

struct his disciples how they may themselves find out the way proper for them...he is only God's usher, and must lead souls in God's way, and not his own."²⁷ Meticulous spiritual hygiene is necessary to keep the teacher's own way from becoming confused with the student's path to the Divine. And, of course, despite the intimacy of the relationship and the possibility of helping a student with crucial and sometimes life-changing work, the teacher is not perfect. Nobody is. Some teachers are very skilled at keeping their flaws and emotional scars far from their spiritual directees, but even a gifted teacher has limits. The tricky part is knowing when and how to express them.

Reb Zalman Schachter-Shalomi was ordained by the Lubavitch Hasidim and served for many years as an emissary of the Lubavitchers. One year, he came to New York from his then home of Winnipeg, and was scheduled to have a meeting with the Lubavitcher Rebbe for spiritual counseling. He went to the Rebbe's assistant at the appointed time but was told that the Rebbe couldn't see him. He went back the next night and was told, again, "not tonight." Finally, on the third night, the Rebbe consented to meet with him. When Reb Zalman was finally granted audience, the Rebbe apologized for having been unavailable the previous two nights and explained that, simply, "There was no one there."²⁸ The Rebbe, it seems, had known that he was not in a mental or spiritual place in which he would have been able to connect effectively with Zalman. It is a testimony to his prowess as a teacher that he knew this, and didn't try to perform a particular kind of magic when he had no magic available.

Not all teachers are as skilled at understanding their own limitations. Some overextend themselves out of a desire to save everyone. Some simply don't know how to say no. Some are so invested in the idea of themselves as spiritual masters that they have trouble admitting that their abilities aren't boundless, that some nights the wise, insightful guide that their students seek needs to be off duty. Some get drunk on the power to affect people's very souls and, consciously or not, exploit their students' feelings of dependence.

Certainly, the sexual and financial abuse scandals that have rocked just about every religious world—implicating priests, ministers, rabbis, Zen masters, imams, and gurus alike—are a direct result of the unequal nature of the teacher–student relationship and the dangers it sometimes poses to the novice aspirant.

Whether in overt or subtle ways, every spiritual teacher's imperfections are eventually revealed. In a healthy teacher–student relationship, this fact doesn't need to be a deal breaker—Reb Zalman and the Rebbe continued to meet for a long time after the night Zalman was refused counsel. Sometimes students idealize a teacher to the degree that even relatively benign displays of weakness—such as the Rebbe's—cause them to become bitterly disillusioned, wondering how they could have relied so heavily on this person for so long. This may be more a result of a student's unrealistic expectations than a true failure on the teacher's part. Sometimes it's the student's job to reassess how much work he was meant to do on his own all along, and perhaps to renegotiate the relationship, if it's healthy and might still be nourishing for the student.

Of course, real exploitation does sometimes happen, and these betrayals are often quite traumatic. In these cases, it's vital that the student not blame herself, but rather gather the courage to speak up. Every effort must be made by the community to help those who have been injured and to address any suspected or confirmed breach of ethics. All too often, a toxic spiritual leader is left unchecked for far too long, and allowed to hurt others without inquiry—even after disturbing rumors (or even initial reports of abuse) have surfaced. Uncritical respect for the glorified sanctity of the teacher should never prevent a student from coming forward or a community from taking serious measures to investigate an allegation.

However, it's hardly true that every time a relationship changes, it's because either teacher or student is in error. Not every teacher keeps all of her students for life, and not every student needs to stay with the same teacher for years on end. Sometimes, things simply

shift. After a year or two at Makor Or, I moved to Los Angeles to begin rabbinical school. At first, I drove back up to San Francisco to
visit my friends almost every chance I had, and each time I'd call
Rabbi Lew's office to make an appointment during his office hours.
He was generous with his time, willing to meet with me on Sunday
mornings and the like, but inevitably I'd leave these meetings dis-
appointed. Something wasn't clicking the way it had. Sometimes
teacher–student relationships weather this sort of evolution, manage to transition from one situation to another well enough to remain effective in some form. This one, for a whole host of reasons,
did not. Of course it wasn't going to be the same as it had been when
I was his congregant, an active part of the Beth Sholom community,
and working with him intensively at Makor Or—but it didn't seem
to find a new incarnation, either. I have a few theories as to why that
is, but it doesn't matter. Rabbi Lew played an important role in my
life, and I will always be grateful to him for that. His teaching is
an important part of who I have become, and he has left an indelible mark on my understanding of Judaism. How could it be any
other way?

At Makor Or, we talked a lot about impermanence—the impermanence of the thoughts and feelings that wander through our
minds, the impermanence of our bodies upon the Earth. Relationships too, of course, shift and change, sometimes emerge and fade
away. I have had many teachers in the years since I left Beth
Sholom, and I've learned important things from each; I've grown
and developed and been transformed as a result of their presence
in my life. My path may cross with that of Rabbi Lew again someday in a meaningful way—but it may not. That's okay.

In Pirke Avot, the Mishnah instructs in the name of Yoshua ben
Perahia, "Make for yourself a teacher, acquire for yourself a friend."[29]
When I got back to San Francisco after my travels, it was clear that
I had a teacher. But in the midst of all of this renunciation, intro-
spection, and enclosure, I wasn't so sure how to become satisfied
socially. I was actually pretty certain that I was going to be doomed
to a life of relative isolation, of lonely Saturdays alone and saying

no to the many things I had somehow stopped enjoying. To my great surprise, however, I stumbled instead into the party next door to the one I'd grown weary of attending. There, I discovered that I wasn't the only one whose idea of fun had shifted and changed, and become something new entirely.

EIGHT

I got the e-mail right after I moved back to San Francisco. The subject was "West Coast Retreat for Young Jewish Social Justice Activists." A well-known Jewish leader from the other side of the country had, evidently, gotten funding to bring thirty people together to talk about religion and politics. The goal was to discuss some of the same questions I'd been having, like how Shabbat changes one's relationship to technology or how paying attention might affect whether one identifies with the woman cleaning the office and what that might mean. It sounded good. I had spent much of the previous year working on an anthology of "next generation" Jewish feminist writing called *Yentl's Revenge*. The idea had been born during my freelancing heyday, mostly out of hunches and suspicions I had about the intellectual peers I hadn't yet met. It was due to be published soon by a press with whom many of my secular feminist comrades had worked, so I put it down on the retreat application. I guess it was enough to qualify me as a "Jewish social justice activist," because I got an e-mail back a month later telling me that I had been given a slot, and should let them know if I needed a ride down.

The weekend took place at a gorgeous retreat center nestled among the Santa Cruz Mountains. When I got there, people were milling around, waiting for the programming to begin. It felt a little like the first day of summer camp; everyone was very excited about

Not PC

meeting everyone else, even if it took a while to get names straight. The "activist" factor was all over the map: There were people who worked with at-risk youth, with prisoners, or with HIV-positive homeless folk. There were union organizers, environmental educators, the creators of a Passover "Seder in the streets," people who ran programs for queer teenagers, the head of a prominent Jewish peace organization, the author of a zine about transgender Jews, and a rabbi who had been part of the WTO demonstrations in Seattle, just to name a few. I did my best not to be too intimidated.

After everyone settled into their rooms, we met for Friday night services. Saul, the prayer leader, used melodies that I had learned in Jerusalem, so I closed my eyes and fell into the music. It's possible that Saul noticed that I knew the liturgy, because afterwards, he asked me if I wanted to say the blessing of the day's sanctification—a couple of paragraphs of text—over the wine before dinner. I demurred: "Oh, I don't know how to do that," I said. He asked somebody else. As soon as the blessing began, however, I realized with a twinge that I actually did know it all by heart after hearing it so many times in synagogue. I could have led it perfectly well myself.

After dinner, we all went into the big communal space for a paired icebreaker exercise, lounging on pillows and switching partners every few minutes. Soon it was my turn to partner with our conference organizer, whose enormous white beard made him look every inch the stereotype wizened rabbi. He leaned on his pillow and smiled warmly at me. "This reminds me of the sixties," he said. "There's an electricity in the air, like something important is starting." It certainly felt like that, at least for me—like I had walked into a new world of promise. Here, for the first time, I began to wonder if something a little bit like integration might actually be possible.

Toward the end of the evening, Saul asked me if I wanted to lead the morning services the next day. Again, I declined—I certainly couldn't lead the full morning services, I definitely didn't know how to do that. But perhaps, I mumbled hurriedly, thinking of my missed opportunity of that evening, perhaps I could lead Musaf, the shorter section toward the end of the service? He shrugged—it wasn't that big a deal to him either way.

I stayed up late with the prayer book, going over the sections. From my current perspective, it's a tiny amount of liturgy to master, but then it was huge. My Hebrew wasn't great, and just about all of my prayer experience had been in places where I had been expected to think of myself more as a follower than as a potential leader; I had never paid close attention to what the leader was supposed to be doing. Even without training or confidence, though, I knew that it was time to cross over into this new role, and I knew that this environment, where everything was lay-led and everyone was so nice and welcoming, was the right place to try—and that here, it would be okay even if I didn't do a wonderful job.

Shabbat morning services that day were very different from what I was used to. The rabbi-organizer's style was much more open and free-flowing than any I'd experienced since my initial Bay Area synagogue search. I found that I had developed a fairly traditional approach to the liturgy; sometimes, when he skipped over things, I said them quietly to myself. That way, I could participate without sacrificing my own understanding of what was supposed to happen.

That morning, after the first part of the service and the Torah reading, people began taking off their prayer shawls and talking about going down to lunch. "But...but...what about Musaf?" I stammered. After all, I was ready, I had practiced! Ten or twelve people offered to stay upstairs and pray with me, to give me a chance to try leading services. I was nervous and hardly elegant in my delivery, but I got through it. It was a huge milestone for me, in a lot of ways—not the least of which is that it shifted my focus from a personal connection to God to a sense of obligation to the community.

This wasn't the first time I had noticed the importance of the collective in prayer. It had been clear even after my mother's death, when I began thinking about why the Mourner's Kaddish can only be recited when there are ten adult Jews present. At the time, I figured that group prayer served a social function, helping to console the mourner and create relationships, and that's definitely part of it. But when I got to Beth Sholom, I began to understand that the power and force of the liturgy itself were proportional to the number of people present, all of whom opened themselves to the Divine through words mumbled, whispered, and sung. Meditation worked the same way—even when I was off floating around my own brain, I was vaguely aware of the presence of the other practice period members, and their company somehow helped me to enter my own meditation in a much more serious way. As Henri Nouwen put it, "think of your community as holding a long line that girds your waist"[1]—a line that keeps you from straying too far from where you need to be.

It wasn't until I began leading prayer, though, that I really began to articulate the ways that community could sustain me—the way that it could keep me tethered to my practice and, simultaneously, encourage me to take risks and push myself in new ways. For a long time, it had been easy enough to stay distant—to drift in and out of synagogues as I traveled, or even just to attend services regularly at Beth Sholom without speaking to the other people there. In Jerusalem, I began to see Shabbat as a communal celebration, but I still thought of myself as a loner who sometimes got Friday night dinner invitations, not as a crucial member of a larger organism. Taking on the mantle of prayer leader helped me to begin regarding my own role in a group as something other than passive.

I found the responsibility of leading others in prayer totally humbling. Over time, I realized that when others placed their trust in my ability to help carry them through worship, I had an obligation to respond with trust in myself, and them. That is to say, I had to lay myself bare. When I tried to make the liturgy beautiful by "performing" well, I usually failed—I was no good, and the energy in the room would be soggy and limp. On the other hand, when I stopped worrying about hitting the right notes and, rather, opened myself to God in front of everyone, when I shared my most private spiritual self and made myself totally vulnerable in front of people who might think that I was completely wacko—that's when the service caught fire. And in a more general sense, I think, this is how community works. It's about matching trust with trust, about creating spaces in which people can let down their guard and reveal what's hidden, about encouraging others to grow in new and challenging ways. And it's also very much about creating the conditions in which this might be able to happen.

The retreat was five days long, each one full but not overly programmed. There were workshops on things like how to mobilize the Jewish community around civic matters, how to think about labor laws through the lens of the command to rest on Shabbat, and how to make Judaism more accessible to Jews of various cultural or economic profiles. When a few folks felt frustrated that certain perspectives were not well addressed, they—veteran educators who had done this sort of thing a million times—put together an impromptu workshop that everyone agreed to attend during one of our free slots.

It wasn't all workshops and "processing," though. Over the course of the week, we had ample time to lie around the grass and sit on the swings. We had time to take long, looping walks in groups of two or three through the redwood forests, to have a late-night dance party, to splash around the pool, and to convene groups of people who wanted to talk about some specific common interest. Two participants who had a fundamental disagreement about an issue were often seen over the course of the retreat locked in intense conversation, trying to come to a mutual understanding.

In short, we bonded.

In this space I found, perhaps for the first time, people with whom I might be able to both pray and play. Most of these folks, in some way or another, shared my struggle to coherently mix secular sensibilities and Jewish devotion. And more than that, I saw a certain ethic of interpersonal relations modeled; here, caring for others was genuinely understood to be sacred work. Granted, I had already learned this from Ariel, Rebecca, Teresa, and company, but it was striking for me to see it enacted in a Jewish context, among relative strangers who weren't invested in preserving old friendships. Here, I saw people tend to one another in a million small ways: Folks stayed to comprise a quorum so that I could lead Musaf, even if they would have been just as happy to skip it and get lunch. They were willing to use their free time to learn about someone else's concerns. Perhaps most strikingly, this ethos was manifest in the two people who stayed up until all hours, hashing through their disagreement rather than shrugging and dismissing the other as wrong and, maybe, a little bit stupid. This was the I-Thou relationship in action: People so committed to seeing each other's wholeness that they would put up with inconvenience or discomfort in order to do so. Folks were genuinely interested in getting to know one another in three dimensions, and as personal confessions emerged over the course of the weekend, it became increasingly clear that there was little that anyone could disclose that would be a deal breaker. I-Thou relationships were, after all, unconditional.

It was marvelous, and a little bewildering.

I made some time for myself during the weekend, as well. I wandered through the forest, open and awe-struck by the trees, the air, this place, my life. I was beginning to see that as faith grows, these feelings of wonder appear and reappear in different forms.

Psalm 150 is heavily punctuated with "halleluyahs." One of the melodies to which it is sung involves chanting the word over and over and over, a dizzying canon of praise to God. Now, alone among the redwoods, I sang "halleluyah" again and again, getting myself drunk on the music and God and the sweet mountain air. I was so grateful, and everything felt so perfect. Praise God.

The end of the retreat was huggy and teary, with lots of promises that we would keep in touch, try to get together as a group the following year. Those of us who lived in the Bay Area had already made plans to hang out in the interim. Our closing exercise was, I suppose, lifted straight from some sort of leadership training course. We stood in a circle, and a ball of yarn was tossed from one person to another. Each one would hold on to the end of the yarn as they tossed and say something nice to the person they were tossing to, and then the next person would hold on to the yarn before tossing it on, thus creating an increasingly complex spider web of string. It was a little hokey, maybe, but it did nonetheless manage to evoke the idea that Martin Luther King Jr. tried to articulate when he said, "All men are caught in an inescapable network of mutuality, tied in a single garment of destiny. Whatever affects one directly affects all indirectly."[2]

People were loving and ample in their admiration of one another, and more than a few people were crying. I waited patiently as this exercise unfolded. As the ball of string got tossed here and there and everyone was lavishly complimented, I began to feel increasingly like I might be the last kid picked for the kickball team. There were only six people left, then five, then four. Then Raf, a hippie kid from Berkeley, got the string and tossed it to me. He smiled.

"I heard you in the woods, singing to the trees," he said. I flinched—how embarrassing! That was supposed to be a private moment!

"It was such a beautiful sound," he said. He continued in that vein for a while, talking about hearing my soul fly, and so forth. After so many years of feeling slightly embarrassed by my faith among my secular friends, after struggling to rein in my enthusiasm for the Divine so that it wouldn't impinge too much upon the rest of my life, it was startling to be seen and valued by a virtual stranger precisely for my deepest longings. I-Thou.

For years, Malcolm X preached racial separatism and declared that he wanted nothing to do with whites. At some point, however, he became disillusioned with the Nation of Islam and, around the same time, made *hajj* (pilgrimage) to Mecca. When he got on the plane to the Middle East, he was shocked to see "throngs of people, obviously Muslims from everywhere, bound on the pilgrimage... hugging and embracing. They were of all complexions, the whole atmosphere was of warmth and friendliness. The feeling hit me that there really wasn't any color problem here." In this new communal space, all of Malcolm X's old assumptions about who he was and how he ought to interact with others were dramatically and suddenly rearranged. His old identities and ideologies were implicitly challenged just by being welcomed on an airplane. "The effect," he writes, "was as though I had just stepped out of prison."[3]

Up to this point, "spirituality," as I'd been thinking of it, had demanded a great deal from me internally. But the retreat helped me to see that despite it all, I hadn't really been accountable to anyone else in my religious life. My closest friends were always happy both to support me and to let me know when I was full of it, and they definitely kept me on the ball in a more general sense. But in the context of Judaism, Torah, and God, I hadn't risked more than superficial relationships, hadn't allowed myself to become embedded in a context where people might really see what I was up to, and might be able to push me to become a better person and a better Jew. Even as I'd been longing for certain kinds of conversations, I had succeeded in avoiding them in any sort of depth.

It was safe and comfortable to keep my distance, even though I was perpetuating a fundamental religious fallacy by doing so—one that is all too common these days.

Cultural theorist bell hooks writes,

I am often struck by the dangerous narcissism fostered by spiritual rhetoric that pays so much attention to individual self-improvement and so little to the practice of love in the context of community. Packaged as a commodity, spirituality becomes no different from an exercise program. While it may leave the consumer feeling better about his or her life, its power to enhance our communion with ourselves and others in a sustained way is inhibited."[4]

But it's no wonder that the model for spirituality in operation today is so highly individualistic. Individual liberty and the pursuit of individual happiness are principles on which America was founded, and, indeed, these ideas have given us many gifts—freedom to dissent, for example, a wide berth for creativity, and the possibility of forging lives other than the ones into which we were born. But relentless individualism has its downsides.

Take the early days of second-wave feminism, for example. In the years before the women's liberation movement emerged in the 1960s, a great many women had been isolated without meaningful connections with one another. Thus, most believed that any struggles they faced were merely their own, reflective of their own weaknesses rather than of a systemic problem. As more and more women came together to discuss their individual experiences, it became clear that the personal really *was* political—that rape, street harassment, job discrimination, unequal pay, and unfair double standards really were endemic to the culture at large. It was only then that these women saw that they could not only support one another in a profound way, but that they needed to mobilize as a group to effect concrete political change.

The dominant culture depends on our sense of isolation. As long as spirituality remains an individualized, personal experience, chances remain good that the inherently revolutionary potential of religious work will sit forever inert and untapped. That is to say, those who practice their spirituality without community are much less likely to demand change in and upheaval to the status quo, or feel that they have the power to do so.

And, of course, in a culture of individualistic spirituality, the boundaries of the self are reinforced, rather than broken down. As the focus has moved to personal improvement, individual ecstactic experiences, and private salvation, the ego that was supposed to dissolve during prayer has become stronger than ever. Saint Francis prayed to God that he would "not so much seek to be consoled as to console; to be understood as to understand; to be loved as to love."[5] Contrast that statement with, for example, the assertion in a recent book called *Essential Spirituality* that "the ultimate aim of spiritual practicices is awakening; that is, to know our true Self."[6] Rather than helping us ask how we can be of service to others—or (ahem) God—our contemporary "spirituality" has become a different kind of code word for self-gratification. As the great sage Hillel famously asked, "If I am only for myself, what am I?"[7] Or, as Gandhi put it, "isolated independence is not the goal. It is voluntary interdependence."[8]

In short, the solitary trip misses a vital part of the religious picture. When the medieval anchoress Julian of Norwich was a young woman, she had an intense and complex vision of the Divine, the meaning of which she pondered for fifteen years. Eventually she understood what God was trying to tell her and wrote, "Know it well, love was His meaning. Who reveals it to you? Love. What did He reveal to you? Love. Why does He reveal it to you? For love. Remain in this, and you will know more of the same. But you will never know different, without end."[9] Many of us experience God as a love that surges through and binds us all, and the way to manifest that radiance in the world is through the giving of love to others. Unfortunately, though, this openheartedness isn't automatic for all of us. Sometimes we need practice learning how to transcend our solitary selves and how to enact empathy, hospitality, compassion. It is by living in community, in part, that we come to see the Divine in others. And in return, we receive love, caring, and connection.

It's not always easy, of course. In a lot of ways, connecting to God seems much less complicated than trying to connect with people. Our fellow human beings are messy, limited, needy, fettered to their own perspectives, and certainly don't always behave as we would like them to. (God doesn't always behave according to our ideas either, but that's another story.) Many have struggled with the desire to dwell only on some lofty spiritual plane and avoid the taxing effort of loving our neighbors as ourselves. But it doesn't work—we can't just stay in the otherworldly zone and forget about trying to get along with our own kind. As it says in I Corinthians, "if I have prophetic powers, and understand all mysteries and all knowledge, and if I have all faith so as to remove mountains, but I have not love, I am nothing."[10] There's a reason that the Ten Commandments appeared on two tablets—five of the commandments concern our obligations to God, and five tell us how to act toward other people.

It's for good reason that Anabaptists (folks like the Amish and Mennonites, who traditionally live in tightly knit communities) have developed an elaborate theology of conflict. Living in close connection with others often means that difficulties will arise. However, as they well know, it's crucial for both individual and communal spiritual growth to face these challenges, rather than running away. As Thomas Merton put it, "Souls are like athletes, that need opponents worthy of them, if they are to be tried and extended and pushed to the full use of their powers, and rewarded according to their capacity."[11] Communities are almost never places of ideal peace and serenity, but natural points of turbulence offer us a chance to address our own anger, impatience, stinginess, and self-ishness in a way we rarely do when left to our own devices. Learn-ing how to love one another is hardly easy. But it is through the imperfect attempt to do so that we become who we were meant to be all along, as individuals and together.

"Thou hast commanded me to love my neighbor," Saint Cather-ine of Genoa says to God, "and I am unable to love anyone but Thee, or to admit any partner with Thee: how then shall I obey Thee?" God answers her that "for the welfare of the neighbor thou shouldst do all that is necessary for his soul and body . . . it is not in himself but in God that the neighbor should be loved."[12] The task is not only to care for the welfare of others, but to see and love that which is most sacred within them.

Our culture's tendency to distinguish "spirituality" from basic communal needs like food or water is exceedingly recent. Every ma-jor religious tradition recognizes in some form that an integral part of the job is securing the basics of sustenence and safety for every-one. Just as "there is no bread without Torah," as one of the ancient rabbinic aphorisms of Pirke Avot instructs, so too "there is no Torah without bread."[13] It's understandably tempting to focus on feeling the Divine love that flows through us and connects us to the peo-ple we know and with whom we feel comfortable. But, of course, refusal to understand that this connection also binds us to AIDS-stricken Africans, exploited child laborors, desperate illegal immi-grants, and the homeless folks we walk by every morning perverts and distorts the meaning and mission of this love.

As Heschel put it, "Few are guilty, but all are responsible."[14]

I returned to San Francisco invigorated. We set up a listserv for the retreat participants and began trying to decide where we would meet for Shabbat dinner. And, to my surprise, I began finding com-munity almost everywhere I went.

It would take a while to get my freelance career going again, so

I began looking for a part-time job to help with my rent checks. A friend of a friend suggested that I contact the head of a program in Berkeley for Jewish teenagers. It was a supplementary education program, offering offbeat classes meant to engage the post–bar mitzvah set: stuff like Theology in Film, Political Torah Commentary, Prayer Through Dance, and even plain old Talmud. High school kids *voluntarily* came out in droves Sunday mornings; evidently they were doing something right. The program director was a warm, funny woman who said she'd give me a whirl even though I had almost no teaching experience. What did I want to teach? I tossed out a few ideas—Jewish sexual ethics, maybe, or perhaps something on the different ways Jewish lore depicts God? She put me in touch with the principals of a few other programs in the area—soon, in addition to my Sunday morning gig, I was teaching Monday and Wednesday evenings on everything from the spirituality of prayer and comparative mysticism to Jewish feminist history.

Teaching was hard, exciting work. I had to figure out how to synthesize everything I'd learned since my religious studies days and spin it in a way that might be interesting to fifteen-year-olds. Fortunately, I was given a pretty wide berth to experiment with tactics and approaches. Some of my ideas were more successful than others, some of my classes more successful than others, and the learning curve was steep—but I loved it. Plus, it turned out that the other teachers in the after-school ed system were, like my retreat buddies, about my age, interesting, socially engaged, and asking hard questions about Judaism and its relationship to the world. More and more, I began to feel like I was finding people who might get my jokes.

I was the youngest member of the Makor Or meditation cadre. Almost everyone else was at least a good ten to fifteen years older, and at a very different stage of life from mine. I often felt like something of a little sister, or perhaps a mascot, tromping in with my big, patched-up army pants and Japanese anime T-shirt. Sure, I sent people into hysterics when they realized that I had sewn cat ears to my hoodie sweatshirt—but here too, genuine friendships began to coalesce.

And, as the publication date of *Yentl's Revenge* drew closer, I started to make phone calls to set up readings and events. It seemed that practically every publicity manager at the bookstores I contacted was in her twenties or early thirties, Jewish, and eager to talk to me about how alienated she felt from spirituality, or how she wished that she could do Judaism in a way that felt coherent with her style, or that she hated feeling like Judaism wasn't compatible with her other interests. These people were looking to me for guidance because they figured that I must know something, having edited a book about it and all. The message became clearer and clearer as the anthology was readied for publication and afterward, when I did readings to promote it: I wasn't alone. I was getting this memo, suddenly, from a lot of different quarters at once. There were a lot of people out there looking for a certain kind of meaningful, engaged Jewish community, and many of us were just beginning to find each other.

Just being able to integrate my disparate selves in a Jewish community of more-or-less peers was a revelation. Suddenly, there were people around who made offhand comments referencing both the Torah portion and some new band, who played gender deconstructionist dreydl, and who screen-printed T-shirts by hand with slogans mashing up Jewish pride and saucy irreverence. One of the women writing for my book had just gotten a grant to launch a new magazine called *Heeb*. Someone else I knew had started up Yid-themed literary readings in a bar in downtown Manhattan. We were, I suppose, at the cusp of what would prove to be a cultural explosion of sorts. Within a few years, a new genre of independent minyanim—prayer communities—would crop up in every American city with any sort of a Jewish population. Websites and blogs catering to folks who lived simultaneously on the inside and the outside of Judaism debuted at an increasingly speedy rate. Klezmer had become a new kind of punk rock.

In the midst of all this, I began to reconnect with the part of me that, at sixteen, had loved running around with purple hair and, at twenty-two, sported sparkly devil's horns. I had been wearing a *kip-*

pah fairly regularly by this point, and I realized there was no rule dictating that my head covering had to be simple and crocheted. My devious mind began to spin—I bought blue fake fur and crafted it into a yarmulke. Onto this I sewed a plastic alien and a few glow-in-the-dark stars to give it that extra-galactic flair. I also bought a plain black yarmulke and, after hot-glue-gunning a gigantic red fake-fur heart to it (I was really into the fake fur back then), I surrounded the whole thing with rhinestones. I had begun thinking about wearing tzitzit—ritual fringes worn on a garment under under one's shirt. When I discovered that Maimonides permitted dyeing them colors, I began plotting an elaborate hot pink and silver extravaganza. Just because I wasn't hanging out with drag queens so much anymore didn't mean that I hadn't retained the aesthetic.

Bouncing around like a Jewish glitter diva provided me hours of crafty amusement and helped me to celebrate the wild silliness that had been too long subsumed by my Serious Religious Questions. It also helped me define myself against what I perceived to be a more mainstream Judaism in which I didn't feel entirely at home. This was a crucial step toward integrating the disparate parts of my life, and helping me to envision the kind of Judaism that I would practice if all of me got to be in the same place. I needed to take this serious part of my life not so seriously, to reclaim the goofiness I feared I had lost forever when I stopped going to Burning Man parties. I'd been undergoing a massive identity shift over a couple of years, and it would take some synthesis before I'd be able to figure out who this new person would be.

Slowly, something of my old attachments to previous incarnations worked their way out of my system. Eventually, my need to advertise all the reasons why I loved fabric shops and toy stores calmed down a bit. Though it was great fun to serve as a walking advertisement for feminist Judaism with a sense of humor, after a while keeping the sparkle level on ten began to feel a little exhausting. As I became increasingly secure in my Judaism and Jewish practice, I found that I didn't want it to have to come with a blinking sign. And, more than that, I found that my choices seemed to have unintended consequences in this new terrain.

It wasn't that I lost my appreciation for creativity gone amok—
to this day, I still visit Lida and inspect her latest costumes with the
awe and reverence demanded by a Mickey Mouse hat done entirely
in Swarovski crystals or a handmade velvet Flamenco dress. But,
whereas in the three-ring circus in which I used to spend my time,
I'd blend unassumingly into the crowd regardless of how bizarrely
I dressed, here, my handicraft ensured that I'd stand out no matter
what. I realized that it was harder to connect with people on any
sort of meaningful level when the plastic alien preceded me, pro-
jecting an image that I didn't necessarily intend to have. Not only
was I really neither all that outgoing or that "wacky" in real life, I
took my Judaism much more seriously than it might perhaps have
seemed at first glance. Over time, I began to wonder why I needed
so much emphasis on the first glance, anyway. I never did go
through with the pink and silver tzitzit. At some point, I realized
that it was radical enough in most religious circles to be a woman
sporting the fringes; God forbid someone might think that I was doing so out of anything but deepest faith in, and service to, the Divine. I didn't want to be some dismissible cartoon character version
of myself, and I didn't want to appear to be screaming when I meant
to speak in a normal tone of voice.

Judaism wasn't just a superficial interest, something that had to
be expressed with kitschy irony or not at all—it was, increasingly,
the pace at which my heart beat. As I began to really internalize the
idea that I could be religious without losing any fundamental parts
of myself, I found that I began to care less and less about expressing my faith in deliberately unusual ways. When I needed sparkle,
I could add rhinestones to my old T-shirts or paint my toes in an
elaborate psychedelic pastiche. The little details, I found, satisfied
me more than enough—and eventually, I'd wake to discover that I
didn't even crave the small doses so much anymore.

My family had been eyeing my religious development warily. As I
began keeping Shabbat and praying all the time, I think they wondered just where this fanaticism would end and what implications
the process would have for them. Would I expect others to hold to

the same standards that I did? Would I stop coming home alto-gether? My refusal to travel on Shabbat had already begun to com-plicate plans when I came home to Chicago. These days, I can sympathize better perhaps than I once did with family who might have been frustrated by my decision to not join them at Shaw's Crab Shack on a Friday night. After all, the desire to take part in "normal" activities had once kept me from deepening my observance of Shabbat, and I had *wanted* to keep Shabbat! I had struggled and ag-onized over my observance level even with the intense yearning for God. For folks without that pull, my actions must have seemed ex-cessive, inflexible, and silly, and my occasional requests for help liv-ing out my religious commitments must have, at times, felt like an undue burden.

During these early negotiations, it was easy enough to get wist-ful about my mother. The dead allow us the privilege of writing their dialogue, and it was all too tempting to fantasize about how my mom would have reacted to my increased observance and religious engagement. She had grown up keeping kosher and had, when I was growing up, spoken nostalgically of her Jewish childhood. To-ward the end of her life, she'd become increasingly interested in the intersection of spirituality and art. Even though my mother didn't choose to practice Judaism as an adult, I think she would have got-ten a kick out of my interest, and even more out of my eventual de-cision to become a rabbi. I suppose it was natural that I indulged in the occasional reverie about her coming to town and joining me at Friday night prayers and Shabbat dinner. More often, though, I tried not to go there; anyway, who knows how she would have reacted in real life? My mother certainly never gave me easy answers about anything when she was alive. Living, breathing humans are always so much more complicated than the words we try to put in their mouths.

The decision by one member of a family to take on a spiritual discipline invariably affects everyone. Even when everyone in the picture is as willing as possible to navigate the shift, there is often some friction as everyone recalibrates their expectations of one another. Over time, my family and I have worked things out—I've figured out what is and isn't fair to ask of them, and they've figured out where they might be willing or able to meet me halfway.

I had given up much of what I previously considered fun and drifted from many of the people who had once populated my social life, but all along I refused to let go of my closest friends—Ariel and Jack and Michael and Lida and Rebecca and the crew. They were, after all, a big part of why I was so happy to be back in San Francisco. Given how much of my life now revolved around Shabbat and Jewish holidays, though, my relationships weren't going to exist in the exact same form that they had before I left town. Most of the things that my friends did on Friday nights and Saturdays were, simply, off limits to me. Nonetheless, sometimes I found ways to meet them on my terms: I figured out that it would take me a leisurely couple of hours—stopping periodically to sit and enjoy the Golden Gate Park through which I was passing—to walk to Ariel and Rebecca's in the Mission District on Shabbat. I could leave at midafternoon, and by the time I got there, it wouldn't be long until sundown and a group of us could go out to dinner or a movie or something. (They were very good sports about lending me cash for the evening and the bus ride home, since I wouldn't be carrying any.)

More than that, though, I began to figure out that not frequenting my friends' world for a big chunk of the weekend didn't mean that I couldn't invite them into mine. I began to host a lot of Friday night dinners at my house, often surprised at how well people from different parts of my life mixed together. They seemed to share a lot of common secular interests, like the nonprofit world, alternative medicine, and certain political causes. And the Jewish factor was amusingly unpredictable; more than once, Ariel and one or two of my retreat buddies exploded into an extended remix (complete with dance moves) of the Zionist hymns of their Jewish summer camp youth. After Yom Kippur I had a gigantic break-the-fast meal at my house that included retreat participants, teachers from the teen ed circuit, Makor Or folk who'd been with me ten blocks away at Beth Sholom, and all of my friends—Jewish or not—from the Ariel-Jack-Teresa crowd. My tiny studio was packed; fortunately, there was plenty of food.

It was hard sometimes when I didn't have the inclination or energy to host, but I also found that I didn't mind a quiet, solitary Shabbat here and there. (I was at Beth Sholom most Shabbat mornings, anyway.) They certainly weren't nearly as lonely as I had feared they would be when I moved back to town. I discovered a hike near my house, along gorgeous cliffs hugging the Pacific, that led me to the beach. I meditated and read. It was quite nice, actually.

My commitment to my friends forced me to develop a complex ethos of pluralism on the ground. I had to find ways to practice Judaism as I understood it while, at the same time, accepting that those around me might not believe or do the exact same things that I did. I had to respect someone's choice to drive to my house on Shabbat, just as I hoped that members of other Jewish communities would respect my choice to wear a yarmulke and tzitzit or to pray in a mixed-gender setting. As Ben Dreyfus, founder of an independent minyan (prayer group) in New York, puts it, "if you want the protections of pluralism, you have to buy into pluralism yourself. This doesn't mean you have to believe that other positions are valid, but it does mean you have to respect their right to exist."[15] My friends had become wonderful about making sure that I was religiously comfortable with the timing of a Saturday night outing or the kashrut level of dinner—Lida even went so far as to buy a whole separate set of dishware for cooking and serving me food. And I tried to give them leeway just as they were willing to give me leeway, to be as flexible as I felt that I could within my understandings of Jewish law.

Somehow, we worked it out. I had decided that, as long as the ingredients themselves were kosher and the cookware clean, I wouldn't refrain from eating in the homes of people I loved. Thus I've been able to pass many a quiet Shabbat visiting Alex and her now-husband, a New Testament professor named Jonathan. I would shop and cook for all of us on Friday (the laws of the "Shabbat goy" are more complicated than many people think, and I wouldn't actually want to have them at my beck and call), and we'd have a lovely dinner peppered with theology talk. Saturday would often be mellow and restful, sometimes with me going to synagogue in the morning, sometimes with Jonathan going off to some activity or another. Though my hosts didn't necessarily refrain from things they would usually do on Saturday, they tried not to harsh my buzz by, say, turning on the TV, which I always appreciated. The fact that they're not Jewish isn't a deal breaker, and goodness knows that my friendship with them both is important enough that I'm willing to find solutions that both preserve my religious integrity and enable me to spend time with them.

All of this community making wasn't perfect, however, and it certainly wasn't instant. In addition to being the only religious Jew among my old peeps, I was also a lot more observant than most of my new Jewish friends. My refusal to, say, travel on Shabbat made getting to a Friday night dinner in Oakland much more complicated. Occasionally I stayed over at someone's house (which was sometimes awkward when I kept Shabbat in a stricter way than they did, and sometimes it was just fine) and just as often I passed up invitations. Sometimes I walked two miles each way to attend a dinner or a lunch in San Francisco. When I stayed in the East Bay, I generally found a way to attend the kinds of services at which I was most comfortable—both traditional and egalitarian—though occasionally I consented to join others in environments that were either more radically improvisational than was my preference or segregated by gender.

I had my limits, however. For example, I accepted the legal and aesthetic opinion that musical instruments were not appropriate for the Sabbath, and thus wouldn't go to services featuring a rock band, though I might meet people who did for dinner afterwards. I didn't need to have the exact same MO as everyone else all the time. Sometimes we can come together, sometimes we can't. Sometimes we can bend our own individual comfort levels to enter a certain communal space, sometimes we can't. As Ben Dreyfus notes, "If I say that [two people's] practice[s] can't coexist in a . . . community, that's not a value judgment about either of their practices; it just means that they're mismatched for this purpose."[16]

Over time, I began to see that I could be an invested citizen of multiple worlds, and that "my" community could be composed of several different communities that fed me in different ways. This multiplicity of identification didn't necessarily mean that I allowed those relationships to be superficial, though. The folks at Makor Or not only encouraged me with my meditation and prayer, but they kept me accountable to it and forced me to live the spiritual discipline I claimed to want. My retreat buddies pushed me to think harder about how I might translate my political ideals into action. My fellow teachers kept me from getting too cocky in the classroom, and from treating my relationships with students like just a day gig. My dearest friends continued to love me, encourage me, and call me to the carpet when it looked like I was shooting for easy answers. As Nouwen puts it, "it is far from easy to keep living where God is. Therefore God gives you people to help to hold you in that place and call you back to it every time you wander off."[17] I discovered that God had given me an awful lot of people, none of whom was terribly shy about letting me know when I might be straying from where I was supposed to be.

I didn't have to force one group to fit all of my needs, but this didn't mean I could or should have gotten away with a consumerist approach to community. That is to say, it wouldn't have worked if I had tried to enjoy the benefits of communal life—fun, connection, having comrades in arms—without doing the work that community demands: Making yourself vulnerable to rejection. Letting the people in your life influence the way you live by allowing their values and opinions to affect your choices. Learning that your individual needs might sometimes have to be secondary to the needs of the greater whole. Bravely excavating sites of potential conflict and committing to transcending separateness, rather than brushing over differences.

Mennonite pastor Shane Hipps suggests that "authentic community involves high degrees of intimacy, permanence and prox-imity. These practices foster shared memories as well as a shared imagination of the future, elements crucial to becoming the people of God."[18] Though I've had friendships that are permanent but not always proximate, Hipps is right that the real work of community takes place when there's time for conversations to unwind however they may, for laughter and touch and tears in one another's physi-cal presence.

I've got a bit of a geeky streak, and I spend my share of time on-line. I'm truly grateful for the ability of e-mail, blogs, and instant messenger media to keep me more involved in the lives of faraway friends; it certainly facilitates keeping in touch. One friend noted that since she and an old college buddy have begun reading each other's online journals, they no longer have to spend the first hour of a phone call going through a laundry list of the recent events in their lives. Rather, the conversation can start up right in the middle of things, as if they had just spoken the week before. I can certainly attest to the value of my little laptop for helping me to maintain ties with those I love when they are far away, and, as is clear with Alex and others, it's also been able to help me develop important new friendships or to continue to be challenged by those who've known me a long time.

But online community is no substitute for the real-life kind. It's difficult to send a hug by phone or to e-mail homemade soup to a sick friend, and prayer is an entirely different experience when one feels the presence of others in the same room. The kind of risk, vul-nerability, and intimacy inherent in face-to-face relationships is simply not possible behind the protection of a monitor screen or (yes, even) cell phone. Life can't be lived in only two dimensions.

Hipps is correct that shared memories and a collective sense of identity are crucial for creating a new vision of the future. As Bud-dhist teacher Thich Nhat Hanh puts it, "the collective insight is al-ways deeper than individual insight."[19] A life lived in real time can slowly build trust and intimate understanding. As discrete individ-uals gradually come together—as is clear in the case of the early feminists—each person not only puts her own life into a collective context, but the group as a whole slowly begins to imagine how the world should look, and how we might get there.

Of course, having a commitment to communal work isn't the same as being obligated to remain stuck in environments that feel problematic or toxic. Not every single member of any community will become your new dearest friend, but the atmosphere needs to feel nurturing to a reasonable degree.

As I stepped out into the Bay Area Jewish world, I met a lot of the "insiders" of the congregations whose services I had sampled four or five years earlier. And I found that a lot of people's communal assumptions and starting points were very different from mine. For example, I passed one Shabbat lunch at the house of the "spiritual leader" of a specific community, known for its highly ecstatic services. I was the only one at the table who wasn't a regular in that scene and a follower of this particular teacher.

At some point in the lunch, some people began speaking ill of folks who came to their services for the first time and didn't want to hug all of the people in their vicinity—as, it seems, was the custom there.

"They're so uptight," one person said. "They just need to open their hearts a little more." There were several murmurs of agreement.

Then a woman piped in.

"No, you don't understand. Sometimes when people have had ... [in a whisper] *bad experiences* ... they find touch to be ... very challenging."

I was incensed.

"Are you suggesting," I asked, "that the only reason someone might not want to hug a total stranger in an entirely foreign context is because she or he is a survivor of sexual abuse?" I thought, but didn't add, What about the possibility that you might smell bad? Or that a person might regard touch as something serious, not to be shared casually? That he or she might just plain not want to, and thus has no obligation to? How dare they judge newcomers who aren't perfectly on board with this agenda of instant intimacy? And yet, for them, I suppose, hugs were a fairly basic means of connection, and I imagine that each of the folks at this lunch had felt a sense of relief to find a congregation in which they would be so warmly welcomed in such a concrete way.

Everyone at the table was perfectly happy operating with, more or less, a shared set of beliefs about ideal behavior and general goals. Everyone but me, that is—in this case, I had most decidedly *not* found my tribe. The people at this lunch didn't espouse my vision of communal conduct any more than the ultra-Orthodox folks in Tzfat did. Communal living offers many worthy challenges to our extreme sense of individualism, but we are, needless to say, not required to do everything that anyone might tell us to do. There is something to be said for a practice of submission and humility that involves allowing others to influence your life in many ways. It's another thing, however, to check one's intuition and common sense at the door.

The line between communal dictates and individual self-awareness can be a blurry one, even in the most ideal of situations. Carol Lee Flinders points out that, for women in particular, the spiritual work of what she calls "self-naughting" has the potential to run counter to many important feminist principles: Find your voice. Tell the truth as you understand it. Establish your self, your identity. Do not annihilate yourself to please others.[20] Self-annihilation can only be expected to bear fruit when the person in question has a firmly established self in the first place. Someone who never learned to express his or her needs, for example, may find that accepting too much input from others has disastrous effects. It's not always easy to determine how much of ourselves to hand over and at what times.

Rabbi Elliot Dorff, a philosopher and interpreter of Jewish law, has said that he always defers to a community standard that's stricter than his own practice, provided that he has no moral problems with doing so. So, for instance, when in Jerusalem, he will abstain from carrying an umbrella in the rain on Shabbat even though his own formidable learning tells him that such an action is per-fectly permissible within the bounds of Jewish law. Many people in Jerusalem understand the law differently—and for Rabbi Dorff, con-necting to others is of greater value than asserting his individual understanding, even if it means getting wet when walking to syn-agogue. His choice to forgo the umbrella is one made from a place of generosity and security. He can afford to stretch a little, and do-ing so enables him to enter the community in a much deeper way.

Sometimes it is vital to give oneself over completely, to allow oneself to be broken down inside the greater whole. But this does-n't mean that there's no room for what's often called "the prophetic tradition," telling the truth and acting from integrity, even at the risk of social alienation—hence Rabbi Dorff's disclaimer that he only follows the community when he believes its behavior to be moral. Does it even need to be said that there are times when one must stand up to the community, and use one's voice in support of an un-popular view? Or that complicity is participation? Sometimes the issue at hand may concern a gross injustice, sometimes it may just be about individual boundaries. Sometimes a dissenting view will be heard and accepted, sometimes it will be ignored. None of this changes our obligation to move through the world with honesty and bravery.

How to know when to submit and when to resist? Our intuition, the part of us that is nurtured through personal spiritual disci-plines—it knows. It knows when, deep down, the reason that we're resisting local standards or the advice of a trusted member of the community is because we're being asked to give up more of our-selves than we can really spare at the moment. And it also knows when we're hearing a difficult truth that we don't particularly *want* to face but must, for our own good.

A strong community is one in which there is room for disagree-ment and dialogue, for its members to grapple and change and grow, and for the collective itself to grow and change its practices, goals, or standards along with the changing needs of its members. In a healthy environment, conflict and diversity offer opportunities for everyone to learn a little bit better how to love. And we need that love in order to have any impact in this world. For, as Thich Nhat Hanh notes,

> You have viewpoints, you have experiences, you have insights. You try to offer the sangha [the community] all that you see and you feel, and you allow all the people in the sangha to have the same opportunity to express their insights, their views, their experiences. So, practicing listening deeply to each other is very important [as is] practicing using the kind of speech that can make other people understand you . . . As you continue to progress on the path of mutual understanding and acceptance, you become an instrument for social and political change . . . People are motivated to do things . . . but without the capacity of listening, of under-standing, of being compassionate, what they do cannot help.[21]

Of course, sharing one's thoughts—dissenting or not—in any sort of context is risky. It opens us up and makes us overwhelmingly vul-nerable. Sometimes it's tempting to hide, to avoid revealing who we are, lest our failures and most secret hopes are set out for evalua-tion. But, of course, in allowing people in, we allow ourselves the most fundamental kind of human connection, and do honor to the Divine image in which we are all created. For, as author Martha Beck wrote, "Whoever said love is blind was dead wrong. Love is the only thing on this earth that lets us see each other with the remotest accuracy."[22]

NINE

Not long after moving back to San Francisco, I had an errand-running day with one of my Makor Or buddies. He had offered to haul some stuff to my new apartment in his truck if I'd help him pick out furniture. After my boxes had been safely deposited onto the floor of my studio, we went to Busvan for Bargains and spent a little too long debating dark versus blond wood and whether extra drawers would be useful. After the grueling work of choosing his new desk and shelves combo, Mark declared that a snack didn't sound half bad; fortunately, there was a taqueria next to the furniture store. Now free of the indecisiveness that had plagued him for the last hour, he immediately ordered a veggie taco. I paused in front of the big menu board, feeling suddenly suspicious. A light bulb went on over my head, and I asked a question that I'd never thought to ask before.

"Excuse me, is your rice totally vegetarian?"

"Well, there's no meat in it, but we do cook it in chicken broth."

Mark had been smiling broadly in anticipation of his taco. His face fell.

He was a recent convert, and was trying to slowly build his Jewish practice. Nonkosher meat is, technically, as forbidden as pork. He had them put the beans and toppings in without the rice, but he was grumpy as he ate it. I wound up not ordering anything, and I was grumpy about that, too. Given that Mexican food was one of

the things that gave my life meaning, it was not good news to realize that I was going to have to start thinking more seriously about
what "keeping kosher" meant.

It seemed that any remaining impulse to segregate my life into
Jewish and non-Jewish compartments was falling away. I had been
wearing a yarmulke, for example, during prayer and formal Torah
study since Jerusalem. As I began teaching Torah in teen ed programs several times a week, the lines between "prayer and Torah
time" and "not prayer and Torah time" became more and more
blurry. It started to feel silly to remove my *kippah* the minute that
class was over, to insist to myself that I drive home bareheaded. It
occurred to me that there was something artificial about the assumption that I wasn't in "service to God" mode even when select-
ing cucumbers at the grocery store. Wasn't this, too, a form of Torah?

Spiritual practice isn't something that just happens once a week
or whenever the mood strikes. Jewish law is designed to affect every
aspect of a practitioner's life; it asks us to mark the doorposts of our
homes and demands that we rend our clothes when a loved one
dies, it instructs in the proper procedure for returning a lost object
and defines the line between friendly chatter and malicious gossip.
The Talmud is famous for an obsession with the tiniest details—the
precise color of a citron fit for ritual use, the exact times by which
certain prayers must be said, the specific kinds of locations designated as communal Shabbat space. In Judaism, the specifics matter, precisely because they show that service to God can be revealed
in every small gesture. Rabbinic scholar Max Kadushin described
the worldview of the Talmudic rabbis as "normal mysticism," utterly
infused with and revealing the sacred through every minute movement, every subtle distinction.

In a famous Sufi story, a teacher, Salih, was known to teach his
students that if a person "knocks at the door of someone constantly,
one day the door must be opened to him." Another Sufi, named Ra-
bia, finally asked him one day, "Salih, how long will you go on
preaching thus, using the future tense, saying 'will be opened'? Was
the door ever closed?"[1] Every small way that we shift ourselves to

live in relation to God helps us not only to knock, but to try to remember that the door is always already open.

I began to ask more and more restaurants whether shrimp were fried in the same oil as the vegetable tempura, or what kind of grease was involved in cooking biscuits. The answers were not always what I had hoped to hear. As usual, it looked like my religious life was going to infringe on the rest of my goings about in ways that were neither comfortable nor convenient; I was just going to have to figure out how to work around, and with, God's demands for my heart and time.

There were almost no kosher eateries in San Francisco, and only a handful of restaurants that didn't serve meat of any kind. I got to know them well: the curry house in Berkeley, the Vietnamese diner in Oakland, the seitan-slinging place in the Mission, the Chinese one in the Richmond with fake meat, a couple of higher-end establishments at which I indulged once or twice. To complicate matters further, Ariel had developed some pretty serious food allergies that precluded her joining me at a couple of the places that put garlic in everything. We found one restaurant where we could both manage to find something on the menu, and we ate there. A lot.

There were more than a few times when I became frustrated with all these restrictions, longed to feed on burritos and Pad Thai with the same careless freedom that I had in the past, when I wished I didn't have to pass up every concert and party that happened on a Friday night or spend a week solid scrubbing my apartment in preparation for Passover. But I kept checking my internal meter—the one from which I tried to discern God's presence—and it kept telling me that, sorry, my decision to be more discriminating was the correct one.

It's not that "stricter" is always "better." There's a sort of machismo that permeates many religious communities that depicts religious practice as sort of an extreme sport. I see this often among people just coming to a spiritual discipline—the famous "zeal of the convert" kicks in and the most restrictive approach to ritual observance is embraced, sometimes with a side order of condescension to those whose practice is more moderate. This attitude might be based in the simple desire to be scrupulous in one's own behavior, or it might have more to do with proving something to oneself or others. In any case, the vibe can be quite contageous, particularly when novices or less informed members of a community believe that authenticity only comes in rigid packages.

This is not to knock a more rigorous maximalist attitude per se. Sometimes, simply, more practice is what's needed in order to serve God better—for me, at this time (and since), there was no question that I had to take my relationship to kashrut deeper, whatever the personal inconvenience. But I couldn't have known that by trying to gauge myself in relation to other Jews, to play a never-winnable match of "too religious" versus "not religious enough." As Buddhist teacher Charlotte Joko Beck notes, "There's a little shade of piety that creeps into practice. You know, 'I have this wonderful practice, I want to share it with everyone.' There's an error in that. You could probably figure it out yourself."[2] Whenever I got caught in the web of comparing myself to others, the results led—without fail—to obsession and neurosis, insecurity, pride, or arrogance. One thinks of the Jewish philosopher Franz Rosenzweig, who, when asked late in his life if he observed a particular commandment, is said to have replied, "Not yet." The issue, for Rosenzweig, was not about the validity of the system, but rather whether one deepened one's practice based on external or internal cues.

When I was able to keep my eyes on my own proverbial exam paper, it was almost always extremely clear what I needed to be doing, and when. The day I began wearing tzitzit, for example, there was no internal wrangling, no drama. I woke up one morning, felt something click, and knew right away that this was the day for me to begin wearing the garment that I had bought several months earlier and ignored up until that morning. I had known for a while that wearing ritual fringes under my regular clothing would someday be the correct next step in my practice, but I hadn't been ready to don them the same day I bought them at my local Judaica shop. It hadn't been time then, but one day, for whatever reason, it was suddenly time.

The early Zionist rabbi Rav Kook notes that "by training yourself to hear the voice of God in everything, the voice reveals itself to your mind as well. Then right in the mind, you discover revelation."[3] Authenticity comes from hearing that Divine voice and following its dictates wherever it might take you—not by taking up the exact same pose as the strictest member of your religious community. What God has to tell you may be very different from whatever God has told him or her. Piling on restrictions in some sort of automatic way, without inner dialogue, can lead to a rigid, robotic practice that offers no real danger of touching the heart. One thinks of a particular rabbi who acknowledged at a rabbinic convention that, until his wife got cancer, he had had a "purely professional relationship with God," as though God had been a figure on the synagogue board whose presence connected only minimally to the religion around which this rabbi had based his life. Needless to say, that's not the goal.

At the same time, however, Psalm 34 tells us to "taste it and see that God is good."[4] There are things that we might not understand about religious practice until we experience them for ourselves. Without a serious, grounded spiritual discipline, it's easy to remain fettered to our attachments, our lazinesses or, more likely, our deeply entrenched blind spots; it is the framework of a well-honed system that helps us to pull ourselves out of our old ways of being and to become new, again and again. The external forms need internal intentions, and the internal intentions need to be expressed and honed with an external practice. Navigating this delicate balance is one of the great, lifelong challenges for every spiritual aspirant.

During this time of increasing care about the kashrut of my food, attempts at rebellion were subverted with maddening predictability. Rebecca had a gigantic blowout bash for her thirtieth birthday; she rented out a venue downtown for about a hundred people. We all got decked out in our glamorous best and stayed out dancing until the very wee hours. Later the next morning, Rebecca, Ariel, and I pulled ourselves out of bed and went out for brunch. All I wanted was eggs. I wanted them so badly, all hot and buttery and cooked by someone besides me. The prospect of a cold salad at this particular moment made me feel deprived and miserable. I ordered the omelet, drowning out the tiny voice telling me that this place was, really, not so kosher. It would be fine! Sure enough, the omelet arrived to the table, and four bites in I found a single cube of ham tucked inadvertently in the middle, sitting there calmly like a sign saying, "Told You So."

As I began to make more of a fuss about restaurants and to check kosher labels on my groceries, I realized that I was thinking more about the food I was ingesting than I ever had before. It was about more than following the rules; after all, one can adhere perfectly to Jewish law and subsist entirely on processed food eaten off of Styrofoam plates. But the Torah says in Deuteronomy that "you shall do that which is right and good in the eyes of God."[5] The medieval commentator Rashi interprets this to mean that one should go beyond the letter of the law, to serve God above and beyond the specifics of ritual adherence. It's about the intersection of the external practice and the awareness of the Divine, about having these laws push us to become better, kinder, more aware, more moral, and more compassionate human beings than we might otherwise be.

Morning prayer was so nourishing.

Not long after waking up, I'd unzip the green velvet bag in which my prayer shawl lived. Still sleepy, I'd murmur its blessing and enfold myself in its soft embrace. I'd take my tefillin out from their casing, bless and secure the prayer box on my bicep, facing my heart, and wrap the strap seven times around my forearm. I'd bless and place the second piece just above my hairline and utter a word of praise to God. Then I'd wrap the arm strap in an intricate pattern around my hand, reciting God's words from the prophet Hosea as I wound:

"I will betroth you to Me forever. I will betroth you to Me with righteousness, with justice, with lovingkindness and with compassion. I will betroth you to Me with faithfulness, and you will know God."[6]

And then I'd begin to pray.

I could get lost for days inside that prayer book when I let myself. I would dip down into the first words, "My God, the soul you have given me is pure," and feel surrounded by the immanent Divine. I'd work through the liturgy—Creation renewing itself, angels calling one to the other, radiant lights surrounding the supernal throne; God as rock, God as redeemer, God as healer, God as lover of justice, God as bringer of peace. Here, everything was slow, sweet, effulgent.

Saying the same words over and over again every morning enabled me to get deeper inside them, to get to know them better. There was something to daily prayer that helped me express things to and about God that I couldn't articulate in any other way. As Reb Zalman Schachter-Shalomi puts it, "It's as if my wife says, 'I love you,' and I say, 'You told me that yesterday.' It's a silly answer because she was not trying to inform me of something that I didn't know. It's a feeling she wants to transmit. It's heart to heart . . . the prayer book is 'heart stuff.' "[7]

The feelings weren't always automatic, though. In any long-term relationship, at some point the swooning infatuation wears off and something more stable must be negotiated. This is also true in religious life, in a committed relationship with the Divine. C. S. Lewis said, "God will look to every soul like its first love because He is its first love."[8] Over time, as the novelty of prayer wore off and I was able to recite parts of the morning service by heart, I found that the blissful feeling of connection didn't always come as easily. What Zen master Shunryu Suzuki Roshi famously called "beginner's mind" was beginning to wear off, and I began the ongoing struggle to engage my prayers with the same sense of surprise and wonder with which I had first encountered them.

Sometimes I'd recite my way through the prayer book, feet all too firmly planted on the ground, and I'd get partway through the liturgy before becoming aware that in the recesses of my heart I was really *praying*. Other times prayer wouldn't seem to have any aesthetic affect. Nonetheless, when it was time to remove my tefillin and get on with the next thing, I'd often find that I had the same feeling as after a passionate morning's prayer—that is to say, I'd feel as though my soul had just had its teeth brushed. There were days when I was irritable and resistant, days when I wanted to do anything in the world besides put on the gear and pray. And I'd pray anyway.

Sometimes when I prayed, I spent more time thinking about, well, pretty much anything but God—what I was going to do that day, the plot of a book I was reading, the errands I still hadn't done, or some random fantasy I'd been nursing about the next chapter of my life. Sometimes I was cranky with Judaism, frustrated by the limits that it placed on my life and angry at God for making everything so complicated sometimes. As in any long-term relationship, ups and downs are par for the course.

This, then, was the importance of practice that had been drilled into me: "Only something we do every day has the power to transform us."[9] If you have a spiritual discipline, I learned over and over, you do it daily whether you feel like it or not. It was, I slowly understood, like the fact that getting into physical shape requires working out regularly, even on the days when the adrenaline high never kicks in—and somehow, even on those days, the muscles still get stronger. Sometimes daily prayer was an exhilarating climb up the mountain. Sometimes it had the sweet familiarity of a neighborhood jog. Some days it just felt like . . . work. A life of relgious commitment isn't about waiting around for inspiration to strike— and that kind of consumerist "it has to be fun for me or I don't want to bother" attitude can be disastrous for a serious practice. It's easy to pray when the mood is right. It's much more difficult to pray when it involves dragging yourself out of bed, focusing on the prayer book when you'd rather be doing anything else, or stopping something you're engrossed in (and possibly enjoying) because it's getting later and you still haven't said the afternoon prayers. But prayer said on those days is still, in the end, prayer.

A committed religious life is not about chasing the next great high. It's not about just having feel-good experiences in which the sky opens up and a chorus of angels sings. It's about staying focused and present and connected to God in all the small moments, the hard moments, the drudge moments—the moments when it feels like a hassle to say the blessing over food before eating it, the moments when it'd be much more tempting to tune out. Even if there isn't a feeling of ecstasy each moment, all of the minute decisions to do this practice anyway are a way of asserting the value of that connection, of worship in its own right. Religious practice is about becoming wrapped in a constant, almost incessant, barrage of connection and service to the Divine. It's about seeing that relationships have obligations. It's about learning how not to confuse sugar highs with real, sustaining nourishment.

Shortly after beginning rabbinical school, I began to worry that I was doing something wrong. Sure, I was still praying multiple times a day—the long morning service and the quicker afternoon and evening ones—and, though I wasn't able to meditate nearly as often, I was studying Torah a whole lot more. You'd think things would be fine, to judge by the scorecard. But I wasn't really having euphoric experiences in my prayer the way I once had. There were times when I felt plugged in, but the fireworks just didn't seem to be going off anymore. I couldn't figure out why. What was I doing wrong? How could I fix it??

After picking at the question for a while, I realized that though I wasn't getting the fancy special effects, I was a lot more aware of the Divine in an everyday way than I had been. There were fewer highs and lows, but my new default setting was actually just fine. And, when I felt far away from God—which still happened more often than not—the process of reconnecting was easier than it had been before. When I remembered to try to reconnect, that is. The extreme nature of my early feelings in this relationship—equal parts, perhaps, infatuation and doubt—had given way to a sweeter, more predictable kind of everyday intimacy. This was, in the long run, much easier to live with.

This is not to say that suddenly things got easy. Not even remotely. Everyone struggles to focus during spiritual practice, at least some of the time, and, for most of us, it's a great deal of the time. Saint Teresa of Avila reports that she wrote *The Way of Perfection*, her guide to the contemplative life, for "souls and minds so scattered they are like wild horses"—that is to say, for everyone.

Sometimes, our roaming thoughts must be reined in like horses or, perhaps, gently but firmly put in their place, as though the mind were a restless puppy that needed to be lovingly told "no" when it wanted to meander.

Sometimes, however, the very ideas that distract can be used as prime spiritual fodder. The Hasidic master the Baal Shem Tov spoke of the necessity of "uplifting" foreign, distracting thoughts during prayer. Though the Baal Shem Tov had most likely been describing thoughts of sin, his great-grandson, Reb Nahman of Bratslav, pushed this idea even further. For, according to Nahman's biographer, his "worst 'alien' thoughts consisted of doubts, both in matters of faith and with regard to his own person and his right to lead a Hasidic community. He thus attempted to 'uplift' and transform these doubts, paradoxically seeking in them the ultimate confirmation of his mission."[10] The things that make it hardest for us to practice—the places where we resist, where we start to wander off and daydream—can be the very things that help us understand who we are and what we're meant to do. The trick, of course, is in identifying the sneaky thoughts as the impediments that they are and in attempting to transform them into offerings to the Divine.

As I tried to meet my own points of resistance to prayer, I began to understand Norman Fischer's statement that perseverance was the attribute he most admired in others. As Saint Teresa notes wryly, "Hardly does our head begin to ache than we stop going to choir, which won't kill us either. We stay away one day because our head ached, another because it was just now aching, and three more so that it won't ache again."[11] Excuses are endless, and one of the great challenges of an ongoing religious life is learning how not to succumb to them.

The more I came to appreciate the value of practice, the more I understood the importance of embedding myself in the religious system in general. Frederica Mathewes-Green's words echoed, stronger than ever: "We can only gain wisdom that transcends time," she had written, "by exiting our time and entering an ancient path, and accepting it on its own terms; we only learn by submitting to something bigger than we are."[12] Most of the time, I began to realize, Jewish law was smarter than I was. Sometimes this was evident: all of those rules forbidding me from doing this thing or that on Shabbat helped open to me a vast, luscious space in which I could hear God quietly pulsing. Given my druthers and desires, there's no doubt that I'd be checking my e-mail every Saturday and popping in a video whenever I didn't want to notice my emotions squirming beneath the surface. Without these options, I was forced, inside the delicate silence, to notice the very things I had been resisting.

I began to see an old wisdom in a lot of the rules, even slightly counterintuitive ones. For example, if a person is forced to miss morning prayers, he or she is supposed to say the Amidah, the central part of the liturgy, twice during the afternoon service. Sure enough, I discovered that if for some reason I was unable to pray in the morning, one round of the liturgy in the afternoon really wasn't enough. I'd be extra itchy and distracted through the first Amidah, and it would only be during the second go-round that I'd start to really become aware of the words and my act of saying them. I saw that the second set of prayers really was necessary.

Over the years, I've come to believe that preexisting religious frameworks help guide us into more sophisticated spiritual practices than we would be able to invent on our own. How can we push ourselves beyond ourselves, mired as we are in our own biases, fears and limitations? Left to our own devices, most of us would indeed create a safe faith that demanded very little from us— something that would certainly not transcend the smallness of everyday comfort and force us into the great, wider beyond.

Jewish law, like most religious practices, is a sort of portable monastery—a structure designed to keep one's focus, on a daily and minute level, on one's relationship to the Divine. It can be difficult to balance the intensity of a monastic focus with the other demands of the world, but this, too, is part of the work. Sitting around the (literal) monastery is hard work, to be sure. But even that is relatively easy, compared to the attempt to negotiate a rigorous spiritual practice when there are a million tugs in every direction.

The Lizensker Rabbi once said that God "appreciates most in a man his zeal in performing a commandment, and his readiness to do it with his whole heart and soul . . . It is, however, almost impossible for a man to concentrate his entire being on the performance of a [commandment], and the enthusiasm with which he commences soon wanes. Hence the actual performance of a [commandment] is necessary to the mind as a stimulus to the effort at pleasing God."[13] In an ideal world, we would be able to retain a keen, meditative connection with the Divine at all times, to keep our hearts in perfect and constant openness. However, given our real-life limitations, we need a robust practice—both to help us concentrate our being on the sacred and as a form of divine service in and of itself. Offering oneself in a myriad of small and large ways (whether or not one feels like doing so in the moment) is about so much more than personal feelings of gratification. As the Benedictine monk Dom Joseph Warrilow puts it, "Doing a thing because you feel wonderful about it—even a work of charity—is in the end a selfish act. We perform the work not to feel wonderful but to know and love the other,"[14] even, or especially, when the object of our love is God.

Jewish law is, as are all ancient religious systems, highly filtered. Over literally thousands of years, generations of people have been working to develop systems of connection between the self and the community and the Divine, propagating effective practices, tweaking them to make them more effective and jettisoning those that fail to get us to the Source. That's why these frameworks are so smart.

At the same time, though, they're hardly foolproof. Every religious system, after all, has been developed by human beings. Those people lived in cultural contexts and historical times and places, and struggled with their own hurts and angers and fears, just as we do. Their wisdom permeates the religions that we have, but their biases do, as well. In Judaism, for example, one can see how the vicissitudes of Jewish history have affected rulings in various times and places about the status of women, of non-Jews, of Jews in some sort of marginalized position. In the cases where we, from our twenty-first-century perspective, find these rulings problematic, there are several ways that we can deal with them.

The first is to renew the ways we engage old modes of thinking. For example, the biblical prohibition against sexual relations with a menstruant carries a long, misogynist textual history in which women are depicted as filthy and polluting—the dark force that must be controlled. In more recent years, however, some Jewish feminists have argued that rather than being problematic for women, the practice is an opportunity—a way both of honoring the body's natural rhythms and of sanctifying intimate relationships. For, as ritual theorist Catherine Bell puts it: "the obvious amibigu-ity or overdetermination of much religious symbolism may even be integral to its efficacy."[15] In other words, rituals—like liturgy, and re-ligious practices more generally—are open to interpretation, and may even work better when they can mean lot of different things at once. Sometimes we can embrace multiple levels at once, and sometimes we can use their multiplicity of meaning to hear the same radio station on different frequencies.

Because I believe that rituals operate simultaneously on innu-merable planes, and that they may serve our needs in different ways now than they have in the past, and because religious prac-tice is a form of divine service—for all these reasons, if I come across some aspect of my religious tradition that I don't like, I tend to be-gin with curiosity. What is this ritual (or rule, or snippet of liturgy) about? What did it do, how did it function, originally? What are some of the core ideas underlying it? How did it get to its current incarnation? How have people understood it in different times and places? The prayer praising God for the resurrection of the dead may have been written as a literal description of the messianic era, but its underlying message about the cyclical nature of life and death is powerful and porous enough to hold both the ancient no-tion and my own musings about the cycles of existence. The lan-guage of the liturgy reveals a truth big enough to carry thousands of years of prayer, and has survived precisely because its wisdom transcends the particulars of time and place. The rabbinic aphorisms of Pirke Avot remind us that with Torah, we must "turn it, and turn it over again, for everything is in it."[16]

Thus, if I see something that seems problematic, my first inclination is to fight with it and to see if I can see it with new eyes—as some feminists have with the menstruation laws. But sometimes that doesn't work. There are plenty of places where I do think that it's incumbent upon our generation and those to come to create space in our religious traditions that may not have always been there. A religion that does not reflect morality at its highest is a failure in our service of God. As our understanding of morality evolves, so should our efforts to make our religious systems embody our understanding of what is right and fair today. "Justice, justice, you shall pursue," implores Deuteronomy 16:20.

Now and again, we find little blind spots in our religious frameworks. There are, unfortunately, places where the importance of bringing every human into a full relationship with the Divine has been sorely underestimated. Jewish philosopher Yeshayahu Leibowitz has said, "what characterizes Judaism as a religion of Mitzvoth is not the set of laws and commandments that was given out at the start, but rather the recognition of a system of precepts as binding, even if their specifics were often determined only with time."[17] The system is binding even as the details, sometimes, need to evolve. It's a huge responsibility to participate in that evolution, one that has the potential to impact others for hundreds of years to come, so even speculation about it must be approached with awe and humility.

The specifics of how change occurs vary from religion to religion, but no faith system today is practiced in the exact same form that it was a thousand years ago—or even, perhaps, a hundred years ago. Structures of authority and hierarchy differ widely among faith systems, as do the mechanisms (official and unofficial) by which change happens—but somehow or another, change does happen. Anyone hoping to take part in the development of his or her religious tradition must, without fail, learn its history and understand how and when things have shifted. Sometimes change can be made from within, and sometimes more radical, revolutionary moves must be undertaken—one thinks, for example, of Rabbi Gershom ben Yehudah's eleventh-century ban on polygamy, which remained controversial for centuries after its declaration. It's worth noting that Rabbeinu Gershom was known as the "light of exile" because of his scholarship and influence; a lesser authority would not have been able to cause such a drastic change to be accepted.

Often, an issue that initially seems monolithic reveals itself, upon further scrutiny, to be much more complex. Demands to increase women's presence in the Jewish public sphere and religious practice, for example, may seem much less radical when one has a thorough mastery of the relevant sources. There's more leeway in the foundational books, like the Talmud, regarding women taking on certain rituals—such as the category of commandments called "time-bound mitzvot" that includes tzitzit and tefillin—than one might think, given some later writings and a history of male-dominated Jewish leadership. There are plenty of ancient sources that make an excellent case for women taking on these practices, and plenty of later rabbis (more than is commonly thought) agreed that doing so is, in fact, permitted. At the same time, some moves to give women full and equal participation in Jewish life demanded a more significant reimagining of the sources themselves, a reading into the "white spaces" of the authoritative texts.

Similarly, while early Buddhism had imparted "eight special rules" decreeing that Buddhist nuns were subservient to monks, women do receive Buddhism's highest levels of ordination in some places today. In some cases, this was possible because of a strange historical twist, such as a Confucian emporor's decree that Buddhist monks and nuns be separated, which had the unintended consequence of providing nuns with a new independence. In other places, the decision by advanced Zen masters to prioritize women's human rights over the eight special rules enabled women access to the most advanced levels of study, ordination, and recognition.[18] In both Judaism and Buddhism, as well as other religions, change happens in highly specialized contexts and is virtually impossible to enact without a mastery of the historical issues and the traditions themselves.

More often than not, the places where it's necessary to mobilize for transformation in religion reflect our contemporary understanding of morality and compassion. There's an ethical imperative inherent in work to enable women to take on leadership roles, to grant rights and status to same-sex relationships and the people in them, or to give space to stigmatized outsiders. There are mechanisms for change in every religion—sometimes it requires a major edict, sometimes it merely requires a more sophisticated reading or new interpretation of our existing texts. Just as I believe it is our duty to fully enter into a tradition, I also believe that it is our duty to fix what is broken. When you have a sprained ankle, you don't cut off your foot—but you also don't pretend that nothing is wrong. Diagnosis is the hard part. Fixing the problem can be challenging, but it is holy work.

There's a tension between agency and humility, between the need to speak out and the need to know your stuff. On the one hand, it can be problematic (or at least ineffective) for someone who doesn't understand the religion that he or she is criticizing to go into attack mode. On the other hand, few of us will ever be as knowledgable and learned as the greatest living minds of our religion—when do we know enough in order to speak, in order to take action? When are we speaking out of arrogance or self-righteousness, and when out of a strong sense that Divine justice is at stake? The answers aren't always clear. Nor is it always clear when it's time to work within the system and when it's time to operate from the prophetic tradition, to reject religious complacency and to follow the seventeenth-century Quaker exhortation to "speak truth to power."

All we can do—all we can ever do—is to follow the voice of God that resounds within. It often knows all too well where and how to carry us.

Religious practice is meant to transform who we are and how we live in relation to the world. One code of Jewish law recommends donating a little bit of money—even just a few coins—to charity every weekday morning before prayer.[19] After I started doing this, I found that it was much harder to pray only for my own personal desires and to forget about what was really needed on a global scale. How much time and energy can I devote to asking for relief of my relatively minor complaints when I've just remembered that war and famine rage outside my door? Of course, awareness of the big picture is packed into the liturgy, but the act of giving imprints itself on my consciousness in a much more concrete way, and it becomes harder to slip back into the familiar litany of me, me, me after confronting the charity box.

The Hindu guru Sant Keshavadas wrote, "Go ahead, light your candles and burn your incense and ring your bells and call out to God, but watch out, because God will come and He will put you on His anvil and fire up His forge and beat you and beat you until He turns brass into pure gold."[20] Intended or not, this process of purification transforms the way we see the world—and it's sometimes about as comfortable as getting hit with a blacksmith's hammer.

Luckily for me, both Alex's seminary and my family were in Chicago—I was able to see her more or less every time I went home to visit. Once during her second year of grad school, I drove down to her part of town to hang out, as usual. She was very agitated all evening, as we walked to and from dinner and returned to the apartment she shared with several classmates. Finally, when we were settled in her room with our mugs of tea, she glanced around as though she thought the place was bugged, shut the door, leaned forward, and confessed in a hurried whisper, "I'm, um, not sure whether I'm exactly 100 percent pro-choice anymore."

Her dirty secret in a liberal denomination. I shrugged—this didn't shock me as much as I guess she was afraid it might. Alex had marched in her share of pro-choice rallies, not to mention the time she had logged stuffing envelopes for the lobbying group NARAL. Even now, she said, she wasn't sure if her feelings were connected to what she thought the laws should be in our present reality so much as the sense that, if the Divine was in everything, didn't it mean *that* as well? And if we were going to build a society based on caring and compassion and reverence for the sacred, wouldn't we want to remove a lot of the root causes that compelled women to undergo abortions in the first place? She became fond of quoting Frederica Mathewes-Green's suggestion that "no one wants an abortion as she wants an ice-cream cone or a Porsche. She wants an abortion as an animal, caught in a trap, wants to gnaw off its own leg."[21]

Alex's spiritual discipline had led her down a path that had radical implications for her understanding of her own politics. She struggled for years with this, trying to figure out how to talk about her growing sense of the interconnectedness of all things without coming across as a crazy fundamentalist who expected women to be baby factories.

It became clear that, on the other side of spiritual transformation, some folks from her old life wouldn't be able to even tell the difference between Alex, now a passionate, feminist Episcopalian, and some of the Christian fundamentalists she had battled in her old clinic defense days—the ones who saw the world in black and white and attempted to impose their understanding of the world onto others. This was a painful realization, but she knew that it couldn't keep her from telling the truth as she understood it. Facing backlash from some of her former acquaintances, Alex noted wryly, "There is, you know, a difference between being judgmental and having judgment." That is to say, it's permitted to contend that one thing might be preferable over another without condemning those who disagree, and it might even be possible to take a stand on something while knowing that what's "preferable" is subject to bias and one's own value system.

Alex set about trying to find common ground between pro-life and pro-choice activists. She began by attempting to define the values and goals that both sides shared, and thinking about how to approach them in a way that would depolarize a complex and highly charged issue. What do low-income women need in order to stay safe and healthy? What kinds of communal resources would any scared, isolated woman (regardless of what she ultimately chooses to do with her pregnancy) need in order to feel supported? What kinds of liturgy would help a woman to work through the many emotions—including grief—that might come up after an abortion?

Her work, to me, echoed a ritual performed by the Yurok and Hupa nations in Northern California. It's called Jump Dance, and it's a ritual enactment of the process of reconciliation among two groups between whom disagreements arise now and then. Dancers representing each of the "sides" take turns as two lead singers and a chorus anchor them to the process. Over a period of several days, the number of dancers and singers increases, until, on the last day, the dancers from both communities join together and the two main singers shift the music into harmony, and all involved feel a sense that balance has been restored among the groups. As Carol Lee Flinders notes, "The beauty of Jump Dance . . . is that it doesn't pretend that one side is right and the other wrong. The burning question is simply: how can we transcend separateness?" [22]

After Malcolm X had his revelation on the plane to Mecca, he began speaking against his old philosophy of militant racial separatism. The pilgrimage had a powerful, indelible impact on his heart—and, as a result, it affected the politics he had held for so long. He wrote to friends from the Muslim holy city, "I've had enough of someone else's propaganda. I'm for truth, no matter who tells it. I'm for justice, no matter who it is for or against. I'm a human being first and foremost, and as such I'm for whoever and whatever benefits humanity *as a whole*." [23]

Religious practice has the potential to change us, dramatically and with a force that we may have heretofore been unable to imagine. Its revolutionary power is nothing short of radical—one is called to think of Gandhi, boarding the trains of colonial India and holding up his hand before their hardly well-off, hardly privileged, riders. He'd raise a finger and tell them that it represented the problem of the treatment of untouchables in India. Another finger—this is economic dependence on the British and the need to begin wearing only homespun clothes. A third: addiction to alcohol and opium. Number four was the Hindu–Muslim conflict, and five, the status of women. [24]

This was the hand, Gandhi told his passengers, with which they could together defeat the British. However, a meaningful victory could only come once India had faced all of the ways in which the country was weak, all of the ways in which the dignity of every human being was compromised.

That is the kind of big-picture thinking that could come only from someone who was aware, on the most primal level possible, that the interconnectedness of everything could never be underestimated. His reverence for each individual life was part and parcel of his reverence for that which is greater than and binds us all. For Gandhi, a society depended on the moral progress of its members, and only a culture based on love and service to others, grounded in the religious impulse and a spiritual discipline, was destined to flourish—for, "so long as the seed of morality is not watered by religion, it cannot sprout. Without water it withers and ultimately perishes."[25] In other words, ethics watered from the small, limited well of a single human is all too easily depleted, but water drawn from the ever-flowing Source can sustain, and help our understanding of who we must be and how to flourish and grow.

At the same time, of course, this morality has to produce results, for, he wrote, "religion which takes no account of practical affairs and does not help to solve them, is no religion."[26] I daresay Gandhi would be horrified by the current state of affairs in this world.

We inhabit the legacy of Margaret Thatcher's 1981 statement that "economics are the method; the object is to change the heart and soul." Thatcher's capitalism and privatization—mirrored powerfully by Reaganomics in the States, where its economic legacy is still felt today—helped to turn people into individuals seeking their individual ends, thus erasing concerns for social welfare that may have lingered in their hearts and souls. As religion scholars Carette and King put it, "Late capitalist societies operate upon the mechanisms of social isolation. They create a social vacuum and an individualized sense of emptiness that consumerism promises, but intrinsically fails, to satisfy."[27] In this culture, people look to buy things to fill the empty spaces once occupied by a robust, nourishing communal life and concern for the welfare of society as a whole. And when people begin to sense that the accumulation of stuff— the next gadget, the latest fashion—isn't enough, they look to spirituality.

However, Carette and King suggest, consumer capitalism has already coopted this move, and is waiting with instructional CDs, amulets, desktop "Zen" gardens, and advice on how to de-stress and how to find bliss in one's daily doings—all while encouraging people to maintain "the materialistic culture that they are ostensibly seeking to resist." In other words, they argue, "capitalist spirituality ...offers personalized packages of meaning...rather than recipes for social change and identification with others.[28]

This ethos is so pervasive in our society that it's almost difficult to identify. Quick steps to enlightenment line the shelves of our bookstores and retreat catalogs invite us to "indulge in an ideal experience of self-care and inner focus."[29] "Improve your life" programs are designed to lure new members to churches and synagogues; the Kabbalah Center promises "the fulfillment you deserve." Self-help spirituality is our cultural white noise, the wallpaper we don't even notice.

Obviously, it's not a bad thing that religious practice transforms us as individuals—this is one of its many difficult blessings, and has always been. But much of what's being sold is, simply, not transformative. It's not designed to push us to confront our own darkest corners and most stubborn points of resistance, let alone to "recall the face of the poorest and the weakest man whom you may have seen, and ask yourself," as Gandhi often did, "if the step you contemplate is going to be of any use to him."[30] We have to heal ourselves, but our doing so must have implications for the most vulnerable members of our society. It's nice to experience ecstatic feelings and to feel better about the life already being lived, but it's simply not enough. Rabbi Rebecca Alpert writes: "The story of Cain and Abel from the book of Genesis teaches...the lesson of social responsibility...The answer to the question 'Am I my brother's keeper?' is a resounding yes."[31]

The thing about this "being present in the moment" business is that it's infectious. Once you start paying attention to where you are, how your breath moves in and out of your body, what you're eating, and how you feel, it gets harder and harder to turn off awareness. It gets harder to walk past a homeless person and not look her in the eye, see that she is human and, probably, hungry. It gets harder not to realize that every purchase you make has a potentially global impact, that it may support a local artisan—or a corporation that trades in sweatshop labor. It gets harder to read newspaper stories about war or capital punishment casually, as though they weren't happening to real people, causing real suffering. It gets harder to be oblivious to the fact that, as Alex had observed years ago, the person cleaning your office is a person, and the reason that she's so tired might have something to do both with you, and with the big picture, with the way that all of these issues are interconnected. It gets harder to forget that 28 million people in America are classified as "working poor"[32] or that 46.6 million people in America go without heath insurance.[33] It gets harder to forget that individuals can come together to change a community, and that communities can come together to make change that's even farther reaching than that. What religion changes is not just our identity, our relationships, our politics, our sense of what the world is and how we move in it, but also, potentially, every small decision that we make. What religion changes, if we let it, is not just ourselves, not just our smaller home culture, but the world as a whole and the power structures that run it.

No wonder that many who expound Thatcherism and views like it would rather that our souls be locked in small, easily controlled packages. Gandhi's personal transformation led to an entire nation overthrowing an imperialist government. Imagine what might happen if we all allowed our souls to be transformed—not by economics, but, rather, by love.

Thomas Merton writes in *The Seven Storey Mountain* that, shortly before he entered a Trappist monastery in Kentucky at age twenty-six, a "life of grace had at last, it seemed, become constant, permanent."[34] Several years later, he is able to say to God, "You have given me peace, and I am beginning to see what it is all about. I am beginning to understand."[35]

It's a lovely way to end the spiritual autobiography that was composed not long after Merton took his vows. Would that real life had complied with his feelings of finality and certainty; his later journals indicate that, perhaps, the story does not end there. In the years that followed the publication of *The Seven Storey Mountain*, Merton continued to struggle with frustration, loneliness, and doubt. Despite his vow of celibacy, he eventually strayed into a six-month love affair with a student nurse. Merton was a great man, but he and his faith were far from perfect. Every time he was drawn away from God, though, he returned—chastened, wiser, more devoted than ever. It even seems that each time he felt his heart broken by doubt, it healed and expanded, made fuller by love. A life of grace is far from fixed, far from linear.

I have no doubt that I will have to learn this over and over as the years unfold.

Spiritual practice is a "practice" in the truest sense of the world—trying, and trying again. Arriving, drifting away, returning always, again and again, to what Merton later in life called "the solitude of the frail, mortal, limited, distressed, rebellious human person, made of his love and fears, facing his own true present."[36]

As a rabbinical student living in Jerusalem, I have a study date every Wednesday afternoon. I meet a friend at the liberal yeshiva he attends—the same one at which I spent a dizzying summer some seven years earlier—and we retire to the study hall. It's crowded even after a full day of classes. I look like a lot of the other students; I'm wearing jeans and a T-shirt. Depending on the day, I've either got a *kippah* or a bandanna on my head, my tzitzit might be swaying in the wind or tucked discreetly in. I grab a copy of the Talmud tractate we're working on and a dictionary for when the Aramaic gets too knotty. I like being in a good study hall; it's comfortable, familiar. Students are hunched in pairs over large books, often wildly animated as they debate what the dense passages mean.

Avi and I have been working our way through the laws of Shabbat and various other topics—the text swerves and digresses. Today, we get to a section in which homiletic stories have been woven into the legal discussions. The rabbis on the page have been talking about what Jews refer to as Revelation, that is, the giving of the

Torah on Mount Sinai described in Exodus 19 and 20. As the sages
are often wont to do, one of them quotes a biblical verse and then
plays with it a bit:

> "And they stood under the mount" (Exod. 19:17). Rav Avidimi, son
> of Hama, son of Hasa said: This verse teaches that the Holy One
> overturned the mountain upon them, like an inverted cask, and
> said to them: If you accept the Torah—it is well, and if not, this
> will be your grave.[37]

The Exodus verse tells us in the Hebrew that, waiting to receive the
Torah, Israel stood b'tachtit the mountain, either right at the mountain's base (as the plain meaning would indicate) or, as Rav Avidimi
dryly suggests, literally underneath it. At first glance, the Deity in
this story seems to be the same angry figment I rejected as an adolescent, the deus who, ex machina, pulls history's strings like a ne-
farious puppeteer.

But on another level, this story seems to be telling us that
Revelation—that encountering the Divine—is not only difficult, it's
dangerous. The text is brutally clear: meeting God is a life-or-death
proposition. It defies every cultural story we have about easy, feel-
good "spirituality," a nice gesture toward self-improvement that's
only slightly more difficult than placing aromatherapy candles
around a bubble bath. Rather, it's absolutely petrifying.

The Islamic prophet Muhammad is said to have once cried,
"Never once did I receive a revelation without thinking that my soul
had been torn away from me."[38] Meeting God is about having our
souls ripped away, having everything we may have ever understood
about who we are pulled out from under our feet—and having to
pick up the pieces afterward. We have to figure out who we are and
what to do once the comfortable and the familliar have been taken
away.

It's terrifying to face the implications of "accepting Torah"—
hearing what God is really asking of us, hearing who God is telling
us that we are. It's more than unnerving to realize how much hard,
grueling work lies ahead for us in order to maintain this relation-

ship. It's alarming, to say the least, to contemplate changing our actions and understandings of the world as a result of this encounter with the Ineffable, with no sense of what kind of long-term impact it may have on our lives and everything we know. It can feel a little like having a mountain hovering over our heads.

It's the feeling that, even if we resist, even if we're resentful, even if it's inconvenient, even if it's scary and hard and will have indelible implications for the rest of our lives—even with all that, we know that aligning our will with God's will may be the only thing that can ultimately save us.

AFTERWORD

My first-ever Rosh Hashanah in San Francisco, I find myself in a synagogue that I've only visited a few times. It's so crowded that I have
to get a seat in the balcony, on the side. I'm carried away by the familiar lilt of the prayers; when the rabbi steps up to the podium to
deliver his sermon, I'm peering down at the top of his head. He knits
a complex web of meaning out of text and politics and God and the
implications of this particular day for who we are. It's language and
theology and truth, and it's delicious. Out of nowhere, a thought
pops into my head: "That's what I want to do." I laugh it away—I had
been an atheist recently enough that the prospect of becoming
clergy is nothing more than amusing—and I turn back to my prayer
book.

But the thought doesn't disappear, not entirely. Somewhere between writing reviews of Internet-themed drag shows and devour-
ing books on Talmudic history, I begin to picture it: a second career.
I imagine working as a writer until my forties and then, somewhere
after marriage and kids, going back to school. I confess my secret
fantasy to Alex right before leaving to travel, and she asks me why
I'd have to wait so long. In Jerusalem, I track down rabbinical students and assault them with questions about their programs, their
paths, their plans. I begin to worry about what it might take to work
for God.

I try, over and over and over again, to come up with another ca-

reer path—this one seems so perilous, so loaded, so full of respon-
sibilities that no mortal should have to handle. Worse, it seems to
demand that I once again leave the San Francisco I love. Couldn't
I just be a journalist who happens to be a religious Jew? Every time
I tune in to the still small voice of the immanent Divine, though, I
hear what sounds disturbingly like an amused chuckle, like God
telling me no, sorry—I actually have to go do this thing. Do I have
to? Yes, God answers patiently, with an irritating consistency.

I have a friend who makes a point of telling her congregants that
God did not bellow from inside her coffee cup that she had to go to
rabbinical school—that, rather, this decision, like every decision,
was something chosen consciously, and was the product of many
other choices along the way. She's right, of course. And yet, on another level, I have felt as though my entering the rabbinate was
much less like pondering Chocolate Mint versus Rocky Road than
like submitting to a call that would give me no peace until I heeded
it, even as I've questioned myself many times along the way. Every-
time I checked my math, the answer always came out the same.

One day, some sort of internal timer went "ding!" and I heard a
now-familiar murmur; this time, however, it said, "It's time." I consulted with Alex and Ariel, had a sizable freakout, and wrote to a
seminary in Los Angeles requesting an application to rabbinical
school. Eight months later I was accepted, and I moved to Southern
California several months after that.

As I write these words, I've completed most of my studies and
lived in Jerusalem for a few years along the way. (It is, I might add,
a much lovelier city than I was able to appreciate as a tourist trying
to sort through the big questions of life.) God willing, by the time
you read this book, I will have been ordained. I've already met and
married my husband—a secular Israeli, of all things. Luckily, by the
time we met I already had years of practice maintaining close ties
with non-Jewish and nonreligious friends. Enacting pluralism and
mutual respect gets easier the more you do it.

How the process of becoming a rabbi has changed me since the
end of this story, and what it's meant to me, is the subject of a whole
other book. The experience has been incredible in so many ways;

intensive study has grounded me in my faith and given it more heft. I've had to learn on many different levels what it means to serve, to put others' needs before my own. I've had to figure out how to set my demons and fears aside when they got in the way of hearing other people clearly. There have been lessons in humility, submission, bravery, trust, and the matchless importance of old-fashioned hard work.

But this book is not about entering the rabbinate. In fact, I chose not to include those experiences in this story for a very specific reason: The fulfillment of religious practice is not in the decision to go professional. The fulfillment of religious practice is in religious practice. And if you keep doing it, it will transform you in ways you never imagined. And then it will transform you again, and again, hopefully over the course of a long and beautiful lifetime. My own personal rabbinic adventure is simply the story of how religion did its work on me in one specific way, of what I happened to have heard when I tuned in to the Divine radio station. But it's a mere subplot in a much bigger tale of one heart, opening slowly. Thank God, this practice doesn't change us all in the same way, but rather sets our feet on the strange and brambly path we didn't know that we'd been trying to find all along.

Everyone with a spiritual discipline must do what it takes to become an educated and empowered member of the community—it's a key part of the work. This, however, hardly requires mass migration to the monasteries and seminaries. Those places are already overcrowded with people who believe that enlightenment can come only from decades on the mountaintop, that knowledge's wealth can only be attained by becoming the expert.

And yet, for every person with a religious résumé and an overinflated sense of self-importance, there will be dozens of layfolk who are slowly learning the opposite to be true. Every day, they find—we all find—that the hard work of a spiritual practice has an indelible effect, that deep change comes gradually. We find that, little by little, this practice takes us back to our work, back into our relationships, our families, our old hobbies, and our slightly revamped ideas of fun. We find that, through the persistence and the tears and the negotiations and the uncertainty and the terrifying moments after something old and familiar has slipped away and before something new and strong has come forward to take its place—through it all, we can feel the sweet presence of Infinity humming below the surface, changing how we see the world and our lives in it. We see that sometimes, the old and new external forms look an awful lot alike, even as the internal content is utterly unrecognizable from what it had once been.

For, even as one undergoes the profound transformation inherent in waking up, real life goes on.

ACKNOWLEDGMENTS

First of all, infinite thanks to my agent, Jill Grinberg, for believing in this project and for her indefatigable work in making it a reality. Thanks to Kirsten Wolf for being excellent in too many ways. Millions of thanks also to my amazing editor, Amy Caldwell, for making everything smarter and better, and to everybody at Beacon Press for the time, attention, and care offered this project.

I also can't say thank you enough to all of the folks who have helped me through this process, supported me, listened patiently as I ranted, offered suggestions on the book in progress, fed me Shabbat dinners, babysat my stuff when I was living abroad, and have generally been way nicer to me than is reasonable.

In particular, big kisses to Kirsten Cowan, Rabbi Haviva Ner-David and the whole Ner-David family, Rabbi Ruth Gan Kagan, Diane Bernbaum, Leora Tanenbaum, Bari Mandelbaum, R. Pickett, Karissa Sellman, Maria Rowan, Eddie Dinel, Janet Leeds, Jen Taylor Friedman, Wendy Love Anderson, Sarah-Katherine Lewis, Doña and Aaron Croston, Rev. Dave Hedges, Laura and Rev. Micah Jackson, Sara Meirowitz, Sarah Ruhl, Tony Charuvastra, and too many other folks to name. Thanks also to all my wonderful hevrutot of the last few years, especially Ari, Ezra, Laurence, Jay, Gila, and Scott, as well as to all of my teachers at the Ziegler School of Rabbinic Studies.

Thanks to Ben, Dad, Irit, Itzik, Guy, and Efrat for much support and general goodness along the way.

Most of all, I am grateful to Nir for his love, encouragement, patience, laughter, companionship, more-than-occasional kicks in the pants, and at least several hundred thousand cups of tea.

NOTES

INTRODUCTION

1. John Cassidy, "No Satisfaction: The Trials of the Shopping Nation," *New Yorker*, January 25, 1999, 88 (consumption figure); Robert H. Frank, *Luxury Fever: Why Money Fails to Satisfy in an Age of Excess* (New York: Free Press, 1999), 46 (debt statistic).

2. Elliot Dorff, *Knowing God: Jewish Journeys to the Unknowable* (Northvale, NJ: Jason Aronson, 1996), 14.

CHAPTER 1

1. Now the idea that a Jewish educator would have asked children to draw God bothers me. I really don't know what that woman was thinking. "You shall not make for you any graven image, or any likeness of any thing that is in heaven above," says Exodus 20:4. Traditionally, Jews take that to mean that drawing crayon pictures of God (or of idols) is right off the list of okay activities.

2. "Music, Part 2," *The Sufi Message of Hazrat Inayat Khan*, http://sufimessage.com/music/musico2.html.

3. "Music, Part 2," *Sufi Message*.

4. Daniel C. Matt, *God and the Big Bang: Discovering Harmony Between Science and Spirituality* (Woodstock, VT: Jewish Lights Publishing, 1996), 38.

5. Jean-Paul Sartre, "Existentialism Is a Humanism," trans. Philip Mairet, in *Existentialism from Dostoyevsky to Sartre,* ed. Walter Kaufman (New York: Meridian Publishing, 1989), 345.

6. Jean-Paul Sartre, *Being and Nothingness,* trans. Hazel E. Barnes (New York: Washington Square Press, 1993), 566; Sartre, "Existentialism Is a Humanism."

7. Jean-Paul Sartre, *The Words: The Autobiography of Jean-Paul Sartre* (New York: Vintage, 1981).

8. Sartre, "Existentialism Is a Humanism."

9. Samuel Enoch Stumpf, *Philosophical Problems: Selected Readings* (New York: McGraw-Hill, 1989), 200.

10. Ron Suskind, "Faith, Certainty, and the Presidency of George B. Bush," *New York Times,* October 17, 2004, www.nytimes.com/2004/ 10/17/magazine/17BUSH.html?ex=1255665600en=890a96189e1620 76ei=5090.

11. A.K.M. Adam, "Stress, Grace, Joy," *AKMA's Random Thoughts,* February 25, 2007, http://akma.disseminary.org/archives/2007/02/ stress_grace_jo.html.

12. John Keats, "Lamia," in *The Norton Anthology of English Literature,* vol. 2, ed. M. H. Abrams (New York: Norton, 1986), 827–44.

CHAPTER 2

1. Knapp, *Appetites: Why Women Want* (New York: Counterpoint, 2003), 13.

2. Geneen Roth, *When You Eat at the Refrigerator, Pull Up a Chair* (New York: Hyperion, 1998), 147.

3. Dante Alighieri, *Paradiso,* trans. Allen Mandelbaum (Berkeley: University of California Press, 1984).

4. Soren Kierkegaard, *Fear and Trembling* (New York: Penguin Classics, 1986), 65.

5. Thanks to the Zen tradition by way of Rami Shapiro for this very apt image.

CHAPTER 3

1. Annie Dillard, *Pilgrim at Tinker Creek* (New York: Harper Perennial, 1988), 269.
2. Suskind, "Faith, Certainty, and the Presidency."
3. Shane Claiborne, *The Irresistible Revolution: Living as an Ordinary Radical* (Grand Rapids, MI: Zondervan, 2006), 39.
4. Zalman Schachter-Shalomi, "On Renewing God," in *Best Contemporary Jewish Writing*, ed. Michael Lerner (San Francisco: Jossey-Bass, 2001), 104.
5. Sifrei Bamidbar, Parshat Shelach, Piska 6, and elsewhere in rabbinic texts.
6. Moses Maimonides, *Mishneh Torah*, Hilchot Yesodei HaTorah 1 (and all over the first third of *Guide for the Perplexed*).
7. Thomas Merton, *The Seven Storey Mountain* (New York: Harcourt Brace, 1948), 174.
8. Anne Lamott, *Traveling Mercies: Some Thoughts on Faith* (New York: Anchor, 2000), 51.
9. Carol Lee Flinders, *Enduring Grace: Living Portraits of Seven Women Mystics* (San Francisco: HarperSanFrancisco, 1993), 153.
10. Arthur Green, "Eco-Kabbalah Spirituality," in *Best Contemporary Jewish Writing*, ed. Michael Lerner (San Francisco: Jossey Bass, 2001), 120.
11. Sally Cunneen, *In Search of Mary: The Woman and the Symbol* (New York: Ballantine, 1996), 189. Thanks to Rev. Micah Jackson for pointing me toward these historical nuggets.
12. Neil Gillman, *Sacred Fragments: Recovering Theology for the Modern Jew* (Philadelphia: Jewish Publication Society, 1990), 81.
13. Sifrei Bamidbar, Parshat Shelach, Piska 6, and elsewhere in rabbinic texts.
14. Shane Hipps, *The Hidden Power of Electronic Culture: How Media*

Shapes Faith, the Gospel, and Church (Grand Rapids, MI: Zondervan, 2005), 94.

15. Monique Wittig, *Les Guérillères*, trans. David Le Vay (Boston: Beacon Press, 1985), 127.

16. Rudolf Otto, *The Idea of the Holy*, trans. John W. Harvey. (London: Oxford University Press, 1973), 12–13.

17. Matt, *God and the Big Bang*, 46.

18. Merton, *Seven Storey Mountain*, 108.

CHAPTER 4

1. Talmud Yerushalmi, Brachot 3:1.

2. Alan Watts, "In My Own Way," in *God in All Worlds: An Anthology of Contemporary Spiritual Writing*, ed. Lucinda Vardey (New York: Pantheon Books, 1995), 398.

3. Roth, *When You Eat at the Refrigerator*, 217.

4. bell hooks, *All About Love: New Visions* (New York: William Morrow, 2000), 224.

5. Green, "Eco-Kabbalah Spirituality," 116.

6. Flinders, *Enduring Grace*, 84.

7. Jeremy Carrette and Richard King, *Selling Spirituality: The Silent Takeover of Religion* (New York: Routledge, 2005), 118, 114.

8. Carol Lee Flinders, *The Values of Belonging* (San Francisco: HarperSanFrancisco, 2002), 205.

9. Genesis Rabba 69:2.

10. Talmud Bavli, Taanit 7a.

11. Conversation with Reiki master Rahel Warshaw-Dadon, August 2006.

12. Rav Pinchas Giller, personal correspondence, April 16, 2007.

13. Donna Rockwell, "True Stories About Sitting Meditation," *Shambhala Sun*, March 2003.

14. Paul Reps and Nyogen Senzaki, eds., *Zen Flesh Zen Bones: A Collection of Zen and Pre-Zen Writings* (Boston: Shambhala Publications, 1994), 125–26.

15. Merton, *Seven Storey Mountain*, 205.

16. St. Augustine, *Confessions*, book 8 (New York: Penguin Books, 1961), 169.

CHAPTER 5

1. Rabbi Alan Lew discusses these ideas at length in his book *Be Still and Get Going: A Jewish Meditation Practice for Real Life* (New York: Little, Brown, 2005), 34–37, 141.

2. Lew, *Be Still and Get Going*, 12.

3. Flinders, *Enduring Grace*, 44.

4. Naomi Wolf, "My Spiritual Path," in *Best Contemporary Jewish Writing*, ed. Michael Lerner (San Francisco: Jossey-Bass, 2001), 97.

5. Wolf, "My Spiritual Path," 98.

6. David Kraemer, *The Mind of the Talmud: An Intellectual History of the Babylonian Talmud* (London: Oxford University Press,1990).

7. Yeshayahu Leibowitz, "Religious Praxis: The Meaning of Halakha," in *Judaism, Human Values and the Jewish State*, ed. Eliezer Goldman (Cambridge, MA: Harvard University Press, 1995), 5.

8. Merton, *Seven Storey Mountain*, 113.

9. Frederica Mathewes-Green, "Should You Design Your Own Religion?" *Utne Reader*, August 1998.

10. Rev. Micah Jackson, personal correspondence, August 2006.

11. The Rema on the Shulchan Aruch, Yoreh Deah 178:1.

12. Yael Shor, "Avodah Zarah from A to Z" (research paper, University of Judaism, Los Angeles, December 2006). Quoted with permission.

13. Pirke Avot 4:1.

14. Tosefta Berachot 4:1.

15. Rachel Naomi Remen, "Consecrating the Ordinary," in *Kitchen Table Wisdom: Stories That Heal* (New York: Riverhead Books, 1997), 282.

16. *Bill Viola*, exhibit catalog (New York: Whitney Museum of American Art, 1998), 143.

17. Abraham Joshua Heschel, *The Sabbath* (New York: Farrar, Strauss and Giroux, 1979), 28.

18. Carol Lee Flinders, *At the Root of This Longing: Reconciling a Spiritual Hunger and a Feminist Thirst* (San Francisco: HarperSanFrancisco, 1998), 71.

19. Knapp, *Appetites,* 15.

20. Stephanie Kaza, "Overcoming the Grip of Consumerism," *Buddhist-Christian Studies* 20 (2000): 23–42.

21. Heschel, *Sabbath,* 28.

22. Flinders, *Enduring Grace,* 167.

23. Henri Nouwen, *The Inner Voice of Love* (New York: Bantam, 1999), 21.

24. Nouwen, *Inner Voice of Love,* 22.

25. Merton, *Seven Storey Mountain,* 232. See Deuteronomy 11:10–11.

CHAPTER 6

1. Yehuda HaLevi, "My Heart Is in the East," in Jane S. Gerber, *The Jews of Spain: A History of the Sephardic Experience* (New York: Free Press, 1992), 73.

2. Genesis 12:1. Translation mine.

3. Lew, *Be Still and Get Going,* 15–16. This was more or less what he had said that night in his sermon.

4. Matt, *God and the Big Bang,* 39.

5. Carrette and King, *Selling Spirituality,* 68.

6. Maura O'Halloran, *Pure Heart, Enlightened Mind: The Zen Journal and Letters of Maura "Soshin" O'Halloran* (New York: Riverhead Books, 1994), 22.

7. Jack Kornfield, *After the Ecstasy, the Laundry: How the Heart Grows Wise on the Spiritual Path* (New York: Bantam, 2001), xiii, 124–25.

8. O'Halloran, *Pure Heart, Enlightened Mind,* 145.

9. Psalm 27:10.

10. Martha Beck, *Expecting Adam: A True Story of Birth, Rebirth, and Everyday Magic* (New York: Crown, 1999), 287.

11. James Fadiman and Robert Frager, eds., *Essential Sufism* (San Francisco: HarperSanFrancisco, 1997), 244.

12. "A Week at Elat Chayyim," *Velveteen Rabbi,* Rachel Berenblat, June 2004, http://velveteenrabbi.blogs.com/blog/2004/06/a_week_at_ elat_.html.

13. Lew, *Be Still and Get Going,* 18.

14. Talmud Bavli, Brachot 57b.

15. Dorff, *Knowing God,* 13.

16. Arthur Green, *Tormented Master: The Life and Spiritual Quest of Rabbi Nahman of Bratslav* (Woodstock, VT: Jewish Lights, 1992), 107.

CHAPTER 7

1. Maimonides, *Mishneh Torah* Hilchot Deot 5:6–9.

2. Pirke Avot 5:9.

3. Nouwen, *Inner Voice of Love,* 23.

4. Flinders, *Enduring Grace,* 112.

5. Danya Ruttenberg, "Striking a Balance: Carol Lee Flinders on Spirituality, Politics, and the Spaces in Between" (interview), *Bitch Magazine* 24 (Spring 2004), 51.

6. Hillary Mayell, "As Consumerism Spreads, Earth Suffers, Study Says," *National Geographic News,* January 12, 2004.

7. Richard Robbins, *Global Problems and the Culture of Capitalism* (Boston: Allyn & Bacon, 1999), 15–16.

8. World Bank, "Growth of Consumption and Investment" (Table 4), *World Development Indicators,* http://devdata.worldbank.org/ wdi2005/Table4_10.htm.

9. Mayell, "As Consumerism Spreads."

10. Barry Schwartz, *The Paradox of Choice: Why More Is Less* (New York: Harper Perennial/Ecco Press, 2004), 12.

11. Susan Fournier and Michael Guiry, "An Emerald Green Jaguar, a House on Nantucket, and an African Safari: Wish Lists and Consumption Dreams in Materialistic Society," *Advances in Consumer Research* 20 (1993), 352–58.

12. Flinders, *Enduring Grace,* 171.

13. V. Vale and Andrea Juno, eds., *Angry Women* (San Francisco: Re/Search Publications, 1992), 184.

14. Flinders, *At the Root*, 77–78.

15. Martin Buber, *Tales of the Hasidim: Later Masters* (New York: Schocken, 1948), 249–50. (Book's translation paraphrased slightly.)

16. Zoketsu Norman Fischer, "How I Got to Where I'm Going," Every-day Zen Foundation website, http://everydayzen.org.

17. Thomas Merton, *Spiritual Direction and Meditation* (Collegeville, MN: Liturgical Press, 1960), 30, 33.

18. Jalal al-Din Rumi, *The Essential Rumi*, Coleman Barks and John Moyne, trans. (San Francisco: HarperSanFrancisco, 1995), 109.

19. Fadiman and Frager, *Essential Sufism*, 228.

20. Nouwen, *Inner Voice of Love*, 27.

21. Merton, *Seven Storey Mountain*, 112.

22. Joanna Macy, "Working Through Environmental Despair," in *Ecopsychology: Restoring the Earth, Healing the Mind*, ed. Allen D. Kanner, Theodore Roszak, and Mary E. Gomes (San Francisco: Sierra Club Books, 1995).

23. Macy, "Working Through Environmental Despair."

24. Rockwell, "True Stories."

25. Talmud Bavli, Brachot 32b.

26. James Carse, *Breakfast at the Victory: The Mysticism of Ordinary Experience* (San Francisco: HarperSanFrancisco, 1994), 70.

27. Merton, *Spiritual Direction and Meditation*, 20–21.

28. Conversation with Rabbi Zalman Schachter-Shalomi, February 4, 2007.

29. Pirke Avot 1:6.

CHAPTER 8

1. Nouwen, *Inner Voice of Love*, 45.

2. Martin Luther King, "Letter from Birmingham City Jail," in *The World Treasury of Modern Religious Thought*, ed. Jaroslav Pelikan (Boston: Little, Brown, 1990), 607.

3. Malcolm X, *The Autobiography of Malcolm X*, with Alex Haley (New York: Ballantine Books, 1999), 328.

4. bell hooks, *All About Love*, 76.

5. Prayer of Saint Francis of Assisi (traditional).

6. Roger Walsh, *Essential Spirituality: The 7 Central Practices to Awaken Heart and Mind* (New York: Wiley, 2000), 4.

7. Pirke Avot 1:15.

8. Lewis Fischer, *Gandhi: His Life and Message for the World* (New York: Signet, 1982), 105.

9. Flinders, *Enduring Grace*, 100.

10. I Corinthians 13:2.

11. Merton, *Seven Storey Mountain*, 83.

12. Flinders, *Enduring Grace*, 148.

13. Pirke Avot 3:21. I did switch the order of the saying for effect.

14. Abraham Joshua Heschel, *The Prophets: An Introduction*, vol. 1 (New York: Harper & Row, 1962), 16.

15. Ben Dreyfus, "Hilchot Pluralism, Part VI: The Limits of Pluralism," *Mah Rabu*, December 29, 2006, http://mahrabu.blogspot.com.

16. Dreyfus, "Hilchot Pluralism."

17. Nouwen, *Inner Voice of Love*, 25.

18. Shane Hipps, *Hidden Power*, 111. (Apparently referencing Mark Lau Branson in the Winter 2003 edition of *Congregations*.)

19. Eloissa Leonna, "An Interview with Thich Nhat Hanh," *In Motion Magazine*, January 25, 2004.

20. Flinders, *At the Root*, 59–98.

21. Leonna, "Interview with Thich Nhat Hanh."

22. Beck, *Expecting Adam*, 220.

CHAPTER 9

1. Fadiman and Frager, *Essential Sufism*, 109.

2. Rockwell, "True Stories."

3. Matt, *God and the Big Bang*, 74.

4. Psalms 34:9.

5. Deuteronomy 6:18.

6. Hosea 2:21–22.

7. Schachter-Shalomi, "On Renewing God," 111.

8. C. S. Lewis, *The Problem of Pain* (San Francisco: HarperSanFrancisco, 2001).

9. Lew, *Be Still and Get Going: A Jewish Meditation Practice for Real Life* (New York: Little, Brown, 2005), 247.

10. Green, *Tormented Master*, 107.

11. Flinders, *Enduring Grace*, 182.

12. Mathewes-Green, "Should You Design."

13. Lewis I. Newman, *The Hasidic Anthology* (New York: Schocken, 1972), 265.

14. Tony Hendra, *Father Joe: The Man Who Saved My Soul* (New York: Random House, 2005), 99.

15. Catherine Bell, *Ritual Theory, Ritual Practice* (New York: Oxford University Press, 1992), 184.

16. Pirke Avot 5:25.

17. Leibowitz, *Religious Praxis*, 3.

18. Grace Jill Schireson, e-mail message, March 23, 2007.

19. Shulchan Aruch, Yoreh Deah 249:14.

20. Kornfield, *After the Ecstasy*, 38.

21. Frederica Mathewes-Green, *Real Choices: Listening to Women, Looking for Alternatives to Abortion* (Ben Lomond, CA: Conciliar Press, 1997).

22. Flinders, *Values of Belonging*, 203.

23. Malcolm X, *Autobiography*, 373.

24. Fischer, *Life of Mahatma Gandhi*, 251.

25. M. K. Gandhi, *Ethical Religion*, chap. 6 (Ahmedabad, India: Navajivan Press, 1930).

26. M. K. Gandhi, article, *Young India*, July 5, 1925.

27. Carrette and King, *Selling Spirituality*, 82–83.

28. Ibid.

29. "Healing Arts," Kripalu Center for Yoga and Health website, www.kripalu.org/healing_arts/49/, accessed March 15, 2007.

30. Pyarelal Nayyar, *Last Phase*, vol. 2 (Ahmedabad, India: Navajivan Publishing House, 1997), 65.

31. Rebecca Alpert, ed., *Voices of the Religious Left: A Contemporary Sourcebook* (Philadelphia: Temple University Press, 2000), 9.

32. Michelle Conlin and Aaron Bernstein, "Working . . . and Poor," *Business Week*, May 31, 2004.

33. "Income, Poverty, and Health Insurance Coverage in the United States: 2005," U.S. Census Bureau, www.census.gov/hhes/www/hlthins/hlthino5.html.

34. Merton, *Seven Storey Mountain*, 277.

35. Ibid., 421.

36. Thomas Merton, *Learning to Love*, ed. Christine M. Bochen (San Francisco: HarperSanFrancisco), 1997.

37. Talmud Bavli, Shabbat 88a.

38. Karen Armstrong, *Muhammad: A Biography of the Prophet* (San Francisco: HarperSanFrancisco, 1992), 89.